T0278086

"The world today is a strange place indeed. In this book, Kevin Ford and Jim Singleton describe our reality and then provide a wealth of wisdom for listening and leading in a fresh, Christ-centered way. Full of real-life pastoral experiences and proven insights, this one book can serve as a reliable guide for both the ministry leader and the church to faithfully make a difference and thrive as a community in this rapidly changing world. It should be read by every pastor and elder."

MaryKate Morse, author, leadership mentor, and professor at Portland Seminary

"With insight (and lots of stories!) borne of their own work consulting, leading, coaching, and teaching leaders across the country, Kevin Ford and Jim Singleton offer us *Attentive Church Leadership*, which exhorts church leaders to discern and truly pay attention to what matters most in a deeply disrupted, often anxious, and rapidly changing world."

Tod Bolsinger, cofounder of AE Sloan Leadership and author of *Tempered Resilience: How Leaders Are Formed in the Crucible of Change*

"We live in a fast-changing world. The leadership principles I used when I was a church planter are no longer relevant in today's world. Technology has advanced rapidly, and the Covid-19 pandemic changed the scorecard of leadership. Churches and leaders must be attentive not only to the changing reality of the world but also to the ways they respond, adapt, and lead in the midst of those changes. In their new book, *Attentive Church Leadership*, Kevin Ford and Jim Singleton provide a great resource for church leaders of the twenty-first century, providing essential insights to help them navigate the rough waters of church leadership in this generation."

Eddy Aleman, general secretary of the Reformed Church in America

"Kevin Ford and Jim Singleton are faithful, experienced leaders in Christ's church who bring unique, insightful understanding into the rapidly changing nature of today's cultural landscape. For the overwhelmed pastor with little time for grasping a wider view of the world, this book provides a wonderful grid for asking the right questions and responding biblically to the churches they lead."

David D. Swanson, senior pastor of First Presbyterian Church of Orlando

"The spiritual practice of paying attention—to what God is doing and what is going on both inside and around us—is hard and holy work. Kevin Ford and Jim Singleton are wise guides on the road to church leadership and sustainable, Spirit-filled ministry, reminding us that the care of our own souls is key to leading a healthy organization. I will be recommending *Attentive Church Leadership* far and wide!"

Courtney Ellis, pastor and author of *Looking Up: A Birder's Guide to Hope Through Grief*

"Brilliant, beautiful, and nourishing, *Attentive Church Leadership* invites you to drink anew of Christ's living water and shows how your church can become a wellspring of God's transforming grace in the world."

Ken Shigematsu, pastor of Tenth Church in Vancouver, British Columbia, and author of *God in My Everything*

"Kevin Ford and Jim Singleton serve as a prophetic voice to challenge us to the same awareness that Paul had in Athens, but within the context we find ourselves in today. *Attentive Church Leadership* will help us all understand that a commitment to the radical transformation of society does not mean that Christians must oppose everything about society, but we need to approach society as if it is God-unaware. Reading this book leaves me wanting to become more attentive to members of my community to make them more aware of Jesus Christ and his kingdom!"

Alan Platt, founder and leader of the Doxa Deo / City Changers Movement

Attentive Church Leadership

Listening and Leading in a World We've Never Known

Kevin G. Ford
and Jim Singleton

Foreword by Ed Stetzer

An imprint of InterVarsity Press
Downers Grove, Illinois

InterVarsity Press
P.O. Box 1400 | Downers Grove, IL 60515-1426
ivpress.com | email@ivpress.com

InterVarsity Press® is the publishing division of InterVarsity Christian Fellowship/USA®. For more information, visit intervarsity.org.

Cover design: David Fassett
Interior design: Jeanna Wiggins
Cover images: Getty Images: © gchutka, © Tarchyshnik

ISBN 978-1-5140-0664-1 (print) | ISBN 978-1-5140-0666-5 (digital)

Printed in the United States of America ♾

Library of Congress Cataloging-in-Publication Data
Names: Ford, Kevin Graham, 1965- author. | Singleton, Jim (Pastor at Gordon-Conwell Theological Seminary), author.
Title: Attentive church leadership : listening and leading in a world we've never known / Kevin G. Ford and Jim Singleton.
Description: Downers Grove, IL : IVP Books, [2024] | Includes bibliographical references.
Identifiers: LCCN 2023042978 (print) | LCCN 2023042979 (ebook) | ISBN 9781514006641 (hardcover) | ISBN 9781514006665 (ebook)
Subjects: LCSH: Christian leadership.
Classification: LCC BV652.1 .F587 2024 (print) | LCC BV652.1 (ebook) | DDC 253–dc23/eng/20231129
LC record available at https://lccn.loc.gov/2023042978
LC ebook record available at https://lccn.loc.gov/2023042979

29 28 27 26 25 24 | 13 12 11 10 9 8 7 6 5 4 3 2 1

Dedicated with much love to both of our fathers, who helped make us the men that we are:

Leighton Ford

J. Martin Singleton

Contents

Foreword

Ed Stetzer

Every generation seems to have iconic moments that shape them. For boomers, these moments include the assassination of President John F. Kennedy and the first moon landing. For my generation (Gen X), there was the Berlin Wall's collapse and the space shuttle *Challenger* disaster. Millennials look to 9/11 and the rise of social media. But for Gen Z and Alpha, they will not forget their school's shutdown due to Covid-19 in the spring of 2020. As Kevin Ford and Jim Singleton state repeatedly, this is a world we've never known. How do we lead in a time like this?

David Brooks wrote in *The Atlantic* about how since 2020, America has been having a moral convulsion, like it has every sixty or so years. The pandemic, protests, and political division create an overwhelming sense of outrage and frustration. This is a time that begs for leaders. And while the Bible is not intended to be a book for our personal leadership growth, it teems with wisdom and examples—both good and bad—of leaders. Jesus showed us the essence of Christian leadership in John's Gospel when he washed the feet of the disciples. Servant leaders like these value relationships.

Ford and Singleton get this, as both the title and subtitle of this book attest. They effectively navigate issues elevated today, from discussions on mental health that offer cogent information and wise counsel, to issues of culture and the "robust cultural narcissism" of our time. You will read countless stories of real leadership case studies in churches and the business world, each of which adds to the collective weight of ideas to help leaders in this novel season.

Pastors will be encouraged and educated to understand and respond to real world situations. This is not a book of theory but of the practical realities of church life. It lays out for the reader a number of valuable constructs to help deal objectively and personally with the diverse challenges leaders currently face.

I encounter more leaders than ever who give more time and attention to conflict resolution, leading themselves, and the specific challenge of developing community in a polarized world. You will find honest and vulnerable help here.

At a crisis point in America—another convulsive time known as the Great Depression—President Franklin Delano Roosevelt gave his inaugural address in 1933. That address is remembered primarily for his famous phrase, "We have nothing to fear but fear itself." What many overlook is how he ended that same sentence, calling the nation "to convert retreat into advance." This is the kind of pivot leaders need to guide us today.

Introduction

What Does It Take to Thrive in a World We've Never Known?

"It felt like a deep grief." That's what Megan Hackman shared when the Covid-19 pandemic in 2020 forced her new church to postpone its launch.

Chapel Hill Church in Gig Harbor, Washington, saw the need for a new congregation in neighboring Port Orchard. They intended to create a new community for the 91 percent of people in Kitsap County who don't regularly practice faith in Jesus. After much prayer and many conversations, Pastors Megan and Larry Hackman decided to launch a new congregation as part of Chapel Hill. Their first Sunday morning service was supposed to be held on Easter Sunday, April 12, 2020, in the auditorium of South Kitsap High School.

"We were less than thrilled to announce a few short weeks later that our first service would be a YouTube broadcast," Megan said. "That Sunday, I cried through most of the broadcast, lamenting the chance to gather and proclaim the gospel. We pivoted in the summer to invest deeply in prayer ministry, the fruit of which we are still being nourished by."

This time of uncertainty, coupled with a new intensity to seek God's face, led them in ways they did not expect by readjusting their plans and refining their purpose. Chapel Hill's leadership team and the local pastors agreed that 2022 would be a good season to launch their new community: Kitsap House, a church with a strengthened local identity and leadership.

"The shutdown set us on a smaller, slower plan for investment in our community," Megan shared. "And doesn't that sound like the kingdom? We remained hopeful and curious." Instead of plowing ahead with their own plans, the Hackmans and their faith community had to discern what God was doing.

A World We've Never Known

This book is not primarily about change. It's about the attentiveness needed to respond effectively to the unending change around us. As we've journeyed with church leaders for decades, the challenge of a changing world is hardly a new thing. But the Covid-19 pandemic brought to a head what many church leaders have been experiencing for years: a world we've never known.

American entertainer and humorist Will Rogers said, "Even if you're on the right track, you'll get run over if you just sit there." A major shift began in the early 1990s from a broadcast culture to a digital one. It started slowly, with people talking about the World Wide Web and America Online (AOL)'s infamous "you've got mail." Email was fun, and by the mid-1990s the internet was an intriguing place to explore trivia, chat with people we'd never seen face-to-face in chat rooms, and find basic information while listening to the rotary dial-up modem. Yet, we still sent snail mail more than we relied on electronic means. In 2001, the United States Postal Services (USPS) had its highest ever volume of first-class mail at 103,656,000 parcels.

In the next twenty years, however, the digital world completely altered communication and commerce. With the advent of more sophisticated connectivity, online possibilities, and a plethora of related developments like texting, smartphones, and Zoom meetings, we became linked in new ways. Car purchases, mortgages, and concert tickets no longer required paper. All could be done instantly from a laptop or phone. By 2020, the volume of mail sent through the USPS dropped by almost half to 52,624,000.

This is a world we've never known! The advances of the digital age, however, are a mixed bag of blessings and curses. Today, if you live in New Jersey, you can see pictures of your high school friend's new baby just minutes after she gives birth in New Mexico. You can make hotel reservations across the world, send flowers to your great-aunt, and donate to your favorite charity without leaving your apartment or picking up the phone—all in your pajamas. On the other hand, marriage counselors report that a main cause of affairs today are old flames who reconnect on social media. What's more, psychologists warn that our brain's activity patterns are being negatively rewired, society has become more impatient, rude, and lacking common respect, and children and teenagers are exposed to pornography, violence, and potential harmful relationships while they sit across the den from their parents glued to their phones. With every cutting-edge invention creating widespread change, we can't just sit there and stare at it—as Rogers says, we may get run over.

A Day of Distractions

The digital world includes a constant barrage of voices. Author Steve Farrar called it a day of mass distraction.[1] Literally millions of tweets, posts, videos, chats, memes, movies, streams, and platforms compete for our attention twenty-four hours a day. People upload approximately 500 hours of video to YouTube every minute. That's 30,000 an hour and 720,000 per day. One year, or 365 days, contains 8,760 hours. So it would take someone more than eighty-two years just to watch the amount of video footage uploaded to YouTube in a single day.

People born in this era grow up in a world where this distraction is normal. However, for most of human history, the constant noise of the digital age was completely abnormal. Remember that a life regularly marked by distraction is the opposite of an attentive one. The apostle Paul warned the Christians in Rome to not "copy the behavior and customs of this world, but let God transform you into a new person by changing the way you think. Then you will learn to know God's will for you, which is good and pleasing and perfect" (Romans 12:2 NLT). The mind and spirit of the believer still wage an age-old battle. Will we let our thinking and reflecting be strangled, shaped, and overwhelmed by the world around us? Or will we resist the world's example and instead cultivate our minds and spirits to be attentive to the Lord? Only then will we be able to listen to his voice, discern his will, and walk in his good and pleasing ways.

The first task of leadership is to discern what needs to be preserved versus what needs to change. We must make changes not to be trendy but to follow God's mission. As churches and organizations we recognize the need for innovation, but we also resist it—not intentionally, but simply because that is our nature. We naturally look for patterns and try to replicate them. In our desire to fit in, we are inclined to conform rather than to grow and change. Instead of asking, "Why?" we tend to reinforce existing norms. Instead of being attentive, we become inattentive.

Attentiveness

The word *attentive* can be defined as "mindful" or "observant."[2] Yet we often stay so busy with activity, so consumed with pleasing people, and so distracted with the opinions of the day that our eyes grow dim and our ears dull. An attentive person is also "courteous" or "devoted."[3] Instead of being self-absorbed, an attentive person focuses on another.

As we work with pastors, ministry leaders, and churches all over the world, we know how easy and natural it is to become distracted with the wrong things. We've also had much experience helping those shepherds and congregations learn to refocus and move forward positively. We are Kevin Ford and Jim Singleton, and together we work with an organization called Leighton Ford Ministries (LFM).

Evangelist Leighton Ford has spent more than seventy years communicating the gospel of Jesus. As a Youth for Christ leader in Canada and later an associate evangelist with the Billy Graham Evangelistic Association, he preached the good news all over the globe. Over the past forty years he has mentored younger leaders worldwide, with a mission to be "an artist of the soul and a friend on the journey." As well as serving as the Honorary Lifetime Chair of the Lausanne Movement, he founded LFM to help young leaders lead more like Jesus, lead more to Jesus, and lead more for Jesus—to be kingdom seekers rather than empire builders. Like a rock thrown into a lake, Leighton has invested his past forty years into having an exponential "ripple effect" on kingdom leaders all over the globe.

In 2019, I (Kevin) joined my dad and LFM as their chief catalyst with a vision for supporting healthy leaders (mentoring) and thriving ministries (visioning, leadership development, governance, and transformation) for the sake of the gospel. After a long career in business with clients including *Fortune* 500s, small businesses, and government agencies, my partners and I sold the company I cofounded, TAG Consulting. I was then able to focus on my passion for ministry. I've facilitated the development of over five hundred strategic plans for organizations, including the redesign of the US Army Staff, the nation's largest employer. Through the years, I've consulted with hundreds of pastors and churches throughout North America. My colleagues and I also crafted the Transforming Church Insight (TCI), a survey for churches that includes over eleven million records in our database.

LFM serves as a catalyst for mentoring healthy leaders who sustain thriving ministries for the sake of the gospel. We are building an international community devoted to mentoring, and we partner with churches to help them navigate the challenges and victories of ministry.

I (Jim) recently completed ten years of teaching as the associate professor of pastoral leadership and evangelism at Gordon-Conwell Theological Seminary near Boston, Massachusetts. I taught both young seminarians new to the church and many students who were coming from careers outside the church but recognizing a call to a new path. In addition, I taught several dozen doctor of ministry students who were already practicing ministry.

Prior to teaching, I pastored congregations in Colorado, Texas, and Washington for thirty years. I first met Kevin when I heard him speak at a conference in Montreat, North Carolina. I knew we needed some help at my church in Colorado Springs. We formed a close friendship during his consultation at my church, so I naturally agreed to partner with him at LFM. I love helping pastors and ministry leaders flourish. With LFM, I serve as executive director of missional leadership, coaching and discipling pastors.

We help ministry leaders and the churches they serve get healthy and learn to thrive. Through our weekly work partnering with people all over the globe, as well as our personal involvement in our own churches and ministries, we encounter the all-too-real challenges of life and ministry in the twenty-first century.

Going forward, to avoid confusion in this book, we will designate which author is speaking by putting one of our names in parentheses.

Listening and Pivoting

My wife and I (Kevin) recently enjoyed a meal at a barbecue restaurant in Boone, North Carolina. We didn't have our phones out, and we spent the time talking and relaxing after a fun day at Grandfather Mountain in Linville. We soon noticed a threesome sitting beside us, who we guessed were two grandparents and their college-aged granddaughter. All three had their heads down and eyes fixed on their phones the entire time. They only talked or lifted their heads to speak to the waiter. This all-too-common occurrence is a sad picture of a society just sitting on the tracks. If we do not pay close attention and practice discernment in this new age, we'll get run over.

Some of our dear friends have faced a world they've never known in more personal ways.

When Daniel discovered that his wife, Dawn, had stage four pancreatic cancer—even though she had been cancer free all her life—leading a church board meeting suddenly seemed so unimportant. He was in a new world, a place he had never been before.

As Susan was leaving her house for church, she couldn't focus on her church responsibilities. Her daughter, Autry, had not come home last night just like many other nights. Was she in jail? The hospital? Dead? Autry had been in some trouble for years, but when she got to high school, her bad behavior suddenly accelerated. Susan and her husband found themselves in a place they had never been before.

When Andrew, the senior pastor of a church, discovered that a youth pastor had been sexually involved with two girls in their youth group, he was brought into a place he had never been before. Lawsuits, unwelcome news coverage, and loss of trust in the congregation overwhelmed him.

Or take our friend Corey Garrity, a young man in his twenties who is a pastor at Redeemer Redwood City in the highly unchurched San Francisco Bay Area:

> Doing ministry here means doing ministry on the margins of society and culture. There is not much of a "best practice" or "how to" in our context. The church in much of the United States still finds itself at the center of culture. Cities and communities see the church and leaders in the church as valid and legitimate sources of authority and direction for life. That narrative is not present in the Bay Area.
>
> The challenges we face are unique and leave us facing a world we've never known. We aren't traditional pastors equipping the saints, but missionaries on the margins called to encourage the saints not to throw in the proverbial towel of faith. These unique challenges also offer beautiful opportunities as well—opportunities to experiment and try non-traditional ministry approaches in order to reach people who don't follow Jesus.
>
> In a ministry world where what's helpful in most places rarely helps us here, life can be challenging. And yet, Jesus continues to lead us into mission toward the people He loves so deeply.

Like these stories from our friends, unforeseen and sometimes unwanted challenges shock us. If we're not careful, they can throw us off our path and lead us into disaster. We might become so distracted with these problems that we start drifting instead of paying attention to where we need to be going.

Covid-19 caught our world's attention in a big way. Like an unforeseen reality check, it forced us to see things we previously ignored. For churches, the problem became even more pronounced. Within a week, most congregations were asking, "How do we do worship online? How do we conduct meetings on Zoom? How do we deliver Communion?" Pastors and congregants who for decades had met and worshiped in person suddenly had to deal with a new reality.

The word we heard most frequently during the pandemic was "pivot." Change typically happens when we encounter an external force. The unexpected pandemic demanded transformational change. If your boss fires you, that imposes a change. If your house burns down, that forces a change. If our pastor retires, a shift occurs whether or not we like it. Internally driven change, however, is more demanding and more important than adjustments forced by circumstances because it lacks an external driver. Why change if nothing is broken? Internal change carries greater significance also because it requires a different posture—a more attentive one. It requires continual questioning. Where is God working? What is he saying? What currently describes our congregation, both above and below the surface? What is happening in the culture? And how should we respond?

Attentive Church Leadership

When I (Kevin) was young, our family used to stay at a friend's home in Highlands, North Carolina. Beautiful waterfalls, rivers, and lakes painted the landscape, offering picturesque views of the splendor of the Blue Ridge Mountains. Temperatures stayed in the seventies there while Charlotte, our hometown, was scorching. We always enjoyed a fabulous time.

One of our favorite activities was an annual trip to the nearby Cullasaja River. Passersby enjoy fantastic views en route to the Waterfall Byway, driving between the towns of Highlands and Franklin. Along a sixty-one-mile road meandering through the Nantahala National Forest, the river includes three waterfalls. We would go "rock hopping," traversing the river by jumping from one rock to the next—probably not the safest activity for a young child. But boy, it was fun! My dad and I were always in search of the perfect swimming hole, a quiet spot on the river where we could see the bottom.

After spending a few minutes in the frigid water, we would get out and skip rocks across the quiet waters of the swimming hole. I was always fascinated by the ripples that emerged each time the rock hit the water and the progression of the rock until it found its final resting spot. Have you ever stood next to a quiet lake on a still summer day and gazed across the water? Even if there's no breeze cooling your face, you will likely still see movement in the water. From massive ocean waves to roaring rivers, ripples can be powerful. But even the quietest pond has ripples caused by the slightest whisper of wind. Like God reaching down into human history, ripples are a divine intersection.

This book is about those divine intersections. This is not a book about step-by-step formulas, but there is a sequence. Rocks skip across the water, creating patches of movement. The ripples are organic, starting at the center and expanding outward in ever-increasing circles. That's how we want you to read this book. Our combined decades of experience supporting healthy leaders and thriving ministries, along with the incredible number of challenges facing church leaders, led us to write *Attentive Church Leadership* together to help Christian leaders in this new day. These three ripples—attentive, church, and leadership—come together to form an intersection.

We've seen churches lose their way because they were inattentive to the most important things. We've seen unhealthy and narcissistic leaders more concerned with their own names than with their church. And we've seen attentive, godly pastors who failed to lead. In this book, we marry these three concepts. A world we've never known requires attentive church leadership.

Navigating Change

Our friend Will Torres and Proclaim Church of Lake Worth, Florida, know about such challenges. They launched in September 2019, six months before the Covid-19 shutdown. In March of 2020, in just a matter of days, the entire country quickly moved into quarantine. "There was no seminary class, breakout session, or book on how to navigate what would ensue," Will said.

After moving from meeting in houses to the local community center, Proclaim Church was out of choices as schools and centers shut down and meeting in homes was not a healthy, feasible option. "As a church planter, you learn to be flexible and make do with less as you venture into understanding God will be with you through the ebb and flow of navigating change," Will said. "You have a prospectus, a plan, but you hold on to it lightly."

Will and his people, like thousands of congregations, had hundreds of questions. Do we stop meeting? Can we gather in a public space, like a park? How do we meet virtually? Will admitted, "I felt scared by the unknown of what we were dealing with and the pressure to figure it out in such a short order. It was overwhelming."

In subsequent months, they prayed, reached out to other pastors and friends, talked, strategized, and then prayed more. Like many churches, they met virtually for a season and had to pivot from a focus on outreach and discipleship to an immediate focus on soul care. They relaunched a public service in the fall of 2020, using another church's facility and navigating the myriad of opinions in the culture about wearing masks and staying healthy. Months later they moved to another location—a school. Battling discouragement from the obstacles of not only church planting but also leading during a pandemic, one Sunday while breaking the room down after a service, Will contemplated closing the church.

How to Read this Book

We wrote this book because we love church leaders and we want to help them be vibrant and lead strong ministries.

In "Part One: Becoming an Attentive Leader," we focus on you—the pastor, staff member, or volunteer leader. We've witnessed time and time again that a thriving ministry won't happen if the leader is not healthy and attentive. But like ripples in the water, when a leader becomes attentive, he or she can have a massive positive impact on the entire system. We'll start with a biblical account that reminds us of where we as church leaders find ourselves today. Healthy leadership starts with taking care of ourselves, and we'll talk about how to become an attentive person. In addition, every leader will deal with anxiety and problematic situations. We'll explore how to respond to anxiety in our churches and how to manage that stress without it overtaking us. And then we'll look at another ripple—how to build trust with our people.

Influencing Your Church

Next, in "Part Two: Leading an Attentive Church," we'll dive deep into specific ways you want to influence your church. First, we'll talk about aspects of attentive churches, including the four qualities of what we call True North. In our narcissistic world, churches must not become self-absorbed but embrace and foster a spirit of community. A community holds together only when the ethos, or internal culture, is compelling. A strong ethos allows us, people created in God's image, to have a desire to belong, to contribute, and to make a difference. We'll talk about how to create that for your congregation. Then we'll look at empowering the people to do ministry. We'll discuss the vital component of facilitating real transformation as we desire to see God continue changing lives. Finally, we'll end with the exhortation to keep on passing the torch of the gospel to other generations as the ripples continue moving out from the center.

The book includes many stories of real pastors and ministry leaders who we've partnered and connected with through the years. In some cases, names of leaders, churches, and cities have been changed for the sake of anonymity. We hope their stories will inspire, encourage, and instruct you as you seek to be an attentive leader and lead an attentive church.

The Adventure Ahead

Change is incredibly difficult. Resistance is strong. The status quo is powerful. All human systems tend toward homeostasis, a state of internal equilibrium. Yet, healthy transformation starts with a posture of attention. We need to observe what God is already doing, starting in our own soul. Then we need to view the congregation with spiritual eyes, desiring to hear from the Lord: "Anyone with ears to hear must listen to the Spirit and understand what he is saying to the churches" (Revelation 3:13 NLT). Finally, we need to pay attention to what's happening in the world around us.

As we practice these habits of becoming attentive, God will lead us through the highs and lows of change into the exciting adventure of being on mission with him. Lives will be changed, and we will be blessed as our Shepherd calls us forward. And the ripples will continue in ever-increasing circles.

Part One

Becoming an Attentive Leader

1

How Did We Get to a World We've Never Known?

In 1964, the year before I (Kevin) was born, Bob Dylan released the song "The Times, They Are A-Changin'." He challenged his audience to learn to sink or swim in a world going through radical shifts. Nearly sixty years after Dylan penned those words, the times are a-changin' once again. Generational theorists say a dominant generation is often followed by a recessive generation. One generation erupts into the spotlight while another one lives in the shadows. In other words, we can expect massive shifts to occur roughly every two generations.

Let's go back to the first part of the twentieth century. My (Kevin's) father, Leighton Ford, lived through massive change. He came into a world in 1931 in which most North American homes did not have a telephone or television, and people received their national news by tuning into a nightly radio broadcast. Dad vividly recalls being glued to the CBC Radio every Saturday, listening to Foster Hewitt's *Hockey Night in Canada*. He tuned in nightly to WXYZ radio station in Detroit to follow the adventures of the Green Hornet, the Lone Ranger, or Jack Armstrong, the American Boy. Dad was born during the Great Depression, which was called the "Dirty Thirties" in Canada. Most people washed their clothes by hand, grew much of their own food, and cooked three meals a day. Only about half of homes used electricity. Widespread economic upheaval resulted in massive political and social changes throughout North America.

In Dad's nine decades, society experienced substantial inventions, innovations, and transformations. If a person traveled in a time machine from the 1930s to the 2020s, the number of advancements in technology, communication, travel, and commerce would overwhelm them.

But change is nothing new. Life cycles through seasons of change.

We are currently living in a massive communication shift from the Broadcast Era to the Digital Era. During the previous era, a few talking heads like Walter Cronkite controlled the flow of news to most of the nation. Today, literally thousands of news options are instantly available. In the old era, three primary television broadcasting companies (ABC, CBS, and NBC) provided at-home entertainment. During the "Sweeps Weeks," each of the three networks put out their best movies and miniseries to compete for viewership. Sixty percent of American households (an estimated 125 million people) watched the series finale of *M*A*S*H* in 1983, and 53 percent (83 million in the United States and an estimated 350 million worldwide) found out who shot J. R. Ewing in 1980. These massive numbers represent the limited options for viewing entertainment at home in the 1980s. Today, due to digital streaming, an uncountable number of companies, options, and services are available to watch at home, in the car, or deep in the woods—as long as you have your phone or tablet. The digital transformation has immensely affected communication, transportation, and production.

Yes, the times, they are a-changin'. Imagine the following account happening today in New York City:

> Marchers filed past the reviewing stand hour after hour. The day was Thursday, June 6, 1946; the place, Prospect Park in Brooklyn, New York. It was two years to the day since the Allies landed on the Normandy beaches, the nation now paused to give thanks and reflect on its collective heritage. But the marchers were not soldiers or war heroes. They were children: little girls in starched pinafores, wearing white dress gloves and carrying bouquets of spring flowers; little boys in neatly ironed white shirts with clip-on bow ties and

> paper hats. Together they marched, accompanied by brass bands and floats, past rows of admiring parents and grandparents. In the reviewing stand, Brooklyn's mayor, the governor of New York, and a justice of the U.S. Supreme Court gave their approval. By public declaration, all schools were closed for the day. In all, approximately ninety thousand youngsters participated. The event was the 117th annual Sunday School Union parade.[1]

Now, it is hard to even imagine a world where public school is canceled for a Sunday school parade, with a Supreme Court Justice on the reviewing stand.

The world described in this Prospect Park vignette seems light years from today. The decade following that event brought the highest church membership and church attendance of any decade in American history. Church buildings went up at an astonishing rate. Many denominations employed a paid architecture department to help with building plans. The GI Generation joined congregations, Kiwanis organizations, and bridge clubs. Suburbs popped up across the American landscape. The church and society were wed together in a form of American Christendom.

That world is gone for many reasons, and we now live in a post-Christian culture. New generations with different value systems have surfaced. Technology brought an acceleration to the changes we face. Throughout this book, we will try to unwrap the dimensions of this new world. Church leaders have never gone this way before. We will also explore what it means to be attentive to God in the midst of such challenges and transitions. We'll invite you to walk with us through a biblical passage in which Joshua encountered enormous change.

Transition: Changing Leaders

Transitions are a normal part of life, but they are rarely easy. In 1998, I (Kevin) cofounded a company called TAG Consulting. We coached leaders and provided organizational development services across virtually every industry in the United States. Our bread and butter, however, came from a handful of large contracts with federal agencies. Following a series of government shutdowns and sequestrations, my partners and I decided it was time to sell the company. We did our best to make sure all of our employees were taken care of in the transition. My partners and I skipped multiple paychecks to take care of our employees. Yet, several of our long-term workers were angry that we were selling the business. It was one of the most difficult transitions in my life. Still, I knew God was involved in that decision. Had we not trusted him then, I never would have been able to join my dad at LFM.

I (Jim) once had the privilege of succeeding a legendary pastor who served that congregation for thirty-six years. I knew I could never fill those shoes. My inadequacy and inexperience would be hard to hide. The congregation was also aware of the difficulty of accepting the change of person and style. The greatest gift I received was the outgoing pastor's unqualified acceptance and encouragement. Serving in that role was the hardest ministry I ever encountered, but I sensed God was behind the whole situation, and I knew he would prevail in spite of me.

The first chapter of Joshua begins with the phrase, "after the death of Moses" (Joshua 1:1). It's impossible for us in the twenty-first century to imagine that difficult juncture. The United States elects a new president every four or eight years. From 1981 to 2021, our country lived under seven different presidents. The people of ancient Israel, however, had the same primary leader for four decades.

The presence, wisdom, and provision of God consistently marked Moses' life and leadership—from challenging the most powerful man in their world and winning, to parting the Red Sea, to miraculously intervening during the Israelites' wilderness wanderings. After Moses' long tenure, it was probably unthinkable to be led by anyone else. And even though the Israelite people did not have the best track record respecting and following a leader, they were accustomed to Moses. They were familiar with his communication style and leadership strategy. They knew what to expect. And humans tend to like the familiar.

Then Moses died, and suddenly, Joshua had to lead two million people. Israel was thrust into its biggest leadership transition in forty years. This was not only a change in leadership but a change in direction. Because of the previous generation's disobedience, the nation "circled the airport" for many years, wandering around in the wilderness near Mount Sinai. But now, God prepared to give them an entirely new set of directions. They were about to enter a completely different phase. They would transform from wanderers to possessors. And the ripples of God's kingdom would continue.

Sometimes change comes to us in the form of an unexpected setback. In January 1983, my (Jim's) wife, Sara, experienced a surprising medical challenge that required immediate emergency surgery. It frightened us on so many fronts. I was finishing my last semester of seminary, and she earned our income as a nurse. After surgery, the doctors told us she could not work for ten weeks while she recuperated. I quickly realized I could not afford to finish school. All tallied, the expenses facing us the next four months until graduation came to $2,322. Today that sum might not seem overwhelming, but to a graduate student in 1983 it was mammoth. In today's dollars, that would be $7,013. I was downcast for many reasons. I would need to drop out and work to support our family of three. It was sobering, compounded with my doubts about entering ministry the following summer.

The next morning, I went to the mailbox and received a letter from my childhood best friend, Dale Boaz. We had not communicated for several months. He had included a check for $2,322, written and mailed three days before Sara went to the hospital. I fell to my knees in awe and wonder. How could this be?

I called Dale, thanked him for the check, and asked why he sent that amount. For weeks he had tried to sell his car unsuccessfully. Dale told God that if he helped him sell his car, he would donate one-third of the amount to someone in ministry. On New Year's Eve, 1982, a drunk driver crashed into his parked car, totaling it. The insurance company gave him $6,966, and one-third of that was exactly $2,322. He then felt compelled to send it to me. Receiving that gift was the signal I needed to continue on my path to ordained ministry.

Isaac Watts wrote the hymn "O God, Our Help in Ages Past" after Queen Anne of England died. The timeless words reminded English Christians of the preeminence of the Lord—he would be with them in the future as he was with past generations:

O God, our help in ages past,

Our hope for years to come,

Our shelter from the stormy blast,

And our eternal home.

Joshua and his people would need to trust that reality without Moses in their midst. God was still their hope for years to come, and they would need to listen to him.

Struggle

Most of us have experienced various transitions—promotions, moves, losses, and disappointments. After each change, we probably knew the next day was going to be different from the previous one. Some transitions are exciting, like the birth of a baby, but others are mostly difficult. We don't know exactly how it will all work out, and we fear letting go of our normal. We embrace a comfortable routine, sometimes forgetting that trials and changes can be blessings in disguise and good tools for our development. In the summer of 2012, through a deep sense of calling, I (Jim) left a wonderful position in a church to begin teaching in a seminary. The dynamics of academic life are quite different from preaching and leading a large congregation. I distinctly remember one dark December afternoon I had no Christmas Eve service to plan for—just papers to grade while a cold wind howled outside my window. I sat there wondering if I had really heard God's call after all. Everything seemed so different from how I thought it would be.

Life coach Dan Miller writes,

> How do you view the struggles in your life? Do you do whatever you can to avoid them? Or do you see them as necessary steps for growth? Do you suspect evil forces are bombarding you? Or could it be that God is allowing the struggles to bring about your transformation? . . . Can you recall a time when you yearned for relief from a tough situation? Did the struggle teach you something important?

He goes on to ask,

> And what about now? Is losing a job or dealing with the pressures of a business limiting your opportunities—or preparing you for a burst of new success? Perhaps you're in the process of entering a new chapter of your life. Don't sabotage your growth with a Band-Aid solution![2]

We are living through several major cultural transitions. So much has been changing for years, but the acceleration of adjustments that came in the early 2020s has shaken many Christian leaders. This recent season of cultural transition has brought much bewilderment. As Israel moved away from their wilderness home, Moses' leadership, and the daily provision of bread, they experienced seven challenges and changes.

Blocked by the Jordan River

In the third chapter of Joshua, the people of Israel camped by the Jordan River. They sat at the edge of the Promised Land after spending forty years in the wilderness. Their wait was not as long as the Chicago Cubs' 108-year wait to win the 2016 World Series. But they waited a long time, wondering when God would fulfill his promise.

They faced one big problem: the Jordan River was at flood stage, and there were no bridges (Joshua 3:15). Nor were there boats to get a huge group of people across. Today it doesn't look very formidable. In the 1930s, the Degania Dam was completed as part of Pinhas Rutenberg's Naharayim hydroelectric power plant project. Then, in 1964, it was repurposed to control water levels flowing from the Sea of Galilee into the Jordan River so as to not flood farmland downstream. As a result, today's

Jordan resembles a calm body of water. But in Joshua's day during harvest time, the river was a mile wide and 150 feet deep at flood stage.

Imagine getting two million people across this river into Canaan on foot. The Lord instructed them to camp out next to the river for three days. Perhaps God wanted the people to stare at their impossibility. He wanted the reality that this task was way beyond their ability to sink deep into their spirits. Remember, God often sets a humanly impossible obstacle in our path before he does a new thing in our lives. Steve Farrar wrote, "God had led them into the crisis. He created the crisis, just as He did for their parents at the Red Sea forty years earlier."[3]

How do you respond when there is a great barrier between you and where you think you are going—especially when you have waited a long time to get there? Surely, the Jewish parents and grandparents remembered and passed down the story of Moses and the Red Sea. It was an essential part of their identity as a people. The Red Sea was an even larger barrier than the Jordan, and Pharaoh pursued them with his entire army. Yet God stepped in, performing one of the Bible's greatest miracles. Whenever the people shared that account during their wilderness wanderings, they were reminded of God's provision. That is why to this day we rehearse biblical texts. They build our trust in the Lord and help us remember.

Remembering faithfully is essential to Christian discipleship. We must habitually focus our minds on true, noble, good, and godly ideas (Philippians 4:8). Remembering helps us to not only react to changing circumstances but also to respond to the reality of the Lord and his truth. But would the Israelites remember correctly now that the Jordan was in front of them? Would they trust God and adapt to this new set of circumstances, or would they give up in fear and uncertainty? And what about us? Will we remember faithfully amid church decline, global events, and political and racial tensions? And will we remember what God has done even ten years from now when we face other challenges? I (Jim) have to regularly remember the gift of Dale Boaz when I face new confusing circumstances.

When we encounter new barriers, we tend to forget basic theological realities: God knows us, he has a plan for our lives, he is not surprised by our problems, and he knows how to get us through or around them. Marriages sometimes get difficult. You and your spouse want to grow together, but then a barrier forms between you both. You can't see how to get past it, and you forget what drew you together in the first place. A good friendship might go through this as well. You and your friend have a good history together, but suddenly a flooded river of misunderstanding arises. Businesses and jobs experience the same thing. An unforeseen problem raises its head, and you don't know how to navigate it.

Today, congregations feel this kind of barrier. Many churches plateaued years ago, and now they feel stuck. Culture has changed drastically, and Christian leaders don't know how to cross the river from where we are to where we want to go. Churches and ministries have tried various approaches, but nothing feels fixed or safe. The troubles of the recent past have uncovered many new cracks in the foundation of congregations around politics, race, religious freedom, and safety. Do we remember God's past faithfulness, or do we stop remembering correctly and grow anxious? It's easy to forget and feel stuck.[4]

I (Jim) have lived long enough to see various institutions at flood stage on this side of the Jordan River. In 1991, I was the pastor of a congregation near Whitworth University in Spokane, Washington. There was so much uncertainty. Morale was low, much like the pay scale. The school's mission swung back and forth for years in the '70s and '80s, depending on the tenure of presidents. Pockets of promise popped up, but a bright future was hard to read. What's more, painful events surrounding the school from 1991 to 1992 felt like a river of grief. Several unusual student deaths occurred that year, and two gruesome murders happened that winter among Whitworth families. A popular professor, Jerry Sittser, lived through a catastrophic accident in which his wife, mother, and daughter all died. I wondered how Whitworth would ever get beyond this river of troubles. However, a year later, an interim president named Phil Eaton arrived. Slowly, encouragement began to grow. Then a new president, Bill Robinson, came to the school and had an immediate impact on students and faculty. The identity of Whitworth was revived, and a long season of thriving occurred. Applications and admissions soared. The climate on campus grew much more vibrant. New dorms were built, classroom buildings were added, and Whitworth's status within the community rose significantly. God was not finished with what he had started.

In our work with pastors and congregations, we often hear of insurmountable barriers. What do we do when the way to God's promise is not clearly accessible? About 65–85 percent of American congregations have plateaued or are declining. Mainline denominations stopped growing around 1965. Some congregations along the way made the painful switch of adding a contemporary service and grew until about 2005. But since then, many congregations have struggled, unsure of how to reach young adults who do not fit historic congregations. Millennials and Gen Z individuals are certainly not flocking to the Christian faith in our country. How do churches relate and adapt to a new day and younger generations?

The Promised Land

The Jordan River was a barrier blocking the entrance to Canaan. While we tend to associate the Promised Land with milk and honey, it also involved a purpose and a mission for Israel. Canaan was to be their home. In Genesis 12, when God promised Abraham to make a great nation, he planned to form a model people in the Promised Land so they would be a "light for the nations" (Isaiah 49:6 ESV). By their collective witness they would draw all nations to the Lord, thereby restoring what was damaged during the fall. God's great design was not only to free them from Egypt but for them to become his light in a dark world.

During the wilderness wandering years, their natural inclinations got in the way of living the life God designed for them. Forty years later, they were a questionable group of untrusting, unfaithful, and disobedient people. But God was ready to take them out of the wilderness and fulfill his promises. He had released them from Egyptian bondage, shaped them during their wanderings, and was now ready to give them victory.

God calls all of us into a marvelous plan for his preferred future. The Promised Land today is not somewhere in the Middle East but wherever

Jesus continues to establish his kingdom. The rule and reign of Jesus in our midst allows us to remember the values he provided so we can walk in those realities. He wants to use our lives to have an ever-increasing ripple effect in our world. Today, the Promised Land might take many shapes and forms. It may even feel like learning how to flourish when we find ourselves in a place we don't want to be. Like the Jewish exiles, we may ask, "How can we sing the songs of the LORD while in a foreign land?" (Psalm 137:4).

Kasr el-Dabar, a congregation in Cairo, is a dynamic church just off the city's main square. We're not sure we've seen a congregation with more regional impact. They host worship in their sanctuary every night of the week. They are not just relaxing in their Promised Land. Their circumstances are hard. Yet, the ministry is flourishing all over their area.

Emmanuel Muhammed, a former Imam with a PhD in Islamic law, was a student of mine (Jim) and is now in Nigeria. Jesus once appeared to him in a profound and mystical way on the road to Abuja, the capital city of Nigeria. He now uses the gospel to reach former Muslims and trains them in the Word of God. He has faced severe persecution and the loss of his birth family. There are daily challenges, but he is focused on the passion of his calling to redeem what is in deep need of repair.

Karen Swanson is one of our mentoring leaders for LFM. She heads the Institute for Prison Ministries at the Wheaton College Billy Graham Center in Wheaton, Illinois. Incarceration can be a terrible experience, one devoid of hope. Through her ministry, Karen gives inmates opportunities to worship, which helps them get their minds off their imprisonment and connect spiritually with other believers and something greater than themselves. "Lost people are drawn in. The unbelievers want what the believers have," she said. These worship opportunities then open doors for the gospel to spread in the prison.[5]

Following the Ark

When you face a barrier, remember that God has a plan and the means to get you across. The Lord instructed Joshua to let the Ark of the Covenant lead their crossing of the Jordan: "When you see the ark of the covenant of the Lord your God, and the Levitical priests carrying it, you are to move out from your positions and follow it" (Joshua 3:3).

God wanted Joshua and the people of Israel to follow the Ark into the river. The Ark was a chest about three feet and nine inches long, and two feet and three inches wide and high, covered with gold both inside and outside. It held the tablets of the law, the Ten Commandments, Aaron's rod, and a jar of manna. A golden lid, decorated with two golden angels, covered it. This was known as the mercy seat, where the Jews believed God's presence resided.

God instructed Moses about the Ark's construction at Mount Sinai. This central piece of the people's worship journeyed with them through all of their wilderness wanderings. Carrying the Ark into the water symbolized God's leading them into the land of promise. The Lord literally was going before them.

Today we do not need the Ark. As believers, we are sealed with the Holy Spirit of promise, a deposit of our spiritual inheritance. We have God's Word preserved through the ages to reveal his truth, purposes, and ways, as he wants to relate to us personally. Jesus, speaking of himself as a Shepherd, said, "The sheep listen to his voice. He calls his own sheep by name and leads them out. When he has brought out all his own, he goes on ahead of them, and his sheep follow him because they know his voice" (John 10:3-4). A basic part of walking with the Lord today is learning not to do our own thing but to follow.

A Way You Have Never Been Before

After telling Joshua to follow the Ark, God said, "Then you will know which way to go, since you have never been this way before. But keep a distance of about two thousand cubits between you and the ark; do not go near it" (Joshua 3:4).

God took these people a way they had not been before. Waging war, conquering enemies, living as landowners, farming the land, and settling down as free people were all new to them. They knew how to be slaves and nomads, but they had never been independent and established. That is an important aspect of the nature of God's leading. Despite his promises to Abraham, Isaac, and Jacob, this generation would be the one to finally take ownership.

Moving from pilgrimage to possession can be scary. When a child leaves home for the first time, she certainly feels excited about new opportunities. But she may also feel angst as she wonders how to journey through the maze of adulthood without the direct support of parents. For Israel, the road ahead was unclear and uncharted. Because of the unknown nature of their journey, they needed to get behind the Lord and follow him.

We don't follow an Ark. Yet, as individuals and collectively as a congregation, we are filled with the Holy Spirit. Following the Holy Spirit reminds us of the way of Jesus and regularly takes us to places we haven't been before. The New Testament gives evidence of an early church through whom the Spirit of God worked. Various preachers through the years have suggested the Acts of the Apostles should actually be named the Acts of the Holy Spirit. Before his death, Jesus assured his disciples of a Helper who would follow, one who would guide and equip them through their pilgrimage.

After pastoring for nearly three decades, I (Jim) was invited to teach at a seminary. It meant learning many new things, and every day I was aware of how far behind I was in certain areas. But I feel great joy and delight because God has led me to train and pour my life into the next generation of pastors. I am going a way I have never been before.

Three years into my new career as a seminary professor, Sara and I became full-time caregivers as grandparents to our two year-old grandson. Living daily with a dynamic child has been a rich experience. I now coach Little League baseball again in my sixties. Chicken nuggets are in our freezer, and Christmas morning starts very early again. We thought we would be entering the empty nester years. Instead, we have never been this way before.

In the eighteenth century, John Wesley and the Methodists brought the church where it had not been before. A Great Awakening began, and a Methodist way emerged that brought life to a tired old church. Small groups known as bands and class meetings began to shape the church in a whole new way, leading to immense growth.

The church in China in 1949 felt defeated when the communist government sent the missionaries home. But they went a way they had not been before and set up underground house churches. Eventually, the church in China exploded with growth.

Becoming a church on mission to our surrounding community requires a new way. I (Kevin) had the privilege of leading worship at Singapore 87, a conference sponsored by the Lausanne Movement for three hundred young evangelical leaders from more than sixty nations. I heard a sermon there I'll never forget. A business owner named Kent Humphreys talked about how frogs wait for food to come to them while lizards seek out their food. Churches today need to be more like lizards and less like frogs. Our call is to go where people live, work, and play with the good news of Jesus. So many churches want to keep things the same and stay inside their buildings. But if we do, we will remain on the east side of the Jordan and miss our opportunity. Following God requires a willingness to go new places. That goes for individuals and congregations.

We have lived through so much change in our culture. The 1960s brought televisions to every home, rock and roll music, the sexual revolution, and racial unrest. The Watts riots occurred in Los Angeles in 1965. The turbulent 1968 Democratic convention in Chicago resembled the chaotic pulse of a country rocked by the assassinations of President Kennedy, Martin Luther King Jr., and Robert Kennedy. Woodstock symbolized bold new expressions of music and sexual freedom. We participated in an unpopular Vietnam War. By the 1970s, we were disillusioned by Watergate and the resignation of a president. Consumerism and individualism became social norms. The roots of a strange kind of cultural narcissism emerged.

The church adapted by creating what we today call the attractional church. We put on great events, hoping for many people from our communities and cities to come hear the gospel. Megachurch leaders like Rick Warren and Bill Hybels as well as the Community Church of Joy developed programmatic church structures with something for everyone. My (Kevin's) uncle, Billy Graham, effectively capitalized on the Broadcast Era to lead millions of people to Jesus. However, it wasn't all positive. Andy Stanley called it the cafeteria approach to church. We offered as many programs for all ages as possible, giving people lots to choose from to keep them happy. Without knowing it, we introduced a Trojan horse of consumerism into the church world. Maybe we followed the Ark well, or perhaps we took a detour.

Today, many churches are struggling. The attractional church, which was crafted for the cultural moment of the baby boomers from the 1970s through the 1990s, has plateaued because it does not fit later generations in the same way. This is a world we've never known.

The loss is not uniform in all regions of the country. There are amazing exceptions, such as the growth of immigrant churches, which are much less consumer-oriented. But for the most part, our congregations have not adapted to this culture because we are conditioned to the attractional model. In this new era, there are new ideas about what the church needs to become. Surely we must be attentive to the leading of God's Spirit, as we do not have a map for this particular region. Instead of entering a promised land, it feels more like entering a period of exile where we do not understand the culture and challenges before us.

Many more changes came with the new millennium. Since 9/11, security protocol at airports, the post office, and government buildings is forever changed. The advent of social media drastically altered the way people communicate. The internet brought significant change to commerce for every industry. The world experienced political polarization unlike anything in recent years. And the Covid-19 pandemic challenged many accepted norms, led to greater health consciousness, and forced society to deal with fear in unprecedented ways.

Our society now is post-Christian. The early church did remarkable evangelism with pre-Christian Rome. But this is a world we've never known. A negative perception of Christianity exists in our culture. Trust in the church has dropped dramatically. There is no designated sacred time when our society makes time for faith. We struggle to afford the buildings that house our worship. And technology has changed the very patterns of communication that transmitted the gospel for several decades.

In larger churches, multisite campuses have become the norm. The advent of podcasting and live streaming makes thousands of church services and sermons instantly available. A family in Ukraine can watch a congregation's worship service in Texas every week. A teen in Atlanta can listen to a podcast recorded weekly in Tel Aviv. There is a move away from the traditional church. People are meeting in homes, coffee shops, and restaurants for Bible study, prayer, and encouragement.

Our hope comes from following the presence of the Lord through his Son Jesus. Step into the Jordan and follow him. Get out of the boat and follow him right onto the water of the unknown. Listen. Trust. Pay attention.

The Miracle of the Water

There comes a time to move and to act. God commanded his people to do the impossible and step into the flooding waters: "Yet as soon as the priests who carried the ark reached the Jordan and their feet touched the water's edge, the water from upstream stopped flowing. It piled up in a heap a great distance away, at a town called Adam in the vicinity of Zarethan" (Joshua 3:15-16).

We cannot explain how a river stopped flowing, allowing thousands of people to walk across a dry riverbed. Where did the water go? How fast was the flow? We don't know these details. We do know the whole group crossed over like their forefathers at the Red Sea. When they finished crossing, the priests took the Ark out of the riverbed. The water started flowing again at flood stage. How did this work? It is part of the mystery of God. Sometimes we shouldn't press the way of miracles.

God did not stop working during biblical times. Today, he wants to do great things for the honor of his name and the good of his people. We don't know what all those things will be. But we do know Jesus wants to restore what is good, beautiful, and true. He's not giving up on the church, and he's not giving up on you. But we will need to be ready to go a new way—right through our own impossibilities.

Stones of Remembrance

Before the priests brought the Ark out of the river, the Lord told Joshua to have representatives from the twelve tribes carry twelve stones out of the riverbed and set them up as a monument. The collected stones were to remind the people of God's intervention. Joshua said, "In the future, when your children ask you, 'What do these stones mean?' tell them that the flow of the Jordan was cut off. . . . These stones are to be a memorial to the people of Israel forever" (Joshua 4:6-7).

God loves to use symbols to trigger our memories. They remind us of greater realities. A cross reminds us of the sacrifice Jesus made for us. A Communion table helps us to recall God's presence among us. An open Bible reminds us of God's Word to us. Lighted candles remind us of the presence of God here in our midst and our call to be the light of the world. We need such symbols to remember God is among us, leading us on a way we have never been before.

The future of the church looked dubious after Peter and Paul were killed in Rome. Christianity seemed like a tough sell as an alternative to the Roman narrative. The future of the church looked doubtful when it got off track just prior to the Reformation. It looked doubtful in 1720 when decadence ruled before a Wesleyan revival came. It looked dubious in 1799 when Timothy Dwight was president of Yale until revival broke out—the Second Great Awakening.

Your life right now may be in a complicated place as you face a river at flood stage. Jesus is beckoning you to step into the water with him and trust. To be attentive.

Questions for Reflection and Discussion

- Take some time to review the transitions you have experienced in your life. Did you resist those times of transition or embrace them?
- In what ways did you experience God's presence amid transition? Do you recognize any unhealthy attitudes within yourself as you went through those transitions?
- Consider the changes in your church or community now. How would you describe your attitude toward change? Are you excited about new possibilities for the gospel as a result of change? Are you frustrated by the greater leadership challenge that change requires?
- In what ways does this season of church feel like there is a huge obstacle in your way?
- What does it mean for your congregation to follow the Spirit and go a way you have never been before?
- Throughout the biblical narrative, God used symbols to help his people remember his faithfulness during times of uncertainty. What pictures or symbols help you remember God's past faithfulness as you face an uncertain future?

2

How Do I Become an Attentive Person?

By most measures, Ken Shigematsu has led a life filled with achievements. The pastor of one of the largest churches in Canada, Ken is a bestselling author and is in demand as a speaker. He earned his doctorate in 2013, graduated from seminary *magna cum laude*, and has studied and worked in business and economics. He is naturally driven to achieve. And, he told us, that is the problem.

Of Japanese descent, Ken was born in Tokyo, one of the busiest, performance-oriented cities in the world. Even though he was raised and educated most of his life in Europe and North America, Ken still naturally struggles with the burden to achieve. Today he pastors Tenth Church in Vancouver, British Columbia.

In a recent conversation, he shared,

> I experienced extreme pressure to perform and achieve success when I was in Tokyo working for Sony. And I still carry it with me in my work as a pastor. The average person may think of ministry as a "spiritual" vocation, less competitive than business. But for me, leaving business for ministry didn't free me from feeling that I needed to achieve. I still felt like I need to do something exceptional with my life, just in a different context.

He then shared about a significant relationship that began moving him into a different understanding of his true self:

> I had the privilege of getting to know Leighton Ford when I was a student at Gordon-Conwell Theological Seminary near Boston in my midtwenties, at the same time I was enrolled in the first year of Leighton's Arrow Leadership Program. This initiative helped develop young, emerging kingdom leaders and still operates today. At the first meeting of our cohort, I'm sure more than one of us compared ourselves to the others, wondering how we would rank.
>
> Though I was one of the younger people in the class with the fewest ministry achievements, I was eager to impress Leighton. I wanted to stand out from the crowd. During one of our classes, I volunteered the summary of an obscure publication by an MIT professor, hoping hard to wow Leighton. What I did not yet realize was that this consummate mentor does not dole out love and approval based on performance.
>
> A few years later, I stumbled as a young Christian leader and got into a conflict with a ministry colleague because of my own emotional immaturity. I was also in a dating relationship where we struggled to maintain healthy boundaries. As Leighton helped me through that season, I discovered through my failures that this globally recognized Christian leader didn't accept me because of my performance or because I could contribute something to his organization. He accepted me and loved me because I was made in God's image. Now, more than twenty-five years later when I'm with him, I feel more at home in my skin than ever before. I feel free to be transparent about my struggles and temptations as well as share without inhibition the joys of my life.

Through that experience, Ken began to understand the need to take care of his own soul and allow others into his life to care for him. He learned that his identity was in who he was, not in what he produced.

Throughout Paul's epistles, the indicative always precedes the imperative. Who we are in Christ precedes what we are challenged to do. As ministry leaders, we need to be attentive to our souls before we can lead others in a world we've never known. There is no road map, but there is a starting point. We need to embrace who we already are in Christ and live out of that.

Ken is not alone in the pressure he feels. Pastors are all over the map in terms of the issues they struggle with. For some, like Ken, it's the need to achieve. For others, it's the need to be accepted. Some tend toward narcissism while others tend toward self-doubt. Regardless of the issue, too many pastors ignore their own soul. Newly revised statistics on pastoral ministry in the United States reveal alarming trends:

- 80% of pastors believe pastoral ministry has negatively affected their families. Many pastor's children do not attend church now because of what the church has done to their parents.
- 65% of pastors feel their family lives in a "glass house" and fear they are not good enough to meet expectations.
- 57% of pastors believe they do not receive a livable wage.
- 52% of pastors feel overworked and cannot meet their church's unrealistic expectations.
- 70% of pastors report they have a lower self-image now than when they first started.
- 70% of pastors do not have someone they consider to be a close friend.
- Over 50% of pastors are unhealthy, overweight, and do not exercise.[1]

Pastoral ministry by nature includes a drive to perform and please others. Success is almost impossible to measure in ministry. Is the missionary who seldom disciples a new believer within an unreached group less successful than the megachurch pastor in America who preaches to thousands weekly? Not in the eyes of the One who matters most. Yet, in a results-oriented society and a success-driven culture, pastors easily jump on the endless treadmill of trying to live up to people's expectations and their own ambitions.

"Being completely absorbed in our work can make us feel fully alive, especially when we are doing what we were put on earth to do," Ken said. "But it can cause us to neglect our most important relationships. It can also lead us to neglect our soul—the part of us that communes with God and determines our true well-being and happiness."

Periodically, we take our cars into a repair shop for a diagnostic test that examines the engine, brakes, transmission, and exhaust system. These significant areas of a car can make or break its long-term usefulness. Similarly, taking care of our inner lives as attentive leaders includes maintaining a watchful eye on several segments of our lives. Just as a vehicle without preventive maintenance will wear out and rust, so too will we crash and burn if we neglect our soul. As we continue to grow in our understanding of what it means to be an attentive church, let us also examine four questions toward becoming an attentive person.

Who Am I?

This is life's most defining question. Who am I? Why do I exist? Am I more than just a conscious being? For centuries, philosophers have explored these mysteries. Existentialist Bertrand Russell said, "I believe that when I die I shall rot, and nothing of my ego will survive."[2] Descartes said, "I think, therefore I am."[3] Aristotle wrote that a soul is "the actuality of a body that has life."[4] For Immanuel Kant, the inner self is comprised of our psychological state and rational intellect.[5] David Hume claimed that the self is "that to which our several impressions and ideas are supposed to have a reference."[6]

Who are you? Think about how you introduce yourself to someone. Early in the conversation, you might mention your role: "I'm a mechanic, nurse, etc." In our mentoring and coaching work with pastors, we find this to be a central problem. Many clergy define themselves by their role as pastor. We often experience the pressure to achieve arising from this role. We may feel like we constantly have to be "on." Volunteer leaders need our help navigating complicated church polity issues. Counselees look to us for answers for a myriad of problems. Each time we lead worship, even if we feel as spiritual as a brick, we have to "perform" anyway. Our spouse needs support from us. Our preschoolers and younger children depend on us for most of their needs. Our teenagers and young adult children look to us to provide for them and help them navigate a complex world. If you serve in a small town, you may feel this pressure even while eating out at a restaurant because someone there will know you're the pastor. The largest performance pressure for most pastors relates to this question: "Can I help this church grow?"

Repeatedly, the Scriptures refer to us as children. The Bible addresses believers as "my little children" (1 John 2:1 ESV). Jesus said, "Let the little children come to me, and do not hinder them, for the kingdom of God belongs to such as these. Truly I tell you, anyone who will not receive the kingdom of God like a little child will never enter it" (Luke 18:16-17). Yet as we grow up and assume adult roles and responsibilities, it becomes easy to ignore our place as children and instead keep performing.

Living out of our core means existing out of a place of being loved perfectly and completely. Ken told us,

> Many of us understand intellectually that we are loved by God, but in our day-to-day experience we continue to measure our value based on our success, our outward appearance, and how others view us. . . . Knowing we are deeply loved by our Creator frees us to pursue a life of significant, enduring achievement—a life that is not driven by fear and anxiety—but one that springs from a deep well of joy and gratitude for the love and grace God has shown us.

Living out of our core—our true identity before God—means embracing by faith the many wonderful promises the Bible makes about who we are in him. One of the apostle Paul's favorite theological phrases in the epistles is "in Christ." He repeatedly reminds believers of all the benefits we receive from simply being in the Lord, adopted as his child. Here are just a few of those blessings:

There is no condemnation for us (Romans 8:1).

We can never be separated from God's love (Romans 8:39).

We are a new creation (2 Corinthians 5:17).

We become God's children (Galatians 3:26; 4:4-7).

We have every spiritual blessing (Ephesians 1:3).

We have the forgiveness of sins (Ephesians 1:7).

We were also chosen (Ephesians 1:11).

We are for the praise of his glory (Ephesians 1:12).

We have been seated in the heavenly realms (Ephesians 2:6).

We've been given the incomparable riches of God's grace (Ephesians 2:7).

We have been brought near to him (Ephesians 2:13).

We are built together as a holy building (Ephesians 2:22).

We may approach God with freedom and confidence (Ephesians 3:12).

We are light (Ephesians 5:8).

We are holy and faithful (Colossians 1:2).

We are rooted and built up (Colossians 2:7).

We have been given the fullness of the deity (Colossians 2:9-10).

Our life is now hidden in Christ (Colossians 3:3).

Stop for a minute. Read through each of the above phrases out loud. All of these things—and much more—are given to you as free gifts simply because you belong to the Lord. You are "in Christ," in the family, a child of God with full rights and privileges.

Ken's mother grew up a very driven person in an impoverished post–World War II Japan. She excelled in school, earning a degree from the University of California at Berkeley and a master's degree at Columbia University in New York. She pushed each of her five children to excel and succeed. When Ken was a teenager, she recommitted her life to Christ, and it changed their home.

Ken said, "As she grew to understand God's gracious love for her, she was free from the need to impress others. My mother became more confident in God's provision for her. . . . She longed that we would follow the way of Christ and become people who faithfully reflect his character." When Ken began applying to universities to study, she gave him a sound piece of advice that reflects her identity. She told him he should not choose a school based on its prestige or the income-earning potential of its graduates. Instead, he should choose a school that would help him fulfill God's calling on his life.

Ken wisely surmised,

> The desire to achieve in academics, music, sports, ministry, or our careers is not intrinsically wrong. These desires can be noble, even birthed by God. But when Christ is at the center of our lives, our primary ambition becomes incomparably greater. We long to know Christ deeply and honor his call to transform our broken world. . . . As our ambition is redeemed, we are freed from the need to succeed in a worldly sense, and empowered to live with depth and integrity.[7]

What Do I Do When the Rug Is Pulled Out from Under Me?

Shane, a pastor we are coaching, leads a large church. A group of long-term members recently began attacking him because they want the church to return to the way it used to be under the founding pastor. Meanwhile, his wife wants to return to their home in Seattle. Shane is deeply committed to the church and to his sense of call. Yet, faced with the enormous stress of constantly trying to please everyone, his response has been withdrawal and isolation. Think back to a stressful time in your ministry. How did you respond?

From a physiological perspective, most of us react to conflict with a fight-or-flight response. Our brains are wired to self-protect in life-threatening situations. But most stressors are not that serious, and many of us overreact to normal stressors. Research suggests long-term stress causes high blood pressure, contributes to the formation of artery-clogging deposits, and creates brain changes often resulting in anxiety, depression, and addiction.

King David, who the Bible describes as a man after God's heart, models a vital spiritual habit for all leaders. In 1 Samuel 30, David and his band of warriors have just returned to Jezreel from the land of the Philistines. Approaching their camp in the valley city of Ziklag, they witness a horrific and gut-wrenching site. The city is destroyed by fire, and all of their wives and children have been taken captive. Waves of immediate, intense grief roll over the army, and they look for someone to blame. That someone is David: "David was greatly distressed because the men were talking of stoning him" (1 Samuel 30:6). This man of God, who developed a heart for the Lord not in the palace but in life's sheepfolds and battle-fields, responds in a telltale manner: "But David strengthened himself in the Lord his God" (1 Samuel 30:6 ESV).

David knew how to let God take care of his soul in the midst of enormous stress. For years he had been developing spiritual habits such as prayer, meditation, singing, silence, and releasing his burdens to God. When the bottom dropped out from his life, his spiritual depth sustained him. The Hebrew word for *strengthened* here can be translated "to prevail, harden, become strong, grow firm, and be resolute." Though David in-dulged in the flesh at other times, he made the right choice in this moment.

Today, we may be tempted as leaders to look for substitutes when our souls grow weary or when we come under intense attack like David. We may turn to surfing the internet, mindless entertainment, alcohol, drugs, pornography, an affair, or other meaningless pursuits in an attempt to divert our attention. A counselor friend of mine (Kevin) said, "We can never get enough of what we really don't need." That's a great definition of addiction. We try to meet our deepest needs with things that will never satisfy.

David knew that intense times required divine empowerment. For years, he had practiced getting in touch with God so that God could touch him. So when he faced this unforeseen challenge, he did not run to poor substitutes. He responded with his spiritual habits.

David built an abiding, reliable relationship with the living God be-cause he understood his identity as a child of God. He did not have to strive for God's approval or acceptance because he already knew he had it. That knowledge freed him to cultivate his intimate relationship with the Lover of his soul. The Psalms often reflect this mindset. David knew he could freely express to the Lord his happiness, pleasure, pain, disappointment, anger, loneliness, frustration, and praise. He understood the Lord as his Shepherd and believed "I shall not want" (Psalm 23:1 ESV). He knew how to get on his face and express love to God—and he also knew how to let the Lord fill him with his love.

Existentialist philosopher and theologian Paul Tillich tells us, "We must accept the fact that we are accepted."[8] This acceptance is key in letting God take care of us. And spiritual guide Henri Nouwen wrote, "The greatest temptations are not money, sex, and power, but self-rejection—because self-rejection contradicts the sacred voice that calls us the beloved."[9]

Letting God take care of our soul starts with acknowledging the gift of grace that we are accepted and beloved. Not that we *could* be accepted, not that we *will* be accepted, but that we *are* accepted. We can never be more loved by God than we are at this moment. It is essential to embrace that reality for the river of God to flow most mightily through our lives. The late Tim Keller said, "To be loved but not known is comforting but superficial. To be known and not loved is our greatest fear. But to be fully known and truly loved is, well, a lot like being loved by God. It is what we need more than anything. It liberates us from pretense, humbles us out of our self-righteousness, and fortifies us for any difficulty life can throw at us."[10] Our friend Ken Shigematsu writes,

> In my experience, I've found that my awareness of grace—of a love that I can't earn and don't deserve—has deepened as I have embraced spiritual practices that create space for God in my life. These life-giving habits leave me feeling less restless and more comfortable in my own skin. I'm stirred to contribute out of deep gratitude for the grace I have been given rather than out of my need to validate myself. As the Holy Spirit works in me through these habits, I am freed to live from approval, instead of for approval.[11]

We hope the concept of spiritual disciplines or habits doesn't conjure up images of a legalistic schoolmaster waiting to punish you if you did not complete your homework. Instead, view them as practices you partake in to spend time with someone you love. If you consistently neglect to spend time with your spouse and children, you grow distant from them and the relationship suffers. Richard Foster accurately writes, "The disciplines allow us to place ourselves before God so he can transform us."[12] It is in his presence, when we are yielded and still, where true change takes place.

The late professor Howard Hendricks at Dallas Theological Seminary performed a study years ago of more than one hundred people in ministry who had engaged in a sexual extramarital affair. The purpose of the study was to discover any common denominators in their lives that led to the sinful behavior. Without exception, every minister had stopped having a daily devotional time with the Lord for the purpose of their soul connecting with God.[13]

Spiritual disciplines like Bible meditation, study and memorization, sabbath and solitude, journaling and learning, prayer as communion, service, stewardship, worship, fasting, and fellowship drive us to the spiritual gas station so that the Holy Spirit can renew and refill us. God created us to need him, and he did not intend for us to live the Christian life nor to serve him out of any other strength and empowerment than his own.

The apostle Paul summarized Christianity in this simple statement: "God is faithful, who has called you into fellowship with his Son, Jesus Christ our Lord" (1 Corinthians 1:9). Paul uses the word *koinōnia* here, which means "fellowship, association, community, communion, joint participation," and even "intercourse."

And Jesus, in his high priestly prayer the night of his arrest, described eternal life in simple terms: "Now this is eternal life: that they know you, the only true God, and Jesus Christ, whom you have sent" (John 17:3). The word "know" here is *ginōskō*, meaning "to learn to know, come to know, get a knowledge of, perceive, feel." In other words, this kind of knowledge is experiential, intensely personal, and emotional.

When Jesus and Paul explained the Christian life, they used simple words to reflect an intimate, ongoing understanding. This involves relationship as much as it involves intellectual knowledge. A preacher once challenged students, "More important than As in the classroom is your intimacy with God in your dorm room." That does not belittle intellectual achievement nor does it embrace emotionalism. But it does remind us that the basic element of the Christian life is a personal friendship with Jesus Christ.

Where Do I Find My Safe Times, Safe Places, and Safe People?

Years ago, I (Kevin) heard a sermon on Mark 6 by Walt Gerber that has stuck with me to this day. In the midst of pressures and demands, Jesus modeled how to stay healthy in ministry when he instructed his disciples, "Come away by yourselves to a secluded place and rest a little while" (Mark 6:31 NASB). After spending time with the crowds, Jesus often retreated to the hills to be alone. He knew he needed a change of place and perspective as well as physical rest. He also needed safe people. He spent time with Mary, Martha, and Lazarus, and he enjoyed a deep relationship with his three closest disciples. Walt Gerber concluded that Jesus needed safe times, safe places, and safe people. We've adopted that as a key phrase in our work at LFM. Leaders, like Jesus, need those safe times, safe places, and safe people.

The first person you must care for is yourself. To some Christians, this sounds anti-gospel. Their understanding of denying self and following Jesus is that we cannot consider ourselves at all. However, Jesus provided a different understanding. After instructing people to love God supremely, he gave what he considered the second greatest commandment: "You shall love your neighbor as yourself" (Mark 12:31 NKJV). He then added a qualifier: "There is no other commandment greater than these."

Implied within Jesus' second command is a subtle but necessary element: you must love yourself. Not in an obsessive, idolatrous, selfish way. But you are to value yourself as a child of God, a masterpiece in his creation. This kind of love includes stewarding or taking care of yourself, otherwise you will not be able to care for others. Stewardship means keeping yourself fresh for the longer run of pastoral ministry. There are times to give and to retreat. There are times to extend yourself greatly. And there are times to refuel. Jesus modeled this rhythm in his ministry.

In the early 1990s, I (Kevin) was doing a series of lectures at a Baptist seminary near San Francisco. I was teaching there in the mornings and at a large church in San Francisco in the evenings. The pastor then asked me to meet with people all afternoon. I told him I couldn't do that. I needed time to refresh. He looked at me sternly and said, "Young man, when your father preached here, he was available to all who had need at any time of the day."

I returned his look and simply said, "And when he came home, he wasn't available to our family." The pastor turned away in a huff.

The attentive leader must learn the vital practice of self-stewardship, caring for oneself. Benefits of such care include being able to operate effectively within your own margin—and being a non-anxious leader in your ministry and community. The book *Resilient Ministry* describes self-stewardship as "a holistic concept that explores how five aspects of one's life are interwoven: the emotional, spiritual, social, intellectual, and physical."[14]

Different personalities have varying capacities for what energizes or drains them. For an introvert, hours alone in the woods or in their home reading a book may be incredibly filling. But for an extrovert, that may seem like punishment. Knowing yourself and your capacity for what fills you and saps you is so important. Today, numerous helpful resources abound to assist in our own self-understanding. Here are just a few that you may find beneficial: the Myers-Briggs Type Indicator (MBTI), the DISC profile, the Enneagram, and the Clifton Strengths Analysis. Understanding ourselves is key to practicing healthy self-stewardship.

Let's revisit Jesus' model.

Safe Times

Pastor Wayne Cordeiro pastored one of the fastest growing churches in the United States. At one point he hit the wall, experiencing an in-his-face burnout and depression that rocked his world. In his book *Leading on Empty*, he writes, "We are never more vulnerable to depression from burnout than when we are totally fatigued and overtired. . . . Schedule rests before your calendar fills up. Rest is not an afterthought; it has to be a primary responsibility. It brings a rhythm back to life and a cadence that makes life sustainable."[15]

Ken Shigematsu also found the weekly rhythm of practicing a sabbath rest is essential to his own well-being personally and professionally:

> A foundational part of my rule is keeping a twenty-four-hour Sabbath once a week. So when my Sabbath "bell" rings, I unplug, stop working, and don't do anything related to my work. The Sabbath enables me to spend time with family and not feel guilty that I am not working, and allows me to work when it is time to work without feeling guilty that I am not with my family. In a very practical way, a rule sets life-giving limits.[16]

Safe Places

I (Kevin) visited Chuck Swindoll's office one time. I will never forget the sign on his desk that said, "You can't beat fun!" Far too few pastors know how to have fun. It's okay to take care of yourself by making time to do what you enjoy. Don't always gear your life toward what you're doing for others. Find a place where you can relax, unwind, and unleash. What's more, healthy people learn how to have several different gears. You can't live in the highest and fastest gear all the time. Safe places help you unwind, shift to a lower gear, and take yourself less seriously. They are places to come out of the public light, let your hair down, and authentically be yourself before the Lord and the people who love you the most. Your safe place may be the mountains, the beach, a lake house, a retreat center, or a vacation home. Wherever it is, it helps you to unwind, relax, and quiet your spirit.

Safe People

The Lord created us for community—for relationships. God models this perfectly in what theologians call the Trinity: the Father, Son, and Spirit living in perfect union. The creation account says, "In the beginning, God [Elohim] created the heavens and the earth" (Genesis 1:1 ESV). This name of God, Elohim, signifies the plurality of God's nature. Together, the Trinity worked to create. If the first recorded image of deity in the Scriptures speaks of God's three-in-one community, is that not a model for how much his people need each other? Sadly, however, many people in ministry—particularly pastors—move toward isolation as the years progress.

Do you have a few people in your life you feel truly safe with? Safe enough to talk about your darkest moments? Safe enough to talk about your doubts and struggles? Safe enough to talk about your family stress? The "role" of pastor often creates a barrier to finding safe people. Think about the number of high-profile pastors who have fallen in recent years. Virtually none of them had safe people in their lives, and that's very sad to us.

When I (Kevin) was a student at University of North Carolina Chapel Hill, I started a Bible study through InterVarsity Christian Fellowship. Four of us ended up rooming together. We shared great times and hard times our last couple of years in college. Dave Grigg had a debilitating bone disease. He broke fifty-two bones by the time he graduated. David Page had to quit the football team after he found out that he had one kidney. Tom Vermillion and I rounded out the group. Tom and I butted heads over groceries and girlfriends, and we developed a strong bond as a result. Through it all, the four of us learned to listen to each other deeply and share our struggles very openly. During our senior year, we vowed a lifelong friendship. We now have a group chat called "Boys for Life" where we seek each other's counsel. When I fall, they pick me up. When I rejoice, they stand beside me. We don't make a major decision in life without checking in with each other first. I am blessed to have these men love me, hold me accountable, and celebrate life with. There's nothing we don't share with each other.

Sometimes pastors and leaders are blessed to have true, deep friendships within their churches and ministries. Many times, however, we find that pastors are wise to develop lasting friendships with others outside of their congregations. These relationships can help pastors with transparency, last longer than their tenure at one church, and be a valuable resource during times of conflict within one's ministry.

LFM is a catalyst for mentoring healthy leaders who sustain thriving ministries. We are intentionally building an international community devoted to "whole-life" mentoring. We don't just help people navigate leadership issues; we are attentive to the whole life of the leader—soul, family, and personal well-being. We help launch and sustain mentoring communities where pastors and spiritual leaders can connect with other like-minded men and women.

Who Are My friends on the Journey?

Jesus mentored twelve men while on this earth. His influence in their lives created a ripple effect that continues two thousand years later. The apostle Paul challenged Timothy to a lifestyle of pouring his life into others, who would then pour *their* lives into others (2 Timothy 2:2). My (Kevin's) father, Leighton Ford, has invested decades of his life in the lives of younger leaders. When he was fifty years old, he sensed the Lord leading him to leave the bright lights of one of the world's leading evangelistic organizations and to begin quietly raising up a younger generation to be led more by Jesus, lead more like Jesus, and lead more to Jesus. In the years since, he has started the Arrow Leadership Program and LFM to help leaders find clarity, community, and confidence for greater kingdom impact.

At the Arrow Leadership Program, Dad made a life-changing discovery. Men and women sat through lectures from great leaders like Colin Powell and Max De Pree. They learned best practices from great pastors. But the real work happened in between sessions, when one of the program attendees asked my dad to go for a walk. Those fifteen-minute walks were often far more meaningful than a week of intense learning. So, in the late 1990s, Dad shifted his focus from programs to people. He decided to become "a friend on the journey," which is his personal mission statement.

Ken Shigematsu has experienced this same kind of spiritual mentoring. When we asked him to tell us about his relationship with Leighton, he said, "For more than two decades, he has been present for me during every crucial turning point of my life, along with many everyday moments. He has listened to my life in a way that has given me the courage to grow more transparent with my temptations and struggles and more honest about my hopes and fears."

Their relationship began through Leighton's intentionality. He asked Ken, a seminary student at the time, to drive him across Massachusetts to the home of a board member. Ken assured the older man that he could sleep during the drive if he wanted. The senior leader crossed his legs and said, "I don't think I'll sleep . . . tell me your life story." That began a relationship spanning over two decades. Ken says Leighton is an "attentive friend on my journey."

Ken recently recounted his early experience at Tenth Church:

> When I first came to Tenth Church in Vancouver, BC in the late 90s, the challenge of pastoring a historic church whose attendance had dwindled from over one thousand to one hundred intimidated me. Tenth had burned through twenty pastors in twenty years. In my first week, the church secretary walked into my office and announced, "If the ship sinks now, everyone will blame you because you were the last captain at the helm." She was trying to motivate me to work harder, but I simply ended up feeling depressed!
>
> A few weeks later, Leighton and I were sitting in my car outside Tenth. I really needed his encouragement, but was too ashamed to ask. I struggled to ask for some counsel or guidance. He was quiet for a minute. He then turned to me and said, "Remember that God is an artist. He will not lead you to copy anyone else. Seek God for his unique vision for this place."
>
> So, I set aside my own goals and began seeking the Lord in prayer. I invited others to do the same. One day, I sensed God saying, "If you will bless those who cannot repay you, I will bless you." A few weeks later, a homeless man died outside our church building on a cold winter's night. It was tragic. But that led us to start a meal and

shelter ministry for the homeless. The Holy Spirit began drawing people of all walks of life to Christ. We met a prostitute who was trying to overcome her drug addictions. We asked her why she came to Tenth and her reply blew us away. She said her pimp recommended the church to her![17]

In our social media culture of instant connection, many people sadly do not get to enjoy deep and meaningful connections with others. A healthy habit to adopt for your own self-care is to seek out older, wiser, and more mature people who can invest deeply in your life. We all need help along life's journey, so we would be wise to link arms with a few people who have gone before us. MaryKate Morse, who is part of the LFM network, says, "We are not meant to be alone. Jesus was not alone, so neither should we expect to do ministry without friendship and supportive mentors."[18]

I (Jim) have talked weekly with a dear friend in ministry, Peter Barnes, for nearly forty years now. That relationship has been absolutely essential for my sustained resilience. What's more, both of us have been deeply shaped by Leighton Ford over the years in much the same way as Ken Shigematsu described.

All these earthly friendships pave the way for understanding God as our friend—which is not natural to many people. Both Abraham and Moses were referred to as God's friends. Jesus told the disciples, "No longer do I call you servants . . . but I have called you friends" (John 15:15 NKJV). Friendship involves closeness, shared interests, and helping one another.

Life is a lonely place without friends. Unfortunately, some spiritual leaders attempt to be lone rangers and do not allow other people into their lives. We are wise to remember the example of Jesus and the apostle Paul, who chose to bring people close to them, did life and ministry with numerous associates, and experienced the ups and downs of life not as solitary figures but together with others.[19] We also see great value in professional people speaking into our lives on a more short-term, need-focused basis. Spiritual directors, life coaches, counselors, and therapists can bring timely help in refocusing, reframing, and redirecting our lives mentally, emotionally, spiritually, relationally, and professionally. I (Kevin) meet regularly with Jim Morgan, a wise business leader who has become a mentor. I've seen a handful of counselors in my lifetime. I still go to Dad for family advice. There is no shame in partnering with these kinds of people. Some pastors would greatly benefit from learning from mental health care professionals, who serve a legitimate need in our self-stewardship. They can help us to minister well and not burn out.

Ken told us that "the individuals or groups of people we choose to expose ourselves to can shape us in significant and often unanticipated ways. . . . If you're not currently in a spiritual friendship that inspires you toward Christ and his call on your life, pray about initiating a connection with someone who might become a friend on the journey."

In this chapter we've explored the inner life of the leader, which provides the foundation for us to lead others from a healthy core. As we attempt to lead others in a world we've never known, with no road map to follow, we at least know the starting point. Healthy, holistic leadership is rooted in our identity in Christ. Jesus declared that he is the abiding and sustaining source for serving and leading others: "I am the vine; you are the branches. If you remain in me and I in you, you will bear much fruit; apart from me you can do nothing" (John 15:5). Next, we will look at how to take that identity and shepherd others as a non-anxious leader who is a vessel or conduit of love, joy, peace, patience, kindness, goodness, faithfulness, gentleness, and self-control (Galatians 5:22-23).

Questions for Reflection and Discussion

- How would you answer the question, Who am I? In what ways does your role as a leader inform the answer to this question?
- Moments of transition or stress elicit either a fight-or-flight response within a leader. Which of these two responses is more natural for you?

- For what reasons are you tempted to believe that you are unacceptable? Have you ever felt like you let God down in your ministry?
- Embracing his acceptance by God, Ken Shigematsu wrote, "I am free to live from approval, instead of for approval." What would your leadership look like if it was based on a statement like this?
- How do you reconcile the call of Jesus to deny yourself with the importance of stewarding yourself?
- Take a personal inventory of three areas: spiritual vitality, family health, and personal wellness. Rate your current state on a scale from 1–10. Ask someone close to you to rate you on those same three areas. Have a conversation with that person based on your answers. What are some self-care practices you know you need to begin?
- Who is investing deeply in you? If you struggle to name someone, ask God to bring someone to mind who you might ask. Are there godly people who knew you before your call to ministry? Are there godly people on the fringes of your life now?

3

How Do I Manage Anxiety?

"Talking him off the ledge" is how Dr. Jim Osterhaus described one of his first coaching sessions with Alan. Jim, a senior leadership coach for LFM, has a wealth of wisdom for navigating interpersonal issues in life and ministry.

After a successful early career in business, Alan Clayton felt called to ministry and went to seminary. In midlife, he started a church in his living room with a handful of people. His experience in business proved valuable in helping him to understand the organizational side of a church and how to manage growth. In time, the church grew to many thousands and a staff numbering in the dozens.

Almost twenty years ago, when Osterhaus began coaching Alan, his church of twenty-five hundred members was meeting in a high school.[1] They needed more space, and the congregation prepared to take a vote to consider their options: purchase property to begin building a new space or stay in the school. The upcoming vote stressed Alan. He thought if they voted no on moving forward, he needed to immediately resign.

Jim challenged him, "I didn't know the vote was about you. I thought you were voting to see if now is the time to go ahead with the church buying property. That's a very different matter."

Alan sat in silence for a moment, letting Jim's words sink in. Jim knew at once that Alan got the message. The vote was not about Alan's competence as the church's leader but whether God wanted them, at that specific time, to take on the responsibility of their own building.

Their conversation served as a pivotal moment for this leader. As Jim told us, "I wasn't talking him off the ledge so much as reframing the situation so he could understand what was actually happening in the church's decision. The reframing helped him to see the crucial difference between a decision for the organization versus him as a person or leader."

Even in a somewhat predictable world, pastors routinely face an enormous amount of anxiety. But leading a congregation in a world we've never known increases that anxiety exponentially. So if the first step is becoming an attentive person, the second step is learning to manage anxiety. Some are able to navigate the stressors in life and ministry without being destroyed by them. Others, sadly, feel habitually warped and wounded by these troubles and irritants.

In this chapter, we focus on the anxiety pastors feel when faced with criticism and conflict. Then we examine how well-defined leaders can stay attentive to God and important realities to help them navigate these pressures without losing themselves. A crucial bonus is that when a pastor grows in self-definition, the congregation also grows in understanding itself.

What Part Do I Play in the System?

Churches and parachurch ministries, like all organizations, are systems. The study of human systems, called systems theory or family systems theory, reveals how groups of people take on predictable patterns over time. These patterns often reflect an attempt to regulate anxiety, typically to preserve the status quo. A conflict begins, resulting in two or three people experiencing discomfort. Very quickly, the anxiety becomes infectious, and discomfort spreads throughout the system. Less mature, or more fragile, members of the group may get caught up in the organization's emotional problems, which then creates more anxiety.

Osterhaus writes, "Emotional reactivity passes like a hot potato between individuals. When one anxious individual succeeds in exciting a second, the first is often relieved. In humans, this phenomenon results in nothing ever getting resolved. The problem that triggered the emotions is never addressed; emotions are merely generated and then circuited and re-circuited through the system."[2]

Disagreements are inevitable among groups of people. The very nature of leadership, which involves moving people toward goals and embracing change, opens the door to some level of conflict. As organizations experience anxiety, one automatic emotional response is triangulation.

I (Kevin) was consulting with a church in the Midwest. The church leadership brought me in to facilitate a visioning process, as the staff lacked clarity of direction and focus. What I discovered, however, was not a vision problem. Rather, the staff felt anxiety about their performance. They tended to hunker down and do their jobs with little teamwork. After a few interviews and focus groups, the staff started to trust me. They confided that the real problem was the senior pastor, Tom. According to them, Tom was a real jerk with an awful temper and never interacted with his colleagues. At least, that's what they told me. So I asked them to give specific examples of Tom's temper. I always received the same surprising response: blank stares. Nobody could give one example of Tom losing his temper or being a jerk. I was very confused.

I sat down with Kara, the executive director, and asked about her passions and experience. She glowed as she told me how much she loved her job. When I asked her to elaborate, she explained she was the fixer on staff. If anyone had a problem with anything or anyone, her door was always open.

Then the light bulb went off for me. She was unintentionally communicating to the staff, "If you have a problem, come to me and don't go to Tom." She never actually said those words, but that's how it was interpreted. They assumed Tom had a terrible temper.

When I spoke with Tom, he wondered why nobody ever knocked on his door. Sure, he could have been more present for the staff. But the perpetuated narrative was that Tom was a villain. And that absolved the system from dealing with the real underlying issues.

Systems create scapegoats to preserve their status quo—even if the status quo is dysfunctional. People almost always choose the known dysfunctional option over the unknown healthy one. Who can they blame for what's going on? When we coach a pastor or consult with a leadership team, we rarely take the "identified problem" as the actual problem. The actual problem is typically rooted within the system.

But what if, like Tom, the senior leader is the identified problem? That's where navigating the structure gets tricky. It is necessary to address this issue because the ripples of change that flow through the system should be positive, not detrimental.

In conflicted systems, three roles often arise: the victim, the persecutor, and the rescuer. Stephen Karpman introduced this concept, known as the Karpman Triangle, in the 1960s. The victim disagrees with a decision, a course of action, or something done to them or someone else. They feel helpless, though they are actually not as vulnerable as they feel. The persecutor pressures, coerces, or initiates action that the victim dislikes. The rescuer intervenes to either ease the tension or help the victim. Quickly, a codependent relationship arises between the victim and the rescuer, with the rescuer taking care of the victim's needs. The rescuer keeps the victim in a dependent state by leaning into their sense of victimhood. In the example above, the rescuer (Kara) unintentionally created the persecutor and victim roles. This drama triangle easily surfaces in a multitude of conflicts. If the people involved do not respond in a healthy manner, triangles can produce a variety of negative results:

A person brought into the triangle feels the need to suddenly fix things or be a peacemaker instead of solving the real problem.

People think worse of the persecutor being blamed.

The victim forms an identity around their supposed victimhood.

Everyone involved may experience much unhealthy stress.

They then may withdraw themselves from the individuals or even the group.[3]

In the example above, Kara came from a dysfunctional family system. During her early years, she witnessed a lot of conflict and emotional abuse between her parents. They divorced when she was a teen, and they continually used her as a pawn in their problems. Kara became the peacemaker in her parents' relationship. She carried that pattern over into other organizations—her college sorority, her first job at a bank, and eventually her role as the church's executive director. Of course, it would be easy to scapegoat Kara instead of Tom. The reality is that the church's dysfunctional system needed Kara to perpetuate the same system that existed under the church's previous leadership. The Old Testament has multiple passages that refer to the "sins of the father." This is an understanding of the nature of human systems from an Old Testament perspective.

In ministry strife, victims often like to draw the leader into the conflict. The victim wants the leader to sympathize with her, validate her victimhood, and become a rescuer. Many times, however, this action does not help in the long run and even adds to the problem.

A further issue in family systems that requires attentiveness to God is overfunctioning and underfunctioning. When the system is anxious, it finds someone to overfunction and solve problems. Many times, that is the pastor. This dynamic often appeals to the pastor's yearning to be needed—a tendency driven by the desire to have something done correctly and the pastor's belief that they are the only one capable. When a pastor overfunctions, it sends a signal that the rest of us do not have to contribute. But when a pastor starts down that road and misses the chance to equip others for all kinds of ministry, the congregation never learns to attend to God's call.

I (Jim) grew up trying to resolve anxiety in my family of origin. That tendency carried right over into my pastoral life. I still remember the conversation during the search process for my first position. I asked two members of the team, "What made the former senior pastor so successful?" They replied, "The same thing that makes any business executive successful. He is not afraid to sacrifice his family for the sake of the church. Can you do the same thing?" I was stunned and said I didn't even intend to try. But before long, I was doing it. My tendency to overwork exhausted me. Yet, I was the one who created my problems. The system then applauded me for overworking. By the time I left my position, I had unintentionally created problems for the next pastor, who never intended to work as hard as I did.

Some questions we must attend to are: How will I respond to the system's anxiety? Will I be involved in triangulation? Will I overfunction? And will I underfunction in many other areas—including my home, health, and emotions?

How Do I Differentiate Myself from My Role?

What if the senior leader is the problem?

When my (Kevin's) children were young, they routinely got mad at me for not allowing them to eat ice cream as often as they wanted. Caroline and I would find empty bowls of ice cream under their beds and in drawers. They didn't like it when I restrained their sweet tooth. As they grew older, we had to set screen time limits and manage curfew. I was called "the worst dad ever" many times. I eventually realized they were mad at my role, not at me. Yes, I thought they were mad at me (and so did they). But in reality, they were reacting to the role of protector I played in the moment. To this day, that's a very difficult distinction for me to manage. As they grew, we wanted them to own their responsibilities for their lives. I have to be reminded of Jesus' words: "Whoever wants to be my disciple must deny themselves and take up their cross daily and follow me" (Luke 9:23).

Sometimes our personhood is not so easily differentiated from our role. For example, we are fathers. That's a part of who we are. It's a role we play. But it's not the primary thing that defines us. When our children react to our roles, they aren't reacting to the primary thing that defines us—that we are children of the King of kings. Others' reactions are often about the roles we play, even when they are roles we didn't choose.

The same pattern occurs in many areas of society. A driver commits a traffic violation and receives a ticket from a police officer. Though the officer may have done nothing wrong and acts with integrity and respect, the offender may quickly assume the role of victim and be mad that the officer enforced the law. The driver is really not mad at the officer as a person. In a different context, they might play ball, enjoy a meal, or attend a concert together. But in this situation, the driver sees the officer through her role as a law enforcer.

You may receive a sweater for Christmas you don't like. When you return it to the department store, the clerk says that because you don't have a receipt, she can only give you $4.97 store credit, even though the original price was $59.99. The absurdity of the small injustice infuriates you, and you may get angry at the clerk. Though she may be a wonderful person, a loving mother, and a fun friend, you are not responding to her as a person. You are reacting to her role as an enforcer of the company's return policy. Meanwhile, she had absolutely nothing to do with creating the policy. If left to her own judgment, she might just give you the full refund.

In my (Jim's) years as a pastor, I initiated significant changes on many occasions. In one instance, I was accused through many emails of "ruining the church." The changes I made were in hopes of freeing the church from older structures that inhibited our mission. But in the minds of angry emailers, this change brought chaos and disruption. My initial instinct was to relent and say, "Just kidding." On the Enneagram I am a seven, meaning I love fun and try hard to avoid pain. Those emails hurt me. Later, Jim Osterhaus would teach me the art of differentiating. He reminded me that critics aimed their comments at the pastor but not really at me individually. I looked again—the emails were addressed to me, but I had conflated my person and role. Slowly, I began to separate the two identities, a process I continue maturing into even now.

How Do I Respond to Unresolved Issues in Self and Others?

To better understand our reactions within a system, we need to unpack two important psychological terms: projection and transference. Projection occurs when people project their unresolved issues onto leaders, or when leaders project their denied issues onto followers.

Projection is a defense mechanism against unresolved issues. A defense mechanism is "a group of mental processes that enables the mind to reach compromise solutions to conflicts that it is unable to resolve. The process is usually unconscious, and the compromise generally involves concealing from oneself internal drives or feelings that threaten to lower self-esteem or provoke anxiety."[4]

This easily occurs among people who live with a "root of rejection." In past relationships, these people experienced a significant rejection. Perhaps their parent abandoned them or sexually abused them, their child rebelled and ran away, or their spouse had an affair and divorced them. If these authentic wounds do not heal properly, they may gradually develop a habitual negative reaction to others. They feel rejected when no one is actually rejecting them. Their brain patterns expect rejection, and they will be convinced of exclusion and rebuff when they are not realities.

We heard of one church member who experienced significant depression triggered by a change in his work schedule that regularly kept him away from his family and friends for days at a time. In his dark state, he felt extremely isolated and began to feel that no one liked him. One Sunday when he attended church, he left in a bad mental state. He told the pastor the next week, "When I went to church, I saw everyone staring at me. No one wanted me there. No one in that church likes me anymore." In reality there was no truth to this, but he believed it to be true. To make matters worse, he became fixated on what he believed to be rejection from the pastor. Eventually, the man had an affair and left the church's fellowship, convinced they had treated him wrongly. In spite of numerous attempts by the pastor and church leadership team to reach out to him, he projected his feelings of rejection onto them.

Projection is "a form of defense in which unwanted feelings are displaced onto another person, where they then appear as a threat from the external world."[5] Simply put, projection involves unresolved issues within myself. What I hate about myself, I put on other people.

Projection's twin sister is transference, which involves my unmet needs from others—my unresolved relational issues. Transference says, "What I needed from an authority figure and never got, I look for in others."

Transference occurs when a wounded person expects the leader to meet their unmet needs. If a woman grew up not feeling accepted by her mother, she goes through life thinking, "Nobody accepts me." When she joins a church, she subconsciously wants the pastor—the leader—to meet her unmet needs of feeling loved and accepted. When the pastor cannot meet this unrealistic expectation, the woman incorrectly thinks, "The pastor does not accept me." In some cases, this wounded person can cause a lot of trouble for the pastor—all in her attempt to punish the leader for not being able to meet her inner needs.

When a leader takes the bait, the dysfunction continues. The pastor can choose to give in to this unhealthy cycle, thereby becoming a rescuer in the triangle. Though it may make the pastor temporarily feel like a hero by stroking their ego, it creates more dysfunction.

In some instances, the pastor's role carries a subtle seduction. Perhaps a church member did not receive strength and affirmation from a parent, teacher, or coach. Throughout their life, they look for an authority figure to provide that affirmation. Often, they expect to receive it from a spouse. But when the spouse isn't able to meet their unmet needs, they may look to a pastor or a therapist instead. This sometimes happens in counseling situations when a vulnerable counselee looks to the counselor to provide emotional stability, which can lead to inappropriate sexual involvement. When pastors start leaning into that allurement, they become vulnerable. Boundary lines become blurred, and they may develop a messiah complex that leads them to take advantage of toxic situations. They start seeing themselves as larger than life.

We remember a pastor who had multiple affairs. Women became romantically interested in him, not because he was charming but because they were trying to fulfill their own unmet needs. They looked to the pastor to meet them. After he left the ministry, he was never sought out by women. Pastors must take care to distinguish between their individual identity versus the pastoral role.

No person can meet or satisfy all of our unmet needs. Instead, our needs are satisfied through right relationship with God as well as our families and communities. Our complex spirits need interaction with God's creation for our inner fulfillment. Crucial in this search for satisfaction is an existence rooted in our identity in Christ.

Every desire in our lives will not be fully met in this life. We will experience disappointments in relationships and longings that seem unmet. It's unrealistic to expect complete healing and redemption in every part of life on this side of eternity. C. S. Lewis famously said, "If I find in myself a desire which no experience in this world can satisfy, the most probable explanation is that I was made for another world. If none of my earthly pleasures satisfy it, that does not prove that the universe is a fraud. Probably earthly pleasures were never meant to satisfy it, but only to arouse it, to suggest the real thing."[6] In our attempts to help people, we are wise to not expect churches and pastors to meet unmeetable needs; rather, we expect them to promote general health and help people flourish individually and in community. Understanding family systems and issues of differentiation, projection, and transference allows the pastor to be more attentive to what God is doing in their ministry.

Am I Attentive in Conflict?

Conflict cannot be avoided. Osterhaus told us, "Conflict is neither a personal failure nor a distraction from your calling as a leader. Conflict is your calling! Conflict cannot be avoided. It's inherent in life itself! If we used just a small portion of the time we waste in avoiding conflict, to learn the skills we need to resolve conflict in our self and with others, the world would be a different place!"[7]

Two types of conflict exist: mission-focused conflict, which we call the blue zone, and person-centered conflict, which we call the red zone. Blue zone issues do not become personal or personality driven. Instead, they focus on issues facing the church.

Red zone issues, however, involve coping mechanisms aimed at avoiding anxiety rather than creating solutions. Here are some distinctions drawn from Osterhaus about these two types of zones:

Table 3.1. Two types of conflict

Red zone	**Blue zone**
This conflict is personal. It's about me! Emotions rule without being acknowledged. I must protect myself because I'm feeling weak. I deny my emotions and therefore project onto others. The situation escalates. **Behaviors:** I disengage. I become easily annoyed. I'm resentful. I procrastinate. I attack others personally. I use alcohol as medication. I avoid people and situations.	This conflict is professional. It's about the business. The mission of the organization rules. I must protect the team and the business. Emotions are understood and acknowledged in myself. The situation is reframed into a more useful construct. **Behaviors:** I am thoughtful. I am reflective. I listen deeply for what the underlying issue might be. I do not see negative intent in the other person.

In the blue zone, the issue is outside the self. Perhaps a congregation is renovating their sanctuary and trying to decide whether they will replace the seating with pews, free-standing chairs, or theater seating. Though opinions and the attached emotions may be strong, the decision-makers keep the conflict objectively focused on pews, chairs, and seats and the accompanying benefits or drawbacks. To operate in the blue zone, leaders must have a common set of values, a shared mission, and clarity of focus. But if they debate seating without these three things, they default to personal preferences and end up back in the red zone. Thus, any issue can become a red zone issue—or remain in the blue zone. Again, attentiveness is required to reframe an issue into the appropriate zone.

Years ago, I (Kevin) was mentoring a young pastor, Mark, at a church in the Bay Area of San Francisco. He told me that he was constantly battling with Tommy, his older associate pastor. The church was growing and had a new strategic focus to create satellite campuses in underserved areas. After a lengthy visioning process, the board was all in favor. The new direction fit the church's mission and vision. But Tommy was not on board. He actively undermined any attempt to move in the new direction with a lot of passive-aggressive behavior in the form of parking lot conversations, subversive emails, and unhealthy alliances.

As Mark was new and had focused his efforts on winning over the board and getting to know the congregation, he hadn't spent much time with Tommy. I encouraged Mark to sit down with Tommy once a week and spend time together, with no agenda, discussing anything but the one topic that was off limits: satellite campuses. Over time as trust grew between them, Tommy shared about his upbringing in Portland. His dad was an alcoholic and left the family when Tommy was twelve. As Mark and I processed this information together, we realized that Tommy's red zone issue was related to abandonment. Meanwhile, Mark was a people pleaser. He longed for Tommy's acceptance.

I encouraged Mark to have a conversation with Tommy. I asked him to be open and honest about his own unreasonable need for Tommy's acceptance. When they had this conversation, Mark was able to explain that the church needed to move forward with their mission. He modeled a shift from the red zone to the blue zone. Progress took a few months. They continued the monthly conversations with no agenda. Eventually, Tommy realized that he was projecting his own abandonment issues onto Mark. The satellite campus strategy had triggered some of his own trauma, leading him to feel that the board and the church were going to abandon him, even though he knew it wasn't logical.

Tommy started seeing a therapist who specialized in eye movement desensitization and reprocessing (EMDR) therapy, which is designed to alleviate the stress of past trauma. Within months, Tommy was a different person. Today, he heads the expansion strategy for that church. Attentiveness is key to identifying what is beneath our conflicts.

If the discussion becomes a red zone issue, the issue at hand morphs into conflict between persons or groups of people. In the red zone, people operate out of their innate drive to preserve or protect one of four core issues:

Survival: "I must take care of myself. The world is full of peril, so I must enjoy the moment."

Acceptance: "I will do anything to be loved and accepted by others. I am a people pleaser."

Control: "The world is a threatening place, and the only way I can feel safe is if I can control every situation and the people around me."

Competence: "I am loved only on the basis of my performance. My performance is never good enough, so I never feel worthy of being loved."[8]

These four underlying felt needs can be driving forces in unhealthy conflict. They become trigger points by which other people can push our buttons. Osterhaus explains,

> Red Zone issues go back to childhood issues, and those you need to resolve on your own. What's important for you to realize is how these issues get pulled into everyday conflicts and totally muck up the process of resolution. You see this everywhere—in political discourse, between husbands and wives, in board rooms, in shops.

> Sufficient to say, if I'm in conflict, and the conflict does not resolve, my Red Zone issue has been triggered as well as with the person with whom I'm conflicted.[9]

Jim Osterhaus and I (Kevin) have been friends since 1987 and have worked together as colleagues for most of that time. In many ways, he is a brother to me. My red zone issue is competence. As the nephew of Billy Graham and son of Leighton Ford, I grew up around very competent people. I've always struggled with my own sense of competence, and I project that onto others. Osterhaus's red zone issue is acceptance. In the early days of launching our consulting firm, I asked him to create an agenda for a client consultation. Osterhaus's background was in listening to people and taking notes—not creating professional-looking documents. When he emailed the agenda to me, I saw the formatting was off with multiple typos. I felt the heat rising in me. *How in the world could we send* this *to the client?* I fumed. *We will look incredibly incompetent.*

I stormed into his office and let him have it. It took a nanosecond for him to give it right back to me. We were in a heated argument and both in the red zone. Was my reaction to the typos proportionate? No way. My competence issue had been triggered. Likewise, Osterhaus's reaction had nothing to do with the agenda. He felt unloved and rejected when I got in his face. His acceptance issue had been triggered.

This is typically how red zone conflict works. We quickly escalate the conflict based on our own unresolved issues—even if our red zone issues are different. He and I eventually worked through the conflict, understanding that we were both triggered by something outside of our own awareness. To this day, he is one of my closest friends. One reason we're so close is that we learned how to have conflict.

Sadly, I (Jim) am a combination of Kevin and Jim Osterhaus in that I have both of their fears. My people pleasing, or acceptance, issue is my stronger trigger to the red zone. Feeling like I am not popular or liked tempts me to cave into the system's anxiousness and overfunction in order to bring about calmness. My attempts at pleasing everyone are always futile—I cannot control others through my charm and cleverness. When I'm in the red zone I rarely lash out; rather, I get depressed and withdraw. As a result, I have to attend to what God is doing in the situation and face the "pain zone" of people's displeasure for the sake of the mission. Yet, my drive to look competent is not far behind people pleasing. One of the most helpful things in leadership is self-awareness, whereby we become attentive to what pulls us toward red zone behavior.

There is one key differentiation between how participants of red zone versus blue zone conflict behave. Leaders in the blue zone accept responsibility for their part of the discussion, issue, or need without becoming the victim or rescuer. In red zone conflicts, individuals act out of the desire to protect and promote themselves—and they look to others to protect them as well.

How Well Do I tolerate the Anxiety of Others?

To manage the anxiety and conflict of others, pastors must take personal responsibility for themselves. Many pastoral types have to be deeply reflective when facing the anxiety of the people in their congregations. Anxiety feeds on ambiguity, and most churches have lots of unclear values, habits, committees, and policies. Reducing ambiguity through strategic processes helps. But the key is to imagine how the pastor can function like a thermostat to regulate the anxiety around them and thus create an ever-increasing movement of healthy, life-changing ripples moving through the system.

Osterhaus shared,

> The chief cause of burnout is not working too much, but getting sucked into other people's problems. Well-defined, non-anxious people resist being triangled, thus influencing others to take responsibility for themselves. Non-anxious leaders are able to tolerate other people's anxiety, thus requiring them to take personal responsibility. Anxiety is thus diffused in the organization, allowing it to function in a healthy way.[10]

Edwin Friedman, a family therapist and leadership consultant, contributed much to the study of family systems theory. In his books, including *Generation to Generation* and *A Failure of Nerve,* he introduced the idea of becoming a non-anxious presence as a twin sister to self-differentiation.

How Can I Become a Non-anxious Presence?

The most effective leader is confident in who God made her as an individual and does not look to her various roles to give her meaning. To draw from a modern term, she values healthy boundaries that separate where her responsibility begins and ends—and where another person's responsibility starts and stops. She can view the issues, decisions, and conflicts facing her organizations separately from her true self. People can only grow and change when they experience a moderate level of anxiety. However, pastors often carry the anxiety for others. While well-intentioned, this is counterproductive. If the leader demonstrates high levels of anxiety, she unwittingly absolves others of their responsibility for growth and change. Instead, when leaders manage their own anxiety, they also allow others to grow.

Friedman explained,

> Differentiation is not about being coercive, manipulative, reactive, pursuing or invasive, but being rooted in the leader's own sense of self rather than focused on that of his or her followers. . . . Furthermore, the power inherent in a leader's presence does not reside in physical or economic strength but in the nature of his or her own being, so that even when leaders are entitled to great power by dint of their office, it is ultimately the nature of their presence that is the source of their real strength. Leaders function as the immune systems of the institutions they lead—not because they ward off enemies, but because they supply the ingredients for the system's integrity.[11]

Self-differentiation allows a leader to become a non-anxious presence. When a leader is in that non-anxious space, she lowers the temperature in the room, allowing others to face and resolve their own issues. This creates an atmosphere for personal growth to occur. But if the leader is highly anxious, she becomes the scapegoat.

Healthy leaders do not allow themselves to get carried along emotionally with the anxiety inherent in their organization. They allow the electricity of the situation to go through them without overloading or diffusing them. Friedman wrote,

> It has far more to do with their presence than with their actions. . . . To the extent that leaders and consultants can maintain a non-anxious presence in a highly energized anxiety field, they can have the same effects on that field that transformers have in an electrical circuit. . . . Anyone can remain non-anxious if they also try to be non-present. The trick is to be both non-anxious and present simultaneously.[12]

A young child may be frightened by a storm, a noise, or a stranger. Often, the child reaches out for the parent's presence. The adult doesn't necessarily have to do or say anything—just as long as they are not visibly scared, the child receives encouragement. In our churches, the non-anxious presence of a leader can stabilize many uncertain moments.

What Does It Look Like to Be Internally Aligned?

One critical quality of a well-defined leader is internal alignment. You may have driven a vehicle whose alignment was out of whack. The car pulled either to the right or the left, and you had to keep both hands firmly on the steering wheel to make sure the vehicle didn't plow into another car or a ditch. It's a pleasure to drive your car after a mechanic performs an alignment. The vehicle seems to sail along the road trouble free.

For the ministry leader, internal alignment reflects integrity. The public self mirrors the private one. Osterhaus says, "Those who lead who are internally aligned with their own values—actions match words—and thus are able to align the organization around its values, mission and vision, are the truly effective leaders."[13]

For example, I (Jim) love helping to develop others in their ministries. But I also love having things done well, which speaks to my competence fear. When I am non-aligned, I tend to overfunction and pick up after a lay person I'm equipping. My anxiety disempowers them. I have to learn to let go of my performance anxiety for the sake of the real value I am trying to affirm—equipping others for ministry. Only when I grasp my internal competing values can I choose the greater missional one. It requires significant self-awareness to keep this before me.

One great challenge of middle age is coming to terms with our true selves—who we really are and not just what we want to be or what others expect us to be. Maturity involves learning to accept ourselves as God made us. Paul advised the Romans prior to listing several spiritual motivational gifts: "Think of yourself with sober judgment, in accordance with the faith God has distributed to each of you" (Romans 12:3). Sober judgment here means a sane estimate. Know who you are and accept who you are—and be all of that for the glory of God.

The well-defined leader continuously pursues internal alignment, embracing their true self before God. They allow the Lord to define who they are more than others' expectations or any organization's apparent successes or failures.

What does a well-defined leader resemble? The following chart[14] compares a healthy leader with a poorly defined one:

Table 3.2. Two types of leader

Poorly defined leader	Well-defined leader
The emotional self rules over the thinking self, thus generating and reacting much more to anxiety and stress in the organization.	The thinking self rules over the emotional self, thus preventing or minimizing the creation of or reaction to anxiety and stress in the organization.
Susceptible to a great deal of emotional stimulation, which makes them excited and adds to the stress they experience rather than diffuses it.	Able to absorb a large amount of stress. Can also be around other excited individuals without becoming emotionally excited, thus diffusing the situation.
Demonstrates much less self-knowledge, which leads to difficulty with decision-making. Because they have less choice between thinking and feeling, more of their choices are emotionally driven.	Demonstrates a great deal of self-knowledge. As they pay close attention to themselves and their reactivity at every level possible, they develop a degree of mastery over themselves and their relationships.
Boundaries are either too porous or too rigid.	Has firm, appropriate personal boundaries.

Is unclear about who they are and their life goals.	Has clarity about their self and their own life goals.
Sacrifices their own position to manage anxiety.	Able to hold their ground in conflict, keeping an eye on the mission.
Focuses on pathology in those around them.	Focuses on strengths, both for their self and their people.
Diagnoses others when problems arise.	Considers self when problems arise.
Is quick to distance from difficult situations.	Is challenged by difficult situations.
Responds poorly to resistance and sabotage, allowing it to distract.	Responds effectively to resistance and sabotage, seeing it as necessary and instructive.
Focuses empathetically on helpless victims.	Has a challenging attitude that encourages responsibility.
	Able to disappoint those dependent on them.
	Seeks enduring change.
	Acknowledges and navigates competing values.
	Welcomes conflict that is focused on the mission and introduces conflicting viewpoints.

What do I need to do to become more self-aware?

Much has been written in leadership literature about the importance of emotional quotient (EQ). One component of a healthy EQ is acute self-awareness—understanding what makes us tick. Osterhaus says that self-awareness includes three critical areas for a leader to be well defined: knowing our natural bent, knowing our story, and knowing our culture.

Knowing our natural bent means understanding how we are uniquely created. Some people call this our element, our sweet spot, our unique talent pool, or our Hedgehog Concept.[15] Whatever you call it, our bent focuses on our unique strengths makeup. We recommend resources like Ken Tucker's *Intentional Difference* to explore this subject more. Osterhaus said,

> When we are functioning in our natural bent, we are extremely focused, lost in the moment. We perform at our peak, getting lost in the process and losing a sense of the passage of time. We can work for hours, and are actually energized rather than depleted by the

> experience. At these times, we are authentically centered in the true sense of ourselves—we are well-defined. We pursue our God-given passions and interests for their own sake, not worrying about the residuals that might flow from its successful prosecution. When we are in that sweet spot, we are re-creating.[16]

Knowing our story involves knowing not only our personal timeline but also our overarching themes, passions, and redeeming qualities. We are unique creations of the Lord. Our lives cover a specific point in history. A careful look inside at ourselves can yield great benefits in helping us to maintain a well-defined life and leadership.

Knowing our culture helps us to remember that we are not just global people. We are born into specific cultures, which Osterhaus calls "the context in which our lives unfold."[17] We experience national culture, local culture, denominational culture, and church or organizational culture. How we view the world, and even how we view Christianity, is colored by our various cultures. A well-defined person takes into consideration his own cultural influences and how they have shaped him.

What Is My WOT?

The greater our self-awareness and internal alignment, the more we can operate within what Dan Siegel calls our window of tolerance (WOT). As leaders, our WOT is the zone where we function most effectively. When we are generally healthy emotionally, mentally, and spiritually, we psychologically operate within a sphere of margin, where we can "readily receive, process, and integrate information and otherwise respond to the demands of everyday life without much difficulty."[18] In this zone our brains function well, and we can respond to the stressors around us—including those within our organizations—without them derailing us.

My WOT increases when I am in a good place with my spirit, mind, body, and emotions. My WOT decreases when I'm in a bad place. The more my WOT decreases, the more likely I am to have red zone reactions to the anxiety around me. The higher my WOT, the more likely I am to have blue zone reactions to those stressors. Keeping an attentive eye on the pulse of my self-awareness helps me keep my WOT open, allowing me to lead out of a place of health and security.

Being a well-defined leader is critical as we navigate anxiety in our organizations. The more secure we are in Christ and in who he made us to be, the more we can be fully present to love and lead. As we step into a world we've never known, we start by becoming attentive people who manage our own anxiety. But how do we begin leading others? The next step in the journey is to build trust within congregations.

Questions for Reflection and Discussion

- How do you respond to anxiety within the church? In what ways do you relate to the story about Tom, Kara, and other staff members at the church?
- As you read about "projection" and "transference," reflect on your leadership. Have you experienced either of these? If you did, what was your response?
- As you read about Kevin and Jim being triggered and responding with red zone conflict, consider your own trigger. Do you think you are more driven by a need for survival, acceptance, control, or competence? Why do you think this is true?
- As you reflect on your leadership, in what ways are you largely internally aligned (what you claim to value lines up with the way you lead)? In what ways are you misaligned?
- What can you do to grow as a self-aware and attentive leader?

4

How Do I Increase My Trust Quotient?

In *The Speed of Trust*, Stephen Covey says, "The first job of a leader—at work or at home—is to inspire trust. It's to bring out the best in people by entrusting them with meaningful stewardships, and to create an environment in which high-trust interaction inspires creativity and possibility."[1] How do you build trust as a leader during seasons of adversity?

Ed Allen helped plant Gateway Church with a small group of people in Northern Virginia in 1998. As they focused on developing authentic Christian community, they grew slowly but healthily for ten years with about 350 people. In the early years, they were nomads meeting at a middle school in Fairfax County, Virginia, about ten miles away from their target community of South Riding in Loudoun County. During that time, every public school in Fairfax County had a church using its facility. Ed's team got the last available one, nowhere close to where God had called them.

Someone then gifted them an undeveloped piece of property in South Riding. At the time there was no sewer, water, or even a completed road to the land. They began a building campaign, until the 2008 recession hit and construction in the area halted, significantly slowing the campaign's progress. On top of that, leadership was marred by a sex scandal and some painful staff dismissals. Ed told us, "That season was deeply discouraging and disconcerting. It was a growing process—but hard."

In 2010, they moved to a middle school closer to their property. Weariness set in. Volunteers tired of setting up and tearing down for church every single week. Attendance shrunk to under two hundred people, and for eight years they did not grow. Occasionally visitors came and a few remained, but just as many people were leaving as were coming, including several significant families who told Ed they didn't see the church going anywhere. It was brutal.

What led the remaining people to stick it out with Ed during difficult seasons? Trust. One way Ed builds trust is through his personal boundaries. "Ed does a good job letting people know what they can expect from him and the church. He manages expectations well," shared one leader at Gateway.

This habit increases the trust factor. Recently, Ed received a long email from a new visitor—a woman with deep emotional needs. He briefly responded with encouragement, to which she replied that she expected a much more thorough response. She told him, "I need to connect personally with the senior pastor in order to connect with a church." He blind copied the elders on his email and responded graciously but firmly: "I truly understand your disappointment. I honestly may not be able to meet your needs." The elders commended him for sticking to his boundaries and not allowing her to manipulate him. A firm but flexible boundary builds, rather than diminishes, healthy trust.

While only one in three American pastors is considered to be healthy in terms of well-being,[2] the leadership of Gateway has helped Ed practice and maintain healthy boundaries—from monitoring his online activities to supporting his sabbath. These small boundaries create the kind of trust required for leaders to create a shared vision. Often, that vision emerges from the people, rather than the pastor, when mutual trust has been established.

In 2013, several key people associated with the church's leadership believed God was stirring them to begin building on their property. Ed said, "This was not at all on my mind. I was not excited and had no vision for this. I didn't even know how to rally the troops and cast vision." But he agreed to go along with the idea, recognizing, "This is God's story. Most of the best things we've done have not been strategic."

They put together a good team of leaders, including a developer in the church, that created a business plan and led Ed step by step through the process. Their goals included doubling in size the first year and opening a preschool. But they needed money for a mortgage. Most banks turn down a church loan if the church has been meeting in a school or theater for more than ten years. So it was no surprise that seven banks turned them down. But then an eighth bank miraculously said yes.

"I had questions through this but leaned on the original indicators" of God's calling, Ed said. "It felt mysterious to me. They trusted me, so I trusted them. We continued to move forward step by step. I didn't see how this was possible until they poured concrete."

As the economy picked up and construction in Loudoun County boomed once again, the church's remote property ended up being on a high volume, four-lane road—the most prominent intersection in the southern part of the county. Ed describes it as an "unbelievable location."

The new facility opened in 2017, and in three months the size of the congregation doubled. In two-and-a-half years, they were nearing nine hundred in worship attendance, with a fully enrolled preschool.

A serendipitous—or providential—event stimulated the growth. Food trucks were in the habit of meeting in the area on Thursday nights, drawing hundreds of families. When the county would not let the vendors continue using a parking lot, the vendors reached out to Gateway Church, which began hosting the event. Fifteen hundred people came on Thursday evenings to their lot and walked through their facilities. Reflecting on this rare and unusual gathering, Ed said, "God dropped it in our laps."

Trust tends to snowball. It starts very small but gains momentum as it extends to more and more people. What started with Ed and the leaders moved through the congregation and eventually into the local community.

Like every church, the pandemic years were not without their obstacles and struggles. But the members of Gateway continue to marvel at what God has done and ask how they can be faithful to steward their blessings.

During their "wilderness years," when the church could not see any way to build and their attendance stayed just under two hundred, the core leadership of about fifty adults stayed. There was deep trust in Ed and the elders—and in one another and their vision of community.

Gateway also works on relational boundaries. Through the years, they have embraced a mindset of proactively handling conflict. One elder shared, "We recognize that conflict is often very messy, and it may not have a neat ending. But that is not necessarily on us. At least we don't avoid it." They have created clear parameters by stating who they help and how much. Ed also works hard at pushing care needs to the small groups. Most hospital visitation and pastoral care needs are handled at the small group level. This small unit is the primary place for relational connections to the church. Small groups do home care visits, offer meals in times of need, and meet practical needs. These practices help keep the staff from trying to meet every need and help prevent people from taking advantage of them.

The members of Gateway recognize the limitations of human beings, including pastors and church staff. They encourage personal and professional counseling as needed for their staff. One of their elders, a professional life coach, regularly speaks to the leadership team about their need for healthy boundaries.

Ed frankly admits, "I am not a great strategic leader, but I am very authentic." And authenticity builds trust.

So far we've looked at various characteristics of an attentive person, including the ability to listen to God and manage anxiety. Leading a church is not a simple task in an entitled world where members often feel privileged. Congregations get confused about who they are serving—themselves or the Lord Jesus? For a pastor to help a church navigate change in a world we've never known, especially when transformation or adaptive challenges are involved, trust is needed. For a congregation to move forward in being attentive to God, they have to trust their leaders. When trust is present, many good things happen. When it is absent, leaders cannot get the people to move forward.

Building Trust

One common way to help children steward money is to set up their own savings account. Through the process, they learn about making deposits and withdrawals. Over time, they see that if they haven't made enough deposits, there won't be money available.

This same simple concept impacts leadership in a church. Leaders cannot make withdrawals—big changes—if they haven't made significant deposits. A pastor needs to earn the trust of his or her congregation by doing ministry in a competent manner over time. Trust is the currency that allows ministry to flow.

Marnie Crumpler of Bethlehem, Pennsylvania, models this accumulation of trust as she practices ministry in a rich and dynamic manner. In her first seven years she faced three major trust-sapping challenges, yet God enabled her to bring the congregation through all three in an amazing fashion. Her first obstacle was leading the congregation to transfer into a different denomination. That decision brought rancor, lawsuits, and eventually the loss of their building, including a classic sanctuary seating eleven hundred people. This drastic change meant taking a large and complex congregation into the wilderness of rented space. It meant massive set up and tear down each Sunday morning for a congregation that had not experienced that world. It meant doing most meetings and ministries in the pastor's living room and backyard. This all meant adaptation after adaptation—some tactical change, some strategic change, and lots of transformational change. Through it all, Marnie built trust.

I (Jim) watched as she tackled her second obstacle: shepherding the congregation through the pandemic. Every church faced massive challenges with the virus and its controversies. Vaccines or no vaccines? Masks or no masks? Gather for worship or do worship only online? In some ways, the earlier changes around the loss of the building prepared the congregation for the Covid-19 phase. The bank account of trust grew as Marnie led through the trying events of the pandemic in ways that allowed the church to thrive.

Marnie's third challenge was mobilizing the congregation to design, finance, and build a new church space. Though she began mobilization for a capital campaign long before Covid-19 arrived, rising inflation-related construction costs required her to do more fundraising during the pandemic years. In our experience helping churches with capital campaigns, we expect a church to raise two or three times their annual budget. However, this Bethlehem church eventually raised $16 million, almost seven times their annual budget. Working together under Marnie's leadership, they constructed an amazing building for the glory of God.

How did this pastor guide her people so well? She cites five major components in building their trust. Over each of these expressions of leadership was God's graciousness, which had been built into Marnie through many years and many mentors.

- First, she said, "**It starts with non-anxious leadership**, combined with steadily equipping the other leaders while guarding your personal boundaries all the way through. I guided them to see their mission and not just the difficulties. Driving home the mission with the people was something I taught at every possible opportunity."
- **Marnie preaches strategically** to catalyze the mission during each trial. A powerful preacher with amazing persuasive power, she dares to see the unseen and believes it will happen. The way she preaches is both biblical and pastoral. This combination propels her into a place that builds trust with the congregation.
- Third, **she maximizes regular communication** with her people. She sends a weekly email to the church that carries a personal message from her heart. The click rate on her emails is 60 percent, which is very high among group email marketing. Communication is one of the spigots that lets trust flow forward.
- She **opens her home** to many meetings and church events. Her hospitality plays an important role in helping people see her life and grow in trust together. Remember how many times Jesus and the early church gathered in people's dwelling places.

- Finally, Marnie knows the importance of **building relationships every day.** She notices people and gives them attention. I (Jim) have walked through her congregation with her many times on a Sunday morning and noticed her remarkable capacity to touch people. She schedules three lunches per week to meet with key people. During the building campaign, she met with every major donor three times each. She kept layering trust by investing in people. Consequently, she has laid a strong foundation on which to build God's vision into the church's reality.

The twenty-first century world is not the same one we experienced years ago. In our current era of ministry, many changes need to be made in our congregations. As we outlined earlier, when Joshua prepared to lead the Israelites into the land of promise, he instructed them to stay about three-quarters of a mile behind the Ark of the Covenant: "Then you will know which way to go, since you have never been this way before" (Joshua 3:4). When a congregation is going in new directions in this complicated world, trust is of paramount importance. The people trusted Joshua to lead them. And as our trust in the Lord grows, so can our people's trust in following us.

Pastor Robert Morgan, writing about this event, shares,

> Your Lord is already in your future, clearing the way, arranging circumstances in advance, and preparing the work you'll do, the burdens you'll bear, and the blessings you'll enjoy. . . . You don't know what the future holds—not even tomorrow. You are heading where you've never been before. But Jesus goes before You with His power, His precepts, and His provisions—all you need to make the most of tomorrow's sunshine or shadows.[3]

Healthy Boundaries

What sustained Ed in Virginia and Marnie in Pennsylvania? Attentiveness to healthy boundaries. A key reality for healthy leaders and thriving ministries is that healthy boundaries create trust. Boundaries are necessary fences marking our physical and emotional limits. As a result, they create zones of responsibility and safety, protect privacy, and differentiate what is yours from what is mine. They show where one thing starts and another ends.

Boundaries require certain actions and provide essential results for leaders and organizations, including the following:

- Establish, clarify, and manage expectations between people
- Create emotional health
- Protect persons from becoming victims
- Clarify roles—who is responsible for what
- Define clear yet flexible lines of authority
- Protect priorities
- Help the church and leaders know when to say yes and no
- Promote a healthy work-life balance

It is very easy and natural to allow boundaries to erode due to seemingly urgent matters. However, doing so creates multiple problems. If boundaries are left unchecked, the ministry will veer from its values, mission, and vision. Resources will not be used according to priorities. Pastors, elders, and staff will eventually operate in a constant state of putting out the next fire.

Jesus did not meet every need. He did not heal every sick person in Judea, feed every hungry child in Nazareth, or raise from the dead every person who died in Bethany. More than any other person in history, his life was driven by his mission. Numerous times in Scripture, he pulled away from the demands of the crowd for more pressing priorities: praying alone with the Father, resting, or having small group time with his disciples. The incarnate Lord lived with healthy boundaries.

Chip, an amiable, sixty-something pastor, loved helping people—and he thrived on the admiration that came from being needed by others. He always kept his cell phone close by in case a church member needed to reach him. Many times, if his personal office phone rang while he was in a conversation or meeting with a staff member at church, he immediately jumped up and said, "Hold on!" He would rush to his office to answer the phone, subtly communicating to the staff member that the incoming call was of greater importance than the current conversation. When church members experienced conflict and talked with him individually, they left the conversation thinking he sided with them. His overwhelming desire to please the person in front of him made it almost impossible for him to communicate and differentiate between opposing ideas. Chip experienced a problem with boundaries, and it ended up costing him the very thing he wanted to keep: trust. One practical boundary-keeping exercise we can practice is turning off our phones during meetings. This ties in directly with attentiveness—being present with the person you are currently with.

Pastors must gain people's trust by showing competence and alignment in the day-to-day acts of ministry. As they do so, their credibility and influence will expand in ever-increasing circles. If the previous pastor was deeply trustworthy, there will be some "borrowed" trust given to the office of the next pastor. If the previous pastor was not trusted or even abused trust, the next pastor will often begin with a trust deficit. The same is true for all leaders, elders, and staff. The process of gaining trust starts with a growing attention to how the congregation trusts. Typically, in seasons of great anxiety and struggle, trust is most needed. We both have watched pastors who sustained great trust in anxious seasons. We've also observed leaders whose trust meter was depleted and could not weather the storm.

Establishing healthy boundaries is essential to building long-term trust. We live in an intrusive world. Thanks in part to technology and social media, people want constant access to us at all times. My boundaries—or fences—communicate where I stop and you begin. They show what I am responsible for and what I am not. Creating and maintaining healthy boundaries respects integrity and fosters authentic trust.

While healthy boundaries are firm but flexible, unhealthy boundaries tend toward the extremes and are either too rigid or too porous. A person with rigid boundaries is completely inflexible. In his poem "Mending Wall," Robert Frost illustrates unnecessary boundaries. His apple trees don't threaten his neighbor's pines, yet the neighbor insists on a fence.[4] We've seen this with pastors who refuse to take calls directly and force all communication through third parties. Sadly, we've even heard of churches that tell their members not to talk to the pastor if they see him in public. Rigid boundaries are impermeable walls that erode trust and often point to a leader who has something to hide. Sometimes the leader is harboring a deep secret. At other times, it may be an emotional wound or insecurity.

We don't want boundaries to be like prison walls. Rather, we want them to be like fences with clear gates for entering and exiting. Fences help define physical space. Likewise, boundaries help shape a person's identity. Leaders with porous boundaries have no sense of self. They tend to say yes to everyone all the time and lose their identity in the process, becoming less available to those who need them the most.

In partnering with hundreds of pastors and churches for leadership development and coaching through the years, we've observed three sets of practices that help a church create healthy boundaries to earn trust. A CEO of a construction company once told us, "If you have a crack in the foundation, it will follow you to the roof." Each of the following areas—governance, the basics, and relationships—needs boundaries. Think of them as building from the foundation to the roof.

Governance

Consider some recent experiences we've had in partnering with church leadership teams.

An elder, upset with the pastor's leadership style, launches a rogue internal survey among the staff.

A senior pastor, in conflict with a lay leader over a mission trip, conducts a secret meeting with elders who she believes are allies.

A long-term member, longing for the good ol' days, circulates a petition among members to overthrow the new leadership team.

A board member routinely calls staff members, demanding immediate answers to his questions.

A pastor purchases a building for the youth, with very little input from the board.

An associate pastor fires several longtime staff members, informing the human resources committee after the fact.

Each of these real examples shares similarities: a well-intentioned person makes a bad decision; enormous leadership conflict spills over into the congregation; someone quits the board or leaves the church; or a staffer gets fired. Every one of these crises could have been resolved through healthy governance boundaries. As with these cases, role confusion creates systemic dysfunction. The typical "solution" is to look for a scapegoat—someone to blame or fire. With a scapegoat, the system doesn't have to change. And the pattern often repeats itself over and over with different people.

The first foundational boundary in every church, regardless of size, involves clarifying governance versus management. All church leadership teams face challenges related to roles, which are another form of boundaries. The concept of playing triple or quadruple roles is unique to the church, compared to a business or a nonprofit. Why? Simply because the church plays at least three roles in the lives of its people. The church, first and foremost, is *a faith community*. People learn to become disciples, worship God, share their faith with others, and make a kingdom difference. At the same time, the church functions as *a family*. People invest in each other's lives. The church marries and buries people. They support each other at the hospital and share meals together. Finally, the church is *an organization*, much like a business. These three functions should work harmoniously. But, because we live in a fallen world in need of redemption, these three roles often function as competing values.

This becomes even more complicated for leaders. The larger a church gets, the greater the tendency to separate out the three—the business stuff belongs to the board while the faith community belongs to the pastors, for example. There is no right or wrong answer here, and it is critical to understand that some of these issues will never be solved—they can only be managed. That is the nature of competing values.

When trust evaporates, people tend to distrust just about everything. Policies, procedures, and protections are put in place to safeguard the church. But while these ground rules manage distrust and clarify expectations, they don't rebuild trust. Rather, trust is built over time through relationships when we not only meet expectations but exceed them. So, a fine line exists between building trust through relationships and managing distrust through rules.

Ron Heifetz, founder of the Kennedy School of Leadership at Harvard, writes, "Authority provides direction. . . . I define authority as conferred power to perform a service."[5] Church leaders can use their authority to serve their people by creating a healthy structure. An essential boundary in any church is providing a clear governing and managing structure that keeps the organization on track with its mission, vision, and values.

We understand that every denomination, association, or entity will have different approaches to polity and governance. A nondenominational church has different ground rules, for example, than a Presbyterian church. Baptists, Methodists, Lutherans, and Episcopalians all appeal to a different form of governance. Regardless of affiliation, a governance structure must be clear and helpful. A church's board must be clear about their mission, vision, and values and make sure all policies and decisions align with those. *What* and *how* are often on the agenda, yet *why* supersedes these items. Once the *why* is understood, questions like the following need to be worked through: Who should be on the board? What expectations are there for selecting board members? To remain engaged? To participate? To be invested in ministry at the church?

Take time answering these questions. Ron Heifetz also introduced us to a very simple model of problem solving: observe, interpret, and intervene. Our nature is to jump quickly to the intervention. But when we do that, today's solutions become tomorrow's problems. For the governance process to be effective, we recommend a slower pace, allowing adequate time for observing and interpreting. This enables leadership to make the best decisions for the long haul.

Once the *why* is clear, the church can begin addressing tactical challenges with more clarity. Perhaps the most significant tactical challenge for many churches is related to authority and decision-making. Frances Hesselbein, former CEO of the Drucker Institute, once said, "Governance is governance. Management is management." Organizations must sharply differentiate "between the two by delineating clear roles, responsibilities, and accountabilities, resulting in a partnership of mutual trust and purpose."[6]

Too many layers of governance and management, which are often added over time to address ad hoc situations, result in confusion. Gaps create communication vacuums or lack of relational connections between the various leadership bodies. Overlapping roles create confusion over authority and decision-making. A good structure, however, eliminates both gaps and overlaps.

Two simple questions are critical for leadership groups to answer: Who governs? And who manages?

Who governs? We often refer church partners to John Carver's Policy Governance model. We also encourage churches to think of Carver's model as one useful tool in the toolbox but not the only tool. Carver's model can be overly rigid, but it's very useful in helping a board define its roles in the tactical mode of leadership. It is less useful in strategic or transformational modes.[7] In Carver's model, the governing body should establish and monitor policies around:

- Executive limitations (for the lead pastor and others who manage)
- Board/staff linkage
- Ends (desired mission and results)
- Means (protections for the church)[8]

Policies, in general, define future decision-making by establishing what we always do and what we never do. This enables many decisions to be made away from the center, creating a culture of empowerment. Policies may be developed out of specific ad hoc situations but should generally be treated as universally applicable.

In a healthy governance model, the top level of leaders—whether elders, the oversight team, pastors, or deacons—should not be a day-to-day decision-making body. The top level of governance ideally establishes policies and determines direction, thereby creating a culture in which decisions, aligned with those polices, can be made throughout ministries. Think of policies as "what we always do or what we never do." Any time a decision needs to be made, it's helpful for a governing board to ask, "Does this decision need a policy?" If not, the decision should be shifted back to those who are tasked with management. Policies need to be established to protect the church as well as clarify levels of authority and processes for feedback and accountability.

Who manages? Depending on the size of the church, management should primarily be in the hands of staff members or volunteers. The governing board should not necessarily be involved in the day-to-day and weekly management of the church. This doesn't mean that members of the governing board can't also be volunteers or on staff. Rather, it is critical to determine which role a board member is playing at what point in time.

Once the church is clear on who governs versus who manages, the church's management structure should align with its True North, which we'll discuss in chapter five.

The Basics

Leaders need to establish order and manage primary tasks. To build trust, they must consistently meet three basic expectations related to financial integrity, preaching, and pastoral care.

Billy Graham observed that most people who morally fail do so in one of three areas: sexual, financial, or pride. We have heard sickening stories of pastors, staff members, or church administrators who embezzled thousands of dollars over many years. Such blatant theft tarnishes the church's name and mission and causes a significant lack of trust in that individual, which in many cases will never be regained.

Most of us will probably never be tempted to steal large sums of money from a ministry. However, we sometimes still practice small or subtle habits that form healthy or unhealthy boundaries, which can cause our trust account with our congregation to either grow or diminish. Here are some healthy habits to practice:

- Meet the budget. Spending within the appropriate categories will cause your stock to increase, particularly among those who manage the church's finances. Especially in your first few years at a church, don't become known as the pastor who habitually busts the budget. Work within your means.
- Pay your personal bills. First Timothy says an overseer should manage his own family well (3:4). This includes your personal finances. Model faithful stewardship for your people by sticking to a personal budget. Many ministries like Crown Financial offer helpful resources to do just that. Not paying your own bills in a timely manner, particularly in a small community, is a surefire way to hurt your reputation, create distrust, and lose credibility. If you need financial counseling, by all means, seek it out. You will be glad you did.
- Live within congregational norms. If most of your people live in $300,000 houses, it's probably not a wise move for your family to immediately purchase an $800,000 one. Like it or not, people notice where you live and what kind of car you drive. That doesn't mean you should not enjoy some nice things. But it does mean that one aspect of incarnational ministry is living like your people.
- Follow, and over time, improve your church's governance when it comes to finances. Don't be like a bull in a china shop your first year on the job—you'll just create unneeded tension and cause your trust bank to diminish. Instead, follow the procedures adopted by the congregation. If they need improving, have the patience to wait it out and slowly introduce healthier systems and practices. Many times, churches do need to change and simplify their process. But you must do it the right way.

Consistency and transparency around financial management are critical for establishing trust. A few years ago we journeyed with First

Church in Orlando, where David Swanson is the senior pastor. The church scored as high as we've ever seen on the financial management dimension of our survey, the Transforming Church Insight (TCI). We dug deeper and discovered that David shares his personal budget with the congregation each year. Every member knows how much he makes and where he spends his money. That simple act has created enormous trust that extends beyond David into leadership as a whole.

Another basic expectation for gaining trust relates to preaching. A pastor is regularly visible to the congregation during the worship service and the time of preaching. Not everyone is equally gifted as a preacher. But when you preach in a way that is faithful to the biblical text and connects people relationally, you build trust. You also need to have something important to say that is both inspiring and engaging.

Here are five simple ways to help build trust through your preaching and teaching:

- Avoid copying sermons from other preachers, and avoid using Artificial Intelligence (AI) to write sermons for you. Doing so can quickly lead to lost trust with congregants. In an internet era, it's easy for someone to check behind you. Most of us who preach are influenced by many sources, as there is nothing new under the sun. It never hurts to give credit to others who influenced you. This can be as simple as saying, "As I studied this week, Dietrich Bonhoeffer's writings helped me tremendously." This creates credibility and shows you don't keep yourself on a high horse.
- Provide a solid layering of biblical teaching and equipping. We are not called to primarily be motivational speakers, leadership gurus, political commentators, or standup comedians. Instead, we are called to preach the Word of God, systematically teaching God's counsel. Reflecting on his ministry in Ephesus, the apostle Paul said, "I did not shrink from declaring to you the whole counsel of God" (Acts 20:27 ESV). This habit requires disciplined study. We must balance our teaching with a plan that encompasses doctrine

and both Old and New Testament passages with the needs of the people.

- Provide illustrations from their worlds. Lazy preachers only use illustrations from their own lives and experiences, which doesn't require any digging and can be thought of almost instantly. Instead, do the hard work of finding relevant, timely, and applicable ways to illuminate your thoughts. We can't emphasize enough the great help of having on hand several books of illustrations and quotations for preachers and public speakers.[9] This can be the difference between sound doctrine floating over your congregation's head and relevant spiritual truth piercing their hearts and being at home in their minds. Through trial and error, you can learn to use the internet to locate good, succinct illustrations without going down too many rabbit holes. What's more, don't gear all of your illustrations toward one audience. Sometimes seminary students leave the academy and want to preach in a rural church in southern Iowa as if they are speaking to an audience of PhD students in biblical languages. One seminary professor wisely told students year after year to contextualize their ministry. And one more piece of advice: don't share stories that always portray you as the hero. People get tired of listening to those!

The third basic expectation people have is for pastoral care. As mentioned in the acknowledgments, my (Jim's) father, a retired pastor, presented the charge at my ordination service. His word was simple: he exhorted me to love and care for the people in my congregation before, and during, the time I tried to fix them. Looking back, I see he was suggesting that I make deposits in the trust bank before I make withdrawals. Sadly, I did not immediately practice his advice. I was an idealistic crusader at that time and far too arrogant. Very slowly, over the years, I began to see the wisdom of his words.

Loving a congregation takes many forms. One of the most mundane but effective ways to build trust is to genuinely care for people. Pastoral care, which often occurs in hospitals, living rooms, and over lunches, involves nurturing people discouraged by life's challenges and supporting them through grief. However, you must be careful not to overfunction or ignore the gifts of other people who are more natural caregivers. Maintaining healthy boundaries means stewarding time to tend to the broken while not embracing a messiah complex that makes you feel like you must meet every need.

Offering an active, attentive presence builds trust. Both Ed and Marnie modeled this with their people. My father and my first senior pastor modeled this for me. I didn't know then that their care for me would increase the trust I would need later to lead that congregation into change.

Eugene Peterson as a young pastor disliked Sunday small talk, which involved standing on the church's steps and engaging with people about the weather, the local football team, or the town's latest news. He thought it was wasted time, desiring only to have deep, spiritual conversations with people. Through experience, however, he learned the value of small talk. Those normal surface interactions offered great ways to slowly build relationships, and sometimes those bridges would lead to deeper and more important conversations.[10] Most pastors who do not build trust simply miss the opportunities right before them. They are not attentive to people.

It fascinated me (Jim) to see this in my ten years as a seminary pastor. As students walked from the library to the dining hall, they often passed each other without speaking. In classroom settings, they did not introduce themselves and get to know their classmates. Many simply took notes and left. I explained that they could not behave like that in church. During my first year of teaching, I told students I expected them to learn the names of every student in the class and discover other aspects of their lives. Where are they from? Who is their family? What are their interests? One student asked, "Will this be on the final exam?" Although I hadn't thought about it, I immediately replied, "Yes." I became notorious on campus for being the professor who expected pastoral investment in the lives of students, and throughout my ten years of teaching, this assignment appeared on the final exam. I did this because I knew it built trust and exhibited competency and attentiveness.

Pastoral care means simply finding time to be with the congregation outside of Sunday morning. I visited my first rural congregation of farmers at various times during the day, trying to understand how their dairy farms and corn crops worked. I learned about their families and connections to the church and community. When I got to my first suburban congregation, they told me they did not want the pastor just dropping by their homes, so I switched the location of my care. Like Marnie, I usually had three to four lunches available during the week and coffee times in the afternoon. Asking a church member to lunch became an avenue to learn their stories. The nurturing was not around a crisis, but it allowed me to know them on a personal level.

In very large congregations, the pastor can't keep up with all the needed care. We often delegate to an associate pastor and deacon ministers. But taking time to sit with those individuals for regular life updates allowed me to offer well-placed phone calls or text messages when the need was high. I also write several handwritten notes each week to build relationships—a ministry very lacking in today's culture.

Relationships

A final way to consistently establish healthy boundaries that will create trust in your ministry is to practice good relationship habits. Your people will not only listen to the sermons you preach; they will read your life. And the latter will probably affect them more positively or negatively than the former. The book of Proverbs says, "Above all else, guard your heart, for everything you do flows from it" (4:23). This heart area has to do with your character and integrity.

Here are a few areas where we can guard our hearts and our character:

- **Anger:** Few things can destroy your potential to lead a congregation as much as a bad temper. Years ago, a seminary president who was qualified in many ways to lead that institution was dismissed by his board for one reason: he could not, or would not, control his temper.

Remember that Moses, though a wonderful man of God, exhibited a habitual problem with anger. In Numbers 20, Moses—in reaction to the people's rebellious attitudes—angrily hits the rock instead of simply speaking to it. God's response is to not allow Moses to enter the Promised Land. Don't allow unresolved anger to steal your land of promise.

- **Coldness:** Some pastors live very aloof lives, rarely allowing anyone to get close to them. Though we certainly understand and can relate to being hurt by other people, we also know the value of friendship. Practice warmth and kindness. Don't take yourself too seriously. Remember the value of a good sense of humor. In his classic book *Spiritual Leadership*, J. Oswald Sanders wrote, "Our sense of humor is a gift from God, which should be controlled as well as cultivated. Clean, wholesome humor will relax tension and relieve difficult situations."[11]
- **Pride:** This natural tendency of humanity has caused problems since the Garden of Eden. Sadly, it has been the downfall of many a pastor and public ministry. Some pastors exhibit unhealthy narcissistic tendencies, which can be destructive to their people. Remember, God did not show up at your church the day you arrived. He was there doing his work long before you came on the scene, and he will continue to do so long after you leave. Young pastors, remind yourselves that some of your people, though they may be simple and perhaps even uneducated, have walked in the fear of the Lord longer than you have been alive. The apostle Paul, who had much reason to be arrogant about his personal credentials and education, wrote, "While knowledge makes us feel important, it is love that strengthens the church" (1 Corinthians 8:1 NLT).
- **Flirtation:** It is important for us as godly people to live lives that please the Lord and honor him, including in the way we relate to the opposite sex. Keeping ourselves under control is a discipline, particularly in a society that flaunts sex on magazine covers,

television ads, and an abundance of digital sources. Refusing to flirt with another person is a habit that must be practiced. In a casual sex society, we should embrace the fidelity that comes from having eyes only for our spouse. This also involves being careful about emotional attachments. In recent years, the Christian world has been rocked by scandals from notable leaders and influencers. In most cases, a healthy accountability structure was lacking, with followers assuming the leaders were "God's anointed" and beyond falling.

- **Reliability**: Nothing will make you lose credibility with people in your church like consistently being unreliable. Missing appointments, forgetting to follow through on promises, being late to meetings, and other bad habits create lots of trust issues. Practice punctuality. There's an old saying: If you are five minutes early, you're on time. If you're on time, you're late. Write things down. Sometimes young pastors want to use their brain to remember everything. Don't try it. The weakest pen is greater than the strongest mind. Remember people's names. Write them personal notes. Develop processes and systems of organization to keep yourself on task. Invest in some quality training in administration. You and your people will be glad you did.

Trust and distrust are not two sides of the same coin. Whether the leader engages in financial impropriety, a sex scandal, or an abuse of power, distrust in the church spreads like wildfire. On the other hand, trust takes time to grow. It must be nurtured. While distrust is like a light switch that instantly throws a room into the dark, trust is more like a dimmer switch that gradually brings a room back into the light. If you're in a situation where trust has been lost, we encourage you to be patient and consistent. Be attentive to the people's expectations around governance, preaching, pastoral care, and relationships. Be reliable. Give it time. Extend trust to the people, and it will typically be reciprocated. Ed and Marnie both built trust by embodying healthy boundaries that consistently increased their credibility. As a result, an organic, positive ripple effect occurred in both congregations.

Billy Graham once said, "I believe integrity can be restored to our society one person at a time. The choice belongs to each of us." As we've seen modeled by pastors like Ed, Marnie, and Clint, setting wise boundaries and living within them helps us to keep our integrity and thus build trust among our followers. As we do, we can make deposits into the trust bank to help us lead. When our trust quotient grows, we can then begin leading people to a clear mission, a compelling vision, and unique values—what we call a church's True North.

Questions for Reflection and Discussion

- What did you learn about building trust in difficult times from Ed's story?
- How did Marnie model healthy leadership that built trust?
- Why is it so difficult in ministry to maintain healthy boundaries? What can you do to intentionally guard the boundaries in your life?
- Jesus did not meet every need. How might you give yourself permission to do the same?
- How might you help your current congregation improve their governance?
- What specific lesson(s) did you glean from this chapter that you would like to work on to build trust among your followers?

Part Two

Leading an Attentive Church

5

Is the Tail Wagging the Dog?

Lord Dundreary: *Now I've got another. Why does a dog wag his tail?*
Flo: *Upon my word, I never inquired.*
Lord Dundreary: *Because the tail can't wag the dog. Ha! Ha!*

TOM TAYLOR, *OUR AMERICAN COUSIN*, 1869

YOU MAY HAVE HEARD THE idiom, "Don't let the tail wag the dog." It usually refers to something really important being driven by something that is really unimportant.

The Dallas Cowboys are nicknamed "America's team," though they have not won a Super Bowl since 1996. They built the AT&T Stadium in Arlington, Texas, considered the crown jewel of football stadiums, in 2009. One of the most expensive sports venues ever built, it cost $1.2 billion and was originally named Cowboys Stadium. According to the Arlington Visitors and Convention Bureau, "everywhere you turn, you will notice the level of detail and luxury that went into creating this world-class stadium."[1] Three thousand LCD video screens, displays, and boards fill the place so that guests can watch the game from luxury suites, concourses, and concession areas. The stadium contains twenty-five thousand square feet of video displays, including one of the largest 1080p HD video display boards in the world weighing 1.2 million pounds. The stadium also hosts a collection of museum-quality contemporary art.

Jerry Jones owns the famous football team. The stadium's website claims, "The Jones family strived from the beginning to create more than a home for the Dallas Cowboys; their dream was to create the next great architectural icon." Indeed, the stadium boasts stunning architecture, art, design, engineering and technology.[2] It normally seats eighty thousand people but can be reconfigured to hold one hundred thousand.

Yet, despite all the brouhaha, the Cowboys have made the playoffs only five times since the stadium opened in 2009. Most seasons, they produce about eight wins and eight losses.

Or take another American standard, the New York Yankees, who consistently have one of the highest payrolls in Major League Baseball—more than $210 million per year. The last time the Yankees won the World Series was in 2009, the same year they opened their new stadium. The $2.3 billion structure includes sixty-eight luxury suites, over 11,000 square feet of team stores, and a seating capacity of over 50,000. The players' dressing area, 3,344 square feet of space, includes a safety deposit box and touch-screen computer with each locker. The ballpark contains 25 permanent concessions stands and 112 floating ones. Since the year of their World Series win and the opening of the new stadium, the Yankees have consistently produced only mediocre results. In contrast, the Boston Red Sox have won four World Series since 2004, yet they play in a stadium that opened in 1912.

The Dallas Cowboys and the Yankees represent all-star clout and high dollars poured out with little results when it comes to winning championships. Sometimes it's easy to major in the minors and miss the point. However, the "minor" things may include spending tons of money, pleasing a lot of people, and invoking much fanfare. At the end of a football or baseball season, billion-dollar stadiums and inflated salaries don't necessarily result in winning games or championships. Could the tail be wagging the dog?

Churches can face similar realities as football and baseball teams. It's possible for a congregation or ministry to throw all or most of their time, effort, and resources into secondary matters like maintaining beautiful buildings, an up-to-date website, or the latest and greatest musical, lighting, and video equipment—while giving little attention to core matters like relational health, maturation of young believers, a spirit of love and trust, and evangelism. Millions of dollars spent on maintaining the church's appearances, comfort, and modern appeal will not necessarily make biblical disciples. In our experience with hundreds of churches, the tail wags the dog far too often. The attentive church, on the other hand, seeks to lead out of its center.

In part one, we looked at how to become attentive leaders. At LFM, we fundamentally believe that healthy leaders can lead thriving ministries. We seek to be a catalyst for mentoring healthy, attentive leaders who sustain such thriving ministries for the sake of the gospel. Now, in Part Two, we will focus on leading attentive churches.

One of the Two or Three Great Churches

First Church of Pittsburgh, Pennsylvania, has a remarkable history. Their impact across the nation and around the world over decades cannot be overestimated. Speaking at the church's two-hundredth anniversary celebration in 1973, Billy Graham called First Church "one of the two or three great churches in America."

Their roots go back to a prayer and praise meeting in 1758, though the church did not officially form until 1773. As the city grew in prominence and influence, First Church became an integral part of Pittsburgh's culture. The heirs of William Penn deeded land to the congregation, where they built their first building. For two centuries, the church thrived as an active beacon for their community. The University of Pittsburgh, Allegheny General Hospital, and Pittsburgh Theological Seminary all had their beginnings in the leadership and ministries of the church. At the turn of the twentieth century, they built a larger building. The new church would not only be a focal point for the spiritual life of the city, but it would also include classrooms and a cafeteria and offer services to workers, minorities, and immigrants nearly around the clock. First Church was a pioneer in Christian camping, establishing a church camp in

Donegal Township in 1914. At one time, the church boasted over two thousand members.

Its breathtaking sanctuary is on the local register of historic places. With its unique collection of Tiffany windows and a magnificent pipe organ, it continues to amaze visitors from around the world. Over time, though, the beautiful, historic cathedral became the church's focus, and they lost much of their attentiveness. When a retired Air Force colonel named Tom Hall became the pastor in 2009, worship attendance was under one hundred people. Service times were literally carved in stone outside the sanctuary. Gradually, the church lost their sense of mission. Members moved to the suburbs. When I (Kevin) consulted with them in Tom's early years, their staff were all contracted workers. It was like they had employees managing the museum.

Recently, however, Tom said, "I don't think the church was stuck on the building so much as it was stuck in the past. I used to say that it had been circling the wagons for so long, the ruts were deeper than the wagons and you could no longer see the sky." The tail was wagging the dog.

Tom remembers my work with them: "You led us in discerning together what God was doing here. The word that came out of our time with you was *relationships*, and it still is the right word. We understand that we have to engage the people of our city. The staff all buys into the vision now. There are no contractors on the staff just punching the clock."

Their ministries now include The Cellar, a joint endeavor with mission partner Youth for Christ to offer a safe place for high school kids to hang out after school. The Walk-In Ministry, shared on a weekly rotating basis with four other downtown churches, operates a food bank and addresses the needs of homeless people downtown. First Church also partners with the Coalition for Christian Outreach to provide a Christian presence on Pittsburgh college campuses. Their Creative Cards ministry prepares personalized greetings to send to our service men and women. And they house the offices of the Coalition to Affirm Real Estate (CARE) Ownership, a nonprofit seeking to restore neighborhoods by renovating properties and to restore lives by equipping disadvantaged people to be responsible homeowners and landlords. These are just a few of the ways First Church is shining the light of Christ into their world.

The people of this congregation are on their way again to being an attentive church. God's river will continue moving and making an impact through their community.

In looking at their dynamic history, we see that First Church lost sight of their first love—what we call True North. This refers to a church's sense of identity, purpose, and direction.

LFM has a congregational survey called the Transforming Church Insight (TCI). The survey was first launched in 2000 and serves as a longitudinal study of the American church. Over more than twenty years, the database has grown to over eleven million records, one of the largest congregational databases in the United States.

The TCI asks more than 130 questions of congregants. The analytics provide interesting insights. For example, some large and fast-growing churches scored low on the TCI, indicating a lack of real health. We concluded that a growing church is not always an indicator of a healthy one. Some of the highest scoring churches on the TCI were small churches, suggesting that health, vitality, and purpose can all be found in congregations of any size.

So, what indicates church health and vitality? Statistically, vision shows up as the most significant factor among the top 10 percent of churches in the database. Respondent rated statements like, "Our leaders effectively establish the church's direction, purpose, and objectives," "This church has a clearly defined vision for the future," and "The church's goals and direction are clear to me" as significant. It is important for people to know where they are heading and to have confidence that leadership is unified around that direction. Vision never showed up as a high score for the bottom 10 percent of the database (based on overall percentile score). These findings suggest that the process of attending to what God is doing in our midst will move us toward health. The more we sense what God is doing and where he wants us to go, the more likely we will be to act in ways that promote health.

In our church partnerships, we use the language of True North to help a congregation clarify vision. We look at two areas to determine a church's True North:

- What we must preserve—our core values and mission
- What we must adapt—our vision and strategy

First Church chose to preserve the wrong thing—their building at the cost of their mission. Instead of making sacrificial decisions to preserve and fulfill their purpose, they made expedient choices. But thankfully, with the right leadership, they got back on track.

The Four Qualities of True North

Churches enjoy a stable and active True North based on four qualities, which help them become and stay attentive. Knowing and understanding these qualities will help any pastor lead an attentive church. These conditions are like the four legs of a table. Each one needs to work for the table to stand. These characteristics can be summarized by four memorable Greek words.

Aretē: the essence that makes you unique. *Aretē* was the first Greek word that I (Kevin) learned in the Classics department at UNC. The professor, a Yale PhD, spent about three weeks on this word. He talked about how difficult it was to translate into English because it is more complicated than any single English word. It speaks of capability and potential as well as virtue. Ancient Greek writers used the term to convey goodness, a gracious act, or uprightness. They also used it to speak of a person's endowment, property, or quality. It was a combination of ability and action. Homer used the term to speak of able warriors, men capable of fighting. To defend their land, they not only needed skill but also enough wealth to afford weapons. *Aretē* included strength and skill, duty and responsibility. Socrates and Plato used it to refer to a person performing in the best way possible. So *aretē* speaks of a person's effectiveness in living up to her full potential. Is she excellent at what she was uniquely created to be?

The apostle Peter used the term several times. In 1 Peter 2:9, he tells the believers that God saved them to proclaim his excellencies (*aretē*). In his second letter, Peter uses the word twice in two verses. First, he again describes the saving power of God, who calls us by "his own glory and excellence" (2 Peter 1:3 ESV). That word *excellence* is the Greek word *aretē*. Then, Peter admonishes Christians to "make every effort to supplement your faith with virtue [*aretē*]" (2 Peter 1:5 ESV). The amazing reality of God choosing to send his Son Jesus to die for our sins and bring us into a relationship with him speaks of his goodness, excellence, and virtue. Peter reminds us that as we follow Christ, we too should add *aretē* to our faith. In Philippians 4, Paul gives one of the best prescriptions for mental and emotional health in all the Bible. While instructing believers of the kinds of thoughts our minds should fix on, he includes the word *aretē*, translated to mean excellent, virtue, or beautiful.

When thinking about healthy congregations, *aretē* speaks of a church's identity, essence, and capability. What is the essence of your church that makes it unique? What is your congregation's identity? What is your church's DNA? In what qualities are you excellent and effective? What are your core values? What are you passionate about, and how do you strive for excellence? Where do you shine, and is it the right place to shine? Is it a dog or its tail? The attentive church is one that listens to God's guidance to keep their focus on their real source of identity.

Apostolos: the mission you are sent on. The missiologist Johannes Blouw used physics terms to describe the difference between an inward and outward congregation. An inward congregation is driven by centripetal force—all feet moving toward the center. But the outward congregation is driven by centrifugal force—a picture of fleeing outward from the center. Blouw said the church is supposed to be centrifugal but often becomes centripetal.[3]

Apostolos speaks of mission, calling, and objective. The word combines the prefix *apo*, "from," with the word *stellō*, "to send." Greek literature uses it to refer to a messenger, envoy, or delegate. An *apostolos* is commissioned by another to represent him or her in some way. The Bible uses this word to refer to an apostle, one who is sent out by Christ to preach the gospel. In Latin it was translated as *missio*, so it is a precursor to our word *missionary*—indicating "being sent." In a practical sense, every Christian, pastor, and church has been sent out by the Lord into this world.

My (Kevin's) dear friend Jim Morgan is on the LFM board and helped turn Krispy Kreme around when he was executive chair and CEO. During breakfast when I asked Jim what his mission was, he recounted, "The mission statement that we created soon after my arrival was 'to touch and enhance lives through the joy that is Krispy Kreme.' My own personal mission was simply a modification of our corporate mission: 'To touch and enhance lives through the joy that is Jesus Christ.'" As I've watched him love everyone he encounters, I've rarely met someone whose words and actions so closely reflect their personal mission. By the way, after our breakfast, I realized it happened to be National Donut Day!

Apostolos speaks of the church's missional calling. The Lord told Abram, our forefather of the faith, "I will bless you . . . and you will be a blessing" (Genesis 12:2). In many ways, this is the first written record of what we call the Great Commission. God blessed Abram, and he eventually gave to Abram's ancestors the Messiah. However, the Savior was not for them alone. They were to take his name into all the world. And so, by faith, Abram began moving into that world. The Bible says, "He was called to go out to a place that he was to receive as an inheritance. And he went out, not knowing where he was going" (Hebrews 11:8 ESV). God sent Abram out so that the blessing would move beyond him to others. Jesus taught this same principle centuries later when he said, "Give, and it will be given to you" (Luke 6:38). The blessing comes as we go, as we give, and as we are sent. Days before the Holy Spirit came at Pentecost, Jesus prepared his followers to receive power, saying, "You will be my witnesses in Jerusalem, and in all Judea and Samaria, and to the ends of the earth" (Acts 1:8). The calling is always beyond ourselves.

Valley Church knew they were facing an uphill battle when their pastors of twenty-nine years, Mark and Cheryl, retired. It was tempting to think their best years were behind them or that they could keep replaying their greatest hits and just hope it would work out. Most churches tend to retreat and focus inward after a long-term pastor retires. In fact, many churches don't survive more than one generation. A group of thirty-year-olds starts a church with a compelling vision. A generation later, that group of young adults retires, and the church fades into oblivion. For Valley Church, this would have been the easiest path. When Mark and Cheryl retired, there was a great deal of fear about the transition.

But that's not what they wanted. This church, set in a redwood grove at the edge of Silicon Valley, wanted to be part of what God is doing now and in the future. They intentionally sought out voices that were different from their White and privileged demographic. They risked being challenged and disrupted in order to allow God to prepare them for what was ahead. The leaders at Valley Church wanted to make a difference in Silicon Valley.

So they took a risk in hiring a new pastor, Jenny Warner. Jenny had never been the senior leader of a church. She was young and inexperienced, but she was a strategic thinker and had a strong sense of her own mission. Like the elders at Valley Church, she was creative. She was also empathetic and paid attention to the people in front of her. The transition, once feared, was seamless. Together, Jenny and the leadership at Valley set out on a journey to craft a new mission. They called in consultants. They conducted focus groups. They listened and prayed. The result not only capitalized on their location and strengths but also gave them a clear sense of mission: "We're a base camp building a more loving world." The base camp image reflects Valley Church's forest location and names what they have always been: a place of beauty, refuge, and respite.

While the place is important, it's not an end unto itself. Valley Church wants their identity to revolve around building a more loving world shaped by Jesus. Their values are unique: slowing down, focusing outward, supporting one another, connecting authentically, and seeking the sacred.

These values are deeply countercultural to the Silicon Valley pace of life. Their new mission and vision have helped to clarify their ministry focus. They now seek to be a hub for Portola Valley through creative arts, spiritual exploration, local service, and personal connections. As they lean into their mission and values, Valley Church is finding that God keeps meeting them. There is a buzz of hope on Sundays and throughout the week as they dream of serving their community as a place for people to gather and hang out. They also seek to strengthen the families and kids in their neighborhood and build new partnerships that allow them to stretch beyond their wooded enclave with authenticity and integrity.

How is your ministry spilling outside of its core? Who on the outside of your building would care if your church shut down? Where is your church's Jerusalem, Samaria, and Judea? Some congregations mostly focus on themselves as if they are a religious club. But attending to God's calling will take us outward in mission as the sent ones.

Telos: the end purpose you are heading for. In my (Kevin's) experience consulting with American businesses, the word *vision* indicates the desired ends. What are we trying to accomplish? Bill Gates's vision was to have a PC in every home by the year 2000. In 1928, Herbert Hoover's campaign vision was "a chicken in every pot and a car in every garage." Years ago, I asked our family friend Truett Cathy what his desire was for Chick-fil-A, which he founded in 1946. Without missing a beat, he responded, "Our vision is to glorify God by being a faithful steward of all that is entrusted to us, and to have a positive influence on all who come in contact with Chick-fil-A."

Aristotle used *telos* to describe the goal of an object or person. The *telos* of a blacksmith was to make a sword, the *telos* of a soldier was to use the sword to wound the enemy, and both the blacksmith and the soldier were submitted to the *telos* of the state to protect its well-being.

The New Testament uses the word *telos* forty-two times. Paul explains that believing in Jesus brings the "end" of trying to be righteous through the law (Romans 10:4)—and that Jesus is the very fulfillment of that law. So, *telos* includes the concept of completion as well as attainment, or realization. In the pastoral epistles, Paul writes that the "aim" of his instruction is love (1 Timothy 1:5). Peter says the end, or goal, of our faith is the salvation of our souls (1 Peter 1:9). And in Colossians 1:28-29, Paul uses this word to describe the maturity of the Christian life.

This word *telos* speaks of direction and a compelling future. A reality greater than the present drives us toward discipline, change, and preparation. *Telos* shows us where we are heading. If we continue with our current habits, structures, and programs, what will be the end? Where will it lead?

What do you want your ministry to look like in the future? What do you believe God wants your church to look like in eighteen months, three years, and five years? How will you know if your ministry has been as effective as it could possibly be?

Stratēgos: the strategy for your leading. When a church knows their *aretē*, *apostolos*, and *telos*, they are ready for the fourth leg of the table. They can define their *stratēgos*, a word combining the Greek words *stratos* (army, or "that which is spread out") and *agos* (leader). A literal definition would be "driving or leading that which is spread out." The board game Stratego lets players act as leaders of two armies by planning how to use their marshals, colonels, captains, scouts, miners, and spies to best defeat their opponent. My (Kevin's) dad and I would play for hours when I was a boy!

Various countries of the classical world used the term to refer to military offices. Philip II of Macedon used it as the title for commanders on detached assignments. Athens had such an office in the sixth century BC. Thrace's Odrysian kingdom was divided into *stratēgoi,* each headed by a *stratēgos.*

Stratēgos speaks of leadership—the ability to harness, administrate, gather, and utilize existing people and resources to accomplish our *telos.* It is the desire and ability to respond to what the Holy Spirit is doing, to understand how a particular church functions best, and to plan and execute procedures that accomplish the goals of the ministry.

Strategy is all about responding to changing conditions and contexts. The digital era ushered in massive differences in the way we communicate and operate. Every organization in North America is adapting to these advancements. As our context changes, we remain steadfast on *aretē* and *apostolos*, but our *telos* and *stratēgos* can and should adapt to changing conditions. Congregations will periodically review their strategy to see if it is effective and timely.

What is our *stratēgos* for being true to our *aretē*, *apostolos*, and *telos*? How are we planning to practically live out these realities? In 2020, as Covid-19 forced many churches to pause in-person gatherings, every leader had to figure out a new *stratēgos*. Some succeeded while others did not. Some were able to adapt while others refused to change.

When a church understands, embraces, and walks in their *aretē*, *apostolos*, *telos*, and *stratēgos*, they thrive in their True North. To excel in the plans God has for you, you must as well. Embracing this reality makes all the difference. Take Moses or Martin, for example.

Moses

In Exodus 5, we meet a frustrated Moses. Things were not turning out as he expected. After receiving and obeying an initial call from God to confront Pharaoh, the most powerful man in the Egyptian world, Moses hit a roadblock. The king did not respond as Moses expected. Instead, Pharaoh made life harder on the Israelites, ordering the slave drivers to stop supplying them with straw for their brick-making: "Let them go and gather their own straw" (Exodus 5:7). When the Jews heard of this sudden turn of events, they understandably became quite agitated with Moses and his brother, Aaron.

Today, many pastors feel the frustration of their own unmet expectations. They obeyed God yet met opposition. People questioned—or attacked—their motives and character. They might have waded through the valley of being misunderstood or misrepresented. The pandemic brought unforeseen challenges to church leaders, leaving many disheartened. That's a tough place to be, especially when we know we serve an infinite God who could change it all in an instant.

Have you ever done that? You thought you heard from the Lord and stepped out in obedience. Instead of improving, matters got worse. In Moses' situation, the Israelites did not understand why things got worse. They blamed their leader. It's an awful, painful thing to be accused of wrongdoing when you have good motives.

Several years ago, I (Kevin) served as a volunteer on the board of directors for a graduate school. A group of students became angry with the president over some decisions he made. As a coach and consultant, I routinely suggest that every leader have a coach to offer perspective, counsel, and a fresh set of eyes. So I made the suggestion to the board chair and the president, even offering my time pro bono. A few weeks later, I received a nasty letter from the board chair telling me I was "out of line" for questioning the president's leadership, and he asked me to resign. I was astonished. Even though I had offered my time and service as a professional coach at no charge and tried to help the president navigate a difficult situation, the board responded with anger.

So, "Moses returned to the LORD and said, 'Why, Lord, why have you brought trouble on this people? Is this why you sent me? Ever since I went to Pharaoh to speak in your name, he has brought trouble on this people, and you have not rescued your people at all'" (Exodus 5:22-23). Moses did what we should all do when we are perplexed: he cried out to God. And the Lord gave an amazing answer:

> "Now you will see what I will do to Pharaoh: Because of my mighty hand he will let them go; because of my mighty hand he will drive them out of his country." God also said to Moses, "I am the LORD. I appeared to Abraham, to Isaac and to Jacob as God Almighty, but by my name the LORD I did not make myself fully known to them. I also established my covenant with them to give them the land of Canaan, where they resided as foreigners. Moreover, I have heard the groaning of the Israelites, whom the Egyptians are enslaving, and I have remembered my covenant." (Exodus 6:1-5)

Notice that God caught Moses' attention through disappointment.

> "Therefore, say to the Israelites: 'I am the LORD, and I will bring you out from under the yoke of the Egyptians. I will free you from being slaves to them, and I will redeem you with an outstretched arm and with mighty acts of judgment. I will take you as my own people, and I will be your God. Then you will know that I am the LORD your God, who brought you out from under the yoke of the Egyptians. And I will bring you to the land I swore with uplifted hand to give to Abraham, to Isaac and to Jacob. I will give it to you as a possession. I am the LORD.'" (Exodus 6:6-8)

We typically expect God to speak to us through the Bible, a messenger, or an answered prayer. In this case, however, God captured Moses' attention by what he did not do. Instead of letting the Israelites go free, Pharaoh made life more difficult for them. In that moment, God did not meet Moses' expectations. Sometimes the Lord does the same thing with us. He captures our attention through unanswered prayer. This is the reality of unmet expectations. Every believer will experience this valley sooner or later.

God wants our attention, and sometimes he gets it by surprising us. Once Moses was listening, the Lord responded by telling his servant what he was about to do.

He would bring them out of slavery.

He would redeem them.

He would display his outstretched arm, symbolizing his power and might.

He would make Israel his own people.

He would be their God.

He would bring them into the land promised to their forefathers.

They would know him experientially as he fulfilled his promises to them.

Notice True North's four qualities in God's revelation of himself:

- *Aretē*—He would be their God and they would be his people.
- *Apostolos*—God would redeem them and bring them out of slavery.

- *Telos*—God would bring them into the Promised Land.
- *Stratēgos*—The unfolding story of how God does the above throughout the Bible.

God was interested in more than just defeating Pharaoh. He wanted to make himself known to his people. Sometimes he puts his people against impossible odds in order to demonstrate what he can do. And when he does, it results in our being in awe of him. Moses and the Jews were about to walk through some of the most jaw-dropping wonders in recorded biblical history. What God planned was much higher and wider than they could have imagined.

God told Moses he would redeem his people. He would free them from the Egyptians. This stream of deliverance and redemption flows through the Bible and continues to this day. When we become followers of Christ, we become a part of his process of seeing lives changed by the power, truth, and presence of the Lord. How as a church are we partnering with God in his redemptive work?

Martin

As he looked at his calendar one morning, Martin dropped his head into his hands. He had a meeting later that day with a group of people who were attempting a hostile takeover. *These things happen with* Fortune *500 companies but not with churches*, he thought. *This isn't how the body of Christ is supposed to live. They will know we are Christians by our fighting? Seriously?*

A few years earlier, Martin Overson had been hired as the new pastor of Desert Hills Church just south of Tucson in Green Valley, Arizona. Green Valley is a retirement community, populated with golf courses, restaurants, and shopping centers and surrounded by miles of desert.

I (Kevin) first met Martin when things were going well. During our first phone call, he relayed most of his story. In the early years, Martin had introduced a new, simple, mission statement. Most churches have one, but Desert Hills is truly *aligned* to theirs. They collectively recite it at all five services each weekend. Walk into their country gospel service on Saturday or a traditional service on Sunday and you'll hear the same thing: "We celebrate grace. We make disciples (starting with ourselves) and we strive to make a difference."

Martin says it has been life changing for people to be part of a church that is unified and focused on a common mission. They hold new member classes four times a year; each includes six sessions and a dinner. They spend three of these sessions discussing who they are as a church, their mission, their values, and their theological underpinnings.

When the church participated in our Transforming Church Insight (TCI), they scored quite high in the eightieth percentile. Even before getting on an airplane for my first visit, I knew this was a special place—an attentive church.

During our initial call, Martin described a hostile takeover attempt by an associate pastor, a council president, and a council vice president. Differing visions had emerged, resulting in polarization among leaders. Martin tried meeting with the associate pastor and even having a denominational mediator intervene, but the associate pastor refused. A small group tried to smear Martin's reputation to various congregation members. He went days without sleep.

Martin shared,

> At my wit's end, I called for a vote of confidence from the council to see if they still wanted me as senior pastor. It passed, but only by one vote. Imagine how much confidence I felt then! Members of the satellite group along with the president and vice president were on the council. Both the president and vice president resigned. I worked believing that my tenure hung by a thread. It was a very dark time. But we began addressing the conflict in healthy ways. We made some changes in leadership. We called in a trusted adviser who helped greatly with the healing process. He helped reframe the situation for me by saying that this kind of conflict was fairly common in healthy churches and that having survived it, my tenure

would be very strong. I did gain much confidence by moving through the lies and betrayals of the event. There were also some wonderfully strong Christian leaders who stepped forward to support me. I tried too long to handle it alone, not knowing that much of the congregation had no clue what was going on.

Things at Desert Hills eventually turned around. The conflict became a distant memory. Martin re-established his leadership, and he learned to lead an attentive church. He brought a sense of humor and joy to every service and every meeting. The dark days were gone. The church grew, with nearly two thousand people attending weekend services and most of them engaged in ministry within the church and the local community.

Martin called us at that point. Approaching retirement, he realized that the church had now become very pastor-centric. Like many large churches, people flocked to hear the dynamic preacher who could supplement his income as a standup comedian if he wanted. A new, more subtle concern emerged: If they moved away from that model, they would lose Martin. If they remained that way, they wouldn't survive once he retired.

Over the last few years, our coaching at Desert Hills has focused on helping them create a shared leadership culture, one where Martin can exercise his wonderful gifts but also celebrate a shared leadership model. Our first step was to help the church create a set of shared values, or *aretē*, that would endure after Martin retired. Through an interactive storytelling process involving many congregation members and every leader, they developed seven unique core values. These values were then displayed in many places throughout their campus and promoted on their website. They provided a grid for all leadership decisions. Martin preached on them. And remarkably, the average church member routinely talked about these values when they spotted them in action. People started paying attention to the church's *aretē*.

Martin has retired now, and Desert Hills is preparing for bright tomorrows with a new pastor named Mike. Mike is drawn to the church because of the clarity of their mission and core values. Specifically, he appreciates the core value "laughter liberates." To me (Kevin), this is a home run. A pastor-centric church moved to being centered around their mission and core values, with Jesus at the true center of it all.

The Desert Hills story demonstrates several important principles. Becoming an attentive church is a journey, not a destination. By definition, an attentive church is always in a posture of thinking ahead, never resting, and never landing. They are habitually reviewing their *aretē*, *apostolos*, *telos*, and *stratēgos* to be faithful to the Lord in their current season and make an ever-expanding ripple effect for the kingdom. We have a series of questions for a congregation to consider once they have clarified their True North. We pose these as questions, rather than imperatives, because no church ever completely arrives:

- Do we have an effective ongoing process for evaluating and revisiting our True North?
- What good things should we say no to because of our True North?
- Do our leadership selection and development process align to our core values?
- Does our budget and stewardship process reflect our strategic priorities and mission?
- Do our facilities support what we are trying to accomplish?
- Do our brand and public identity reflect our core values?
- Does our internal culture align with what we say is most important?

These questions function as a guide on the journey. But the journey takes time.

Survey Says!

Earlier we mentioned the TCI, a tool we use to assess congregations.[4] Vision—or *telos*—is the most important of all fifteen facets. But a church's vision must be embraced by the congregation, not just proclaimed by the pastor.

I (Kevin) was debriefing a church leadership team on their TCI results. Interestingly, they scored fairly high on questions related to the clarity of the church's vision, yet they scored low on a few other vision questions: "I believe our church is heading in the right direction," "I'm excited about where the church is heading in the next few years," and "I have a clear understanding of my role in fulfilling the church's mission." The leaders were perplexed by the high scores on the first set of vision questions and the low scores on the second set. It was a great chance to talk about the difference between a clear vision and a compelling vision. For years, the elders worked together successfully to do long range planning. They were crystal clear about goals and objectives. They were great at implementation and project planning. But that wasn't the issue. The congregation knew the plans but were quite uninspired by them. The plans were clear but not engaging.

When I asked the leaders about their most recent five-year plan, they bragged about how successful they had been in accomplishing over 90 percent of their objectives: new technology in the sanctuary, a remodeled fellowship hall, a larger conference room. Nothing in their visioning process spoke to the *why*. In fact, the buildings and facilities had become too important for them. The tail was wagging the dog. When the vision is clear *and* compelling, people will find a way to align to it.

Lee Bolman and Terrence Deal describe the importance of a consistent objective in lessons learned from an aircraft carrier in their book *Reframing Organizations:*

> "It may look like chaos, but we always know what is going on," says Lt. Cdr. Gary Deal, a naval officer who once served aboard the aircraft carrier USS Kennedy. When equipped for deployment, the Kennedy is home to more than five thousand men and women. About half of these people are assigned to the ship, the other half to the air wing. The ship is organized into nineteen departments, including operations, engineering, supply, navigation, and air. The air wing is organized into nine squadrons. Each squadron ensures that its flight crews and aircraft are ready to conduct an assigned

> mission at any time. The flight deck is responsible for the safe and efficient launch and recovery of the aircraft. Fifty functional roles are involved in the process. Individuals' functions are immediately obvious from their uniforms: blue for "grunts," red for weapons and fire-control personnel, brown for those who direct the taxiing and towing of aircraft, and purple for fuelers. Supervisory personnel wear yellow, while safety personnel wear white. The captain has overall command of the ship, while the commander of the air group is responsible for the air wing.
>
> In combat, the USS Kennedy's primary goal is clear: bombs on target. To reach that goal, all functions have to work together. Anything anyone does affects everyone else, especially in close quarters under battle conditions. Individuals know their own job even if they are unaware of the big picture.

This illustration points to a core premise of the need for a structural frame. Clear, well-understood roles and relationships and adequate coordination are key to how well an organization performs.[5]

Bolman and Deal go on to share several assumptions that undergird a successful structural framework for an organization. The primary one is, "Organizations exist to achieve established goals and objectives."

The book of Proverbs says it like this: "Where there is no vision, the people are unrestrained" (Proverbs 29:18 NASB). Centuries later, when standing before King Agrippa, the apostle Paul dramatically declared, "I was not disobedient to the vision from heaven" (Acts 26:19). Throughout his life, he faithfully fulfilled his purpose of declaring the gospel to the Jews and Gentiles. Having, knowing, and implementing your *telos*—aim, goal, purpose, and vision—is absolutely essential to leading attentive churches. If not, as Eugene Peterson said, "If people can't see what God is doing, they stumble all over themselves" (Proverbs 29:18 MSG).

In our TCI research, we see that an emphasis on buildings, finances, and implementation is common among lower-scoring churches. In other words, these churches become victims of the tail wagging the dog. The maintenance of the church overcomes the church's mission and vision. We're not suggesting a church should demolish its facilities and throw the budgeting process to the wind. But we are recommending an essential order that starts with a clear and compelling vision.

Becoming an attentive church is not an easy journey, but it is one worth taking. The positive impact you will have on others is worth the cost. Are you ready to take the next step?

Questions for Reflection and Discussion

- This chapter begins by contrasting sports teams that focused their attention and resources on secondary matters versus those that were attentive to the core mission of the organization: winning championships. In what ways have you witnessed a similar contrast in churches? What are some of the secondary matters some churches focus on? How would you describe the core mission of the church?
- What was the most important thing you learned from the story of Martin and Desert Hills Church? How do you see that learning affecting your congregation?
- What has God used to get your attention during important junctures in your life? How could you imagine God getting the attention of your congregation?
- What struck you most about the patterns the authors saw in the TCI survey data?
- How open is your congregation to change?
- What ministries or functions need to be realigned in light of your True North?

6

How Do We Create Community in a Narcissistic World?

In Greek mythology, Narcissus was a beautiful young man who was a hunter. He habitually showed disdain and contempt for people who showed him affection. Seeing his own reflection in a pool one day, he fell in love with himself, which led to his ultimate destruction.[1]

Self-absorption is the exact opposite of Christian discipleship. Instead of a free-flowing river, narcissism creates a stagnated pool. Stating the cost of following him, Jesus said, "If anyone would come after me, let him deny himself and take up his cross daily and follow me" (Luke 9:23 ESV). Community, however, is part of God's very essence. In the Trinity, the Father, Son, and Spirit dwell together in divine community. The Lord was not satisfied to only enjoy that tribunal community; he also wanted to share a relationship with his creation. The Bible makes an amazing statement in 1 Corinthians 1:9: "God is faithful, who has called you into fellowship with his Son, Jesus Christ our Lord." The calling to be a Christian includes the call to share life with Jesus and commune with him.

Yet many churches, shaped by today's culture of narcissism, don't reflect his relational design very well. Consumerism is "the situation in which too much attention is given to buying and owning things."[2] Often, this consumption is viewed "as a vehicle for personal satisfaction."[3] The unquenchable thirst to satisfy self has grown far beyond only material items. Today, much of our culture, including church culture, is driven to use organizations, services, or entities to satisfy personal needs. This creates monumental challenges for pastors and ministry leaders wanting to lead attentive churches. One vital aspect of leading attentive churches is learning to create a spirit of interdependent community in a world of self-driven consumption.

Several years ago, I (Kevin) was hired to consult with Hope Chapel in Arizona. The pastor, a gregarious man with a charming personality, had been an entertainer in Atlantic City before becoming a Christian. In 2002, the church moved to a seventy-five-acre campus with a four-thousand–seat sanctuary. His charismatic and warm transparency drew people to him instantly. He lit up a room when he entered. He attracted a star-studded leadership team. It's no wonder his infectious passion helped them become one of the country's largest churches.

When I first visited in 2012, they averaged about twenty-five thousand people weekly on multiple campuses. Their holiday light show drew a quarter of a million people yearly. Their Christian-themed amusement park was well known across the state. Dan, the pastor, had resonated with one of my books and invited me to fly in for a few days to help them think through their effectiveness in the church's mission statement: "To make disciples."

In our meetings those days, a red flag became obvious to me. The church and staff put Dan on a precarious pedestal. I cautioned them that their work needed to take on more of a collaborative effort. One of the young staffers angrily pushed back, saying, "He is our shepherd. We do whatever he says! Kevin, you are out of line." Others in the room echoed his sentiment. They attributed most of their success to having a dynamic pastor who was special and anointed by God to grow the church. In their minds, to question him was to subvert God's established authority.

I stood firm in my advice, but so did they. Leaving our meeting discouraged and concerned, I pondered a system clearly rooted in glorifying their pastor. I worried that their outward success blinded them to the call to become an attentive church. They needed to listen to God more than a single charismatic leader. An attentive church builds community. An attentive church equips and empowers each person to grow and serve. Many times, our church partners send us a follow-up phone call or email for another consultation. But I heard nothing from this one after our meeting.

Sadly, like many rock star pastors before him, Dan resigned several years later amid allegations of misconduct. A sex scandal ensued, which shook the church. In the following months, the church's board wrestled with their dynamics. Their strategy of focusing on meeting self-centered desires by creating exciting programs led by a celebrity pastor—rather than attentively building community—had been doomed to fail from the beginning.

The Roots of Consumerism

The early church drove home three major lessons on how to be a Christian in a pre-Christian Roman culture. Those three keys were believing, belonging, and behaving.[4] As Christendom swept over Western Europe, the church sought to transmit the value of believing. It was also vital to teach the value of behaving in a pre-Christian culture where so much challenged the values of the kingdom of God. Yet, while belonging was one of the most evangelistically significant features of the early church, it diminished during the Middle Ages. The lack of emphasis on belonging became the precursor to the Modern Era, which then became the precursor to the consumer-driven culture we live in today.

Following the Middle Ages, the Modern Era represented a marriage between the Renaissance and the Enlightenment. The Renaissance rediscovered early Greek philosophy with renewed attention on the autonomous self. Protagoras said, "Man is the measure of all things." Fast forward to the Enlightenment when René Descartes said, "I think, therefore I am." In other words, I can't be sure of anything other than the fact that I am thinking.

The Enlightenment was the age of reason. The scientific method became the filter for understanding truth. Francis Bacon, who was at the forefront of the scientific method, advocated for a reasoned, empirical, and observational method of understanding reality. He challenged metaphysical speculation. We should note that he was a religious man and believed his work would only help us understand God's design. The

Modern Era began to move Western culture away from the mystery of God to the certainty of science.

So, the Modern Era gave us the "thinking self." This gave rise to some wonderful social changes focused on human rights. The United States became the "Enlightenment Project" with "liberty and justice for all." Ultimately, this focus on individual rights led to the abolition of slavery, women's suffrage, freedom of speech, and a host of other protections for the individual.

If the movement away from belonging in the Middle Ages was the precursor to the Modern Era, we suggest that the focus on individualism in the Modern Era was the precursor to elitism in today's world. Individual rights, for several centuries, were understood within the context of the common good. But the last eighty years have stripped away any sense of the common good. Individual rights now exist only for the benefit of the individual. We are arguably experiencing the most consumer-oriented culture in human history. Consumerism is an economic theory that encourages a never-ending escalation in the attainment of products, services, and entertainment. It is individualism on steroids. The ordinary American is now shaped to have an unquenchable thirst for more things.

The Roaring Twenties birthed this phenomenon, but it did not really take root until the 1960s and 1970s. New technologies and workplaces created the first wave of latchkey kids—children with nothing to do after school. Historically, children worked on the farm or in the family shop. But for the first time in human history, teenagers had enormous amounts of discretionary time. Personal entertainment became an unquenchable thirst.

And that's the problem with the very premise of consumerism as an economic model. We can never get enough of what we really don't need. Consumerism, combined with the rise of social media, has resulted in a culture of narcissism. Whether it's video games or "likes" on social media, our self-centered desires are unquenchable. Churches that continue to pursue a consumer-driven strategy will find they can never meet the needs of their consumers. In the early church, people related to each other as family in a culture where they were strangers and exiles. The sense of being adopted into the family of faith was profound. Recapturing this understanding of belonging will dramatically affect the church of today. And it will take deep focus and real work.

The Customer Is Always Right

In recent decades the West has become obsessed with self. Restaurants, department stores, and online retailers cater to the individual. An oft-repeated phrase in retail stores is, "The customer is always right." This inadvertently produces an attitude of elitism. In our experience working with hundreds of American churches, the same mindset is alive and well.

John Micklethwait and Adrian Wooldridge describe the state of the American church as the "Disneyfication of God," seeking to make Christianity attractive, palatable, and entertaining for—you guessed it—the customer. In 1985, Neil Postman published a prophetic book titled *Amusing Ourselves to Death.* He wrote, "Americans no longer talk to each other, they entertain each other. They do not exchange ideas, they exchange images. They do not argue with propositions; they argue with good looks, celebrities and commercials."[5] And that was 1985, twenty-two years before the first iPhone was released.

Elitism isn't always about mimicking what culture gives us. It's not always about having great music, coffee shops, or Zumba classes. And there's nothing wrong with any of those things by themselves. However, elitism occurs when my personal preferences outweigh our shared mission. Several years ago, I (Kevin) was helping a church outside of Indianapolis through a pastoral transition. The previous pastor was a wonderful expository preacher. The church attracted thousands of people to their weekend services, with Bibles thoroughly marked up and highlighted. Unfortunately, after a comprehensive assessment, we learned that the expositional preaching rarely resulted in any real life change. Church members were mesmerized by the pastor's ability to exegete Scripture. His knowledge of Hebrew, Greek, and Aramaic almost put church members in a trance as he preached. After our assessment, however, it was clear that the church was much more focused on the pastor and his preaching than on Jesus. The church had little interest in missions or evangelism. As they looked for a new pastor, they were intent only on one thing: someone to satiate their appetite for expository preaching.

So how do we begin making headway against this current? We have to move people toward community.

The Rise of Cultural Narcissism

Over the last several decades, the evolution of individualism, consumerism, and social media have together created a robust cultural narcissism. The use of social media platforms such as Facebook and Twitter has dramatically increased in recent years and has even drawn the attention of scholarly research. A number of these studies seek to show a correlation between the use of social media and narcissistic tendencies.[6] These platforms, which have been called a "pervasive presence in our society," cannot be underemphasized in the development of self-absorption in our culture.[7] Some researchers even speculate a link between social media, narcissism, and violent, aggressive behavior.[8]

In her article "Cultural Narcissism: Is Social Media Making Us Narcissists?" Kathryn Carver writes, "Selfie sticks and their related behaviors are a potential sign of a society becoming increasingly self-centered." She identifies cultural narcissism as "woven into the very fabric of our culture in insidious, subtle, and incremental ways. It inhibits character growth, leading to dysfunction, and the more dysfunctional individuals populating our society, the more detriment there is to that society, causing real problems at every level."[9]

The fascination with taking selfies, comparing our experiences to those of other people on social media, and posting pictures has created a tsunami of self-centeredness. For younger generations, an experience as simple as going out to eat with friends or attending a ball game doesn't seem real, validated, or complete unless there are pictures to post, boasting of what a great time you had. Prior to social media, families would go on vacation or visit a theme park together without feeling any need to show their adventures to anyone else! They could just enjoy the time for what it was in the moment—without the need to compare or boast.

The reality of addiction to social media and the underlying reasons are causes for great concern. Neurologically, the use of social media appeals to our brain circuitry related to reward. More specifically, it involves hyperactivation of the striatum and ventral tegmental area (VTA), which include neuron clusters designed for reward, motivation, and cognition.[10] Dopamine is a hormone that naturally makes us feel good. It is released in the body when we experience and even anticipate pleasurable activities such as good food, sex, recreation, or just about anything we genuinely enjoy. Some people, however, can become dopamine addicts and thus are compelled to habitually practice behaviors that release dopamine.[11]

I (Kevin) remember how exciting it was as a child to go to an arcade. Children could spend hours there, popping quarters into games like *Space Invaders*, *Ms. Pac-Man*, *Centipede*, *Frogger*, and *Tetris*. Following the rush of excitement (and dopamine) of playing one game was the urge to play another. Likewise, when game consoles became popular in homes, children could experience that rush again. However, there was a notable difference between video games of those days and modern ones. In my childhood, video games had a clear beginning and a clear ending. When it was over, it was over. Today, however, video game developers use neurological science to create addictive behavior. Most games never really end. They have multiple levels of achievement, and players can jump in and out of ongoing games with other virtual players. This modern approach to gaming is in itself extremely addictive.[12]

The advent of social media presents a new challenge in discipleship. What does it mean to follow Jesus in the virtual world of social media? How can we promote health in these areas? How can we set our "minds on things that are above, not on things that are on earth" (Colossians 3:2 ESV) and prepare our "minds for action . . . being sober-minded" (1 Peter 1:13 ESV)? As the *Journal of Science* warns, "It is of upmost importance to recognize the way these platforms exploit our brain psychology in a drug-like manner."[13]

The Bible often talks about the believer in light of the entire Christian community. The many "one another" passages in the New Testament are not simply instructions for individual Christians to practice privately. They are admonitions to be obeyed and embraced in the context of community. Unfortunately, the advent of social networking services (SNS) has resulted in a greater emphasis on self rather than community. Carver says,

> Over the past few decades, **we have switched from focusing on the greater good to concentrating on oneself**, leading to the Self-Esteem Movement, which asserted that self-esteem is the key to a successful, happy life. This shift led to a **rise in entitlement and individualization**, which emphasized self-reliance, subsequently eradicating the need for social support or meaningful connection. Along with this modernization of society came a valuation of fame, wealth, and beauty above all else.[14]

Dr. Archibald Hart and Dr. Sylvia Frejd wrote a thoroughly researched book called *The Digital Invasion: How Technology is Shaping You and Your Relationships*. Dr. Hart was the dean emeritus of the school of psychology at Fuller Theological Seminary. As a professor of PhD students, he realized significant changes among students in the latter years he taught. He said students did not want to be challenged to "reason anything or figure out a problem anymore." They just wanted the answers. He wrote,

> Our ability to reflect and reason seems to be declining. It appears that while modern technology is fantastic in being able to give us instant answers, this easy access to a lot of information is also reshaping our creativity, inventiveness, and ingenuity. The result? According to Dr. Nicholas Carr, an expert in the area, it is making us shallow thinkers. And he is also convinced that shallow thinking will lead to shallow living.[15]

The cultural tendency toward narcissism is a result of this type of shallow thinking. Attentive Christians, like King David, lift their eyes off themselves, understanding their own smallness in light of the magnificence of their Creator. The psalmist declared, "O Lord, our Lord, your majestic name fills the earth! Your glory is higher than the heavens. . . . When I look at the night sky and see the work of your fingers . . . what are mere mortals that you should think about them?" (Psalm 8:1, 3-4 NLT).

Sadly, the church is not exempt from the dangers of narcissism. In his book *When Narcissism Comes to Church*, Chuck DeGroat discusses narcissistic pastors:

> The church becomes an extension of his narcissistic ego, and its ups and downs lead to seasons of ego inflation and ego deflation for this pastor. Today social media platforms add to this mix. Because his sense of identity is bound up in external realities, his sense of mission is wavering and unmoored, often manifesting in constantly shifting visions and programs, frequent dissatisfaction with the status quo, and anxious engagement with staff and members.[16]

Another danger of the digital world is how easy it is to maintain superficial relationships that we call "connecting" online, while never really making mental, emotional, spiritual, and psychological connections with other human beings on a face-to-face, deep level. This reliance on pseudo connections has led in part to the rise of loneliness, anger, and depression among many young people. Years ago, teenagers rarely struggled with depression. Sadly, that is no longer the case. The Mayo Clinic calls teen depression a "serious mental health problem."[17] Pew Research reveals that the number of teens experiencing depression increased by 59 percent in one recent ten-year period.[18] The Centers for Disease Control and Prevention (CDC) reports that teen mental health is in crisis.[19]

A healthy, attentive church works to create community for its people—safe places where relationships can thrive. An overabundance of virtual platforms does not replace how God intended for humans to connect. And in the atmosphere of real connection, many of the hurts, frustrations, and fears of life receive genuine help, peace, safety, and reconciliation. Again, Hart and Frejd wrote that the virtual world does not offer "the face-to-face relationships that God intended. If our social connections are not in-the-flesh, face-to-face social connections, we will feel increasingly lonely. Our wonderful brain responds better to reality and face-to-face connectivity more than to any other form of social connection."[20]

Creating Community

We were created in God's image, the *imago Dei*. This means we share some similarities with God that don't exist in other creatures. The very first thing we learn about God is that he is creative: "In the beginning God created the heavens and the earth" (Genesis 1:1). To bear God's image is to be creative. Dorothy Sayers wrote a wonderful book, published in 1941, called *The Mind of the Maker*. She describes the creative process inherent in humans as a reflection of the creative interaction of the Trinity. To be created in God's image is to have the stamp of producing creative work. "To create" is the opposite of "to consume." Churches who primarily pursue a customer-driven strategy will always struggle to unleash the creative contributions of their people. The second thing we learn about God in the creation narrative is that he exists in community: "Then God said, 'Let us make human beings in our image, to be like us. . . .' So God created human beings in his own image. In the image of God he created them; male and female he created them" (Genesis 1:26-27 NLT).

From eternity past, the Father, Son, and Spirit dwelt together, sharing, existing, and collaborating. Their awesome power worked together at creation (Colossians 1:15-20). The Bible's first two chapters present Elohim—the three-in-one creative force—establishing family as the first community and emphasizing the importance of connectedness. God declared, "It is not good for the man to be alone," and he created a counterpart for Adam (Genesis 2:18 AMP). Throughout biblical history, God desired for his people to dwell and thrive in community with others. One of the simplest statements about this reality is in Paul's description of the Christian calling: "God is faithful, who has called you into fellowship with his Son, Jesus Christ, our Lord." (1 Corinthians 1:9). Sometimes people in ministry talk about calling primarily in terms of tasks: a call to preaching, evangelism, music ministry, etc. But here, the primary calling from God is to relationship—sharing life together in Christ and being a creative community.

The Clergy and Laity

One obstacle to creating healthy community that has persisted throughout church history is the false dichotomy between the clergy and the laity. Stretching back to the early church, hierarchical divisions have existed between the professional ordained elders, pastors, and bishops and the ordinary lay members of the church. The emergence of "an organized, duly ordained clergy, as a closed 'status' over against the 'laos,' the people," created a shift in focus. The ordained were the ones tasked with doing ministry. The congregation became the passive receivers, expected to "pray, pay, and obey." However, biblically, every believer possesses a priesthood, giftedness, and calling to use his or her gifts, passions, and abilities to serve others, meet needs, and thus do ministry.[21]

Many who were part of the priestly system in the Roman Catholic Church during the medieval era were viewed as the experts on spiritual matters. The laity, on the other hand, were characterized by secular work, resulting in a devaluation of their world, their interests, and their occupations. As Hendrik Kraemer wrote in his book *A Theology of the Laity,* "The laity so to speak were taken for granted," and they "inevitably fell into a lesser category of saintliness." Though the Reformation urged the recognition of the "priesthood of all believers," the division of clergy and laity did not change much. This unhealthy wall of distinction keeps individual believers from developing their gifts and engaging in ministry. Instead of expecting the Spirit to speak and manifest Christ through the individual members of the congregation, the expectation became to put the ordained few on a high pedestal, thus stifling true biblical community.[22] This causes the clergy to overfunction and encourages the laity to underfunction. How does a congregation truly attend to what God is saying if the clergy are too dominant?

Another roadblock in the way of healthy community is our modern self-absorbed culture. Churches miss the mark when they focus only on meeting people's felt needs instead of building biblical community. It's a mistake to think the church can adopt a customer-driven strategy, reach people, and then convert them into a close-knit community. This has become one of the legacies of Covid-19 as congregations had to pivot to online worship. When the pandemic began to wane and congregations came back together, many people realized it was still easier to stay at home and watch the service in pajamas, coffee mug in hand. Many churches had a hard time wooing part of their congregation back into physical community. Yet we were created for community—not spiritual consumption or elitism. When churches teach their members a self-centered way to enjoy the faith, they become resistant to adopting a greater commitment to community. And when the focus is on self, it becomes almost impossible to lead a church to become attentive.

There are two fatal flaws in this failed strategy. First, narcissism resists change. You can lure them in, but a self-oriented strategy will fail to transform them. Second, the consumer is never satisfied. Rather than be transformed into a life of sacrifice and service, they will demand more and more of others. In his book *I Am a Church Member,* Thom Rainer says, "With a country club membership you pay others to do the work for you. With church membership, everyone has a role or function. That is why some are hands, feet, ears, or eyes. We are all different, but we are necessary parts of the whole."[23]

I (Jim) have faced this clergy-laity divide and found it perplexing during my years in the pastorate. Early in my ministry I read authors like Bruce Larsen, Keith Miller, Greg Ogden, and Stan Grenz. I saw what Ephesians 4 said about equipping saints for the work of ministry. I was convinced these authors were right about needing a "New Reformation" (Ogden).[24] But inside I found significance in being the biblical expert in my domain. I knew the original languages in a way that was both helpful and distancing from my congregation. I loved leading and teaching in ways that drew people in. I also fell for the adulation from people who suggested my vital importance to the success of the congregation. Yet, I often heard comments about how the congregation paid me and the other staff to do these things well. As a result, it was easy to become complicit in the undoing of the laity's development. Ironically, my own competence enabled me to avoid equipping others. How do we stay attentive to God's work when our egos are being stroked to overfunction as do-it-all pastors? Sadly, I know what it is like to cooperate with the undoing of God's plan for community.

One healthy corrective is to not have full-time vocational pastors and instead have a mix of bivocational pastors and volunteer leadership, in the context of team leadership that doesn't elevate a singular superstar pastor. The church in Antioch in Acts 13 seems to have been led by a team of several people rather than one superstar. One of our very healthy cohorts at LFM, through our partnership with Church United in South Florida, consists primarily of bivocational pastors. As the demographics in North America continue changing, it is likely that more churches and more pastors—out of necessity—will need to entertain the reality of part-time and bivocational pastors.

A Lonely World

Everything in our culture points to the need to integrate this community focus throughout the entire vision and values of a congregation. One of my (Kevin's) seminary professors, Stan Grenz, shared in his book *Created for Community*,

> God is at work in our world, we declare. And God's purpose in this activity is the establishment of community—a reconciled people who enjoy fellowship with Him, with one another, and ultimately with all creation. Why community? Because the focus on community encapsulates the biblical message, it stands at the heart of the theological heritage of the church, and it speaks to the aspirations and the sensed needs of people in our world today. In short, as we realize that we are created for community, we are in a position to connect Christian belief with Christian living.[25]

We live in a terribly lonely world. In spite of social media and instant connection, many people close their eyes at night without having experienced any deep and meaningful interaction with others. An astounding statistic from a Barna study captured in Don Everts's book *The Reluctant Witness* reveals that the majority of church goers have fewer than ten spiritual conversations with anyone in a year.[26] Our world and congregations yearn for community, and God designed the body of Christ to address this need for connection.

If you comb the bottom of a creek or riverbed, you will likely find hundreds of smooth stones. The Lord does not intend for us to be one lone rock in the river. He wants many stones to create a multitude of ripple effects in ever-increasing circles.

Our Transforming Church Insight (TCI) survey research has over eleven million records. Over the course of the first twenty years, the national scores didn't change much. So after Covid-19, we got curious. We assumed that, because of the effect of the pandemic, we would see lower national averages across the board. Wow, were we wrong. We compared five years of data prior to March 2020 with the data of all churches that completed the survey after March 2020. All fifteen scales saw a meaningful increase in our national database. Which ones increased the most? The community scales! The survey measures four scales related to community:

Relationships: People rate things like warmth, caring, and fellowship.

Support: This reflects how well people feel cared for and ministered to, reflecting personal growth and support from the church.

Ownership: This scale measures whether or not people feel they have ownership and can make a difference at the church. They believe that they count.

Connectedness: People experience connectedness to a church in many ways. When newcomers quickly connect and the church has an effective assimilation process for all, people will understand and engage in the mission of the church beyond just the weekend worship service. Further, when people are connected, they will more readily embrace change.

As we looked at the scores on these four scales after March 2020, we saw an average increase of 7.44 percentage points. The most significant increase was in "connectedness" with an overall increase of 9.91 percentage points!

Or course, we were shocked. We expected Covid-19 to have a negative impact on our church health scores. As with any survey, the data simply gives us observations, not interpretations. So we had to translate the numbers qualitatively. Our best understanding is that Covid-19 may have been a turning point in moving churches away from entitlement and toward community. Churches are still experimenting with new ways to build a culture of connections. Are we on the cusp of rediscovering how to create community? We hope so. Let's take a look at a few questions to help move us toward becoming a creative community.

As a Pastor or Ministry Leader, How Does My Role Either Stifle or Create Community?

Healthy leaders are unifiers and communicators. Abusive leaders polarize people; healthy leaders build bridges. Unlike the insecure or narcissistic pastor, a healthy one measures success by the growth, maturity, development, and spiritual fruit of their people. At their core they are not just completing tasks and projects but mobilizing people to become a creative community. Leadership author Max De Pree said, "Leaders need to foster environments and work processes within which people can develop high quality relationships."[27]

In our narcissistic culture, it is tempting to measure success by the unquenchable thirst of church growth. Of course, we want to reach as many people with the gospel as possible. But if we have church growth at the expense of church health, we have simply created entitled customers.

One of the dangers of the rock star pastor mentality is that it works against the creative nature of building community and relationships. Ed Stetzer comments,

> If the church life revolves around one person's speaking gift, it is incredibly difficult to move to community. A community "won" to a single voice is not won to community but to spectatorship. . . . If you

> get thousands sitting in rows but can't move them to sitting in circles, true community is hard to find. . . . A gifted communicator can draw a crowd, but biblical community will sustain a congregation.[28]

To resist the slippery slope of succumbing to entitlement, pastors are wise to take a hard look at the biblical role of the shepherd-leader. The past several decades we've seen a plethora of resources aimed at making people better leaders. Many of these books, podcasts, and conferences are helpful and worthwhile. The Bible most often uses the word *shepherd* to refer to those who led others, whether spiritually or in society. As spiritual leaders, we must not divorce our understanding of leadership from the biblical role of shepherd.

Jesus used a shepherd as one of his main pictures of spiritual leadership in John 10, which is sometimes called the Twenty-Third Psalm of the New Testament. He described the connection the shepherd had with his sheep: "The one who enters by the gate is the shepherd of the sheep. The gatekeeper opens the gate for him, and the sheep listen to his voice. He calls his own sheep by name and leads them out. When he has brought out all his own, he goes on ahead of them, and his sheep follow him because they know his voice" (John 10:2-4).

Healthy pastors adopt a model of shepherding, not just management or vision-casting. The aim is to edify and build people, not just to use them to accomplish the leader or organization's purpose. Pastoral identity must be grounded in the biblical metaphors of ministry. At the heart of the biblical understanding of shepherding is taking care of the people entrusted to you.

In some megachurch settings, the untouchable pastor flies high above the common church members, creating a culture that adheres to their lone voice. This can create an atmosphere in the church that indicates the success of the congregation is primarily measured by how many people come to hear the pastor preach, how many books they sell, and how in demand they are to speak at cool church conferences around the country.

Another notable church in a different part of the country lost their celebrity pastor after a months-long affair was exposed. Before the fall, the pastor rarely mingled with church members. On Sundays, volunteers worked hard to keep people from him and kept him secure in the green room, fully stocked with "a lavish catering spread and changes of clothes" to fit his many tastes. When high-profile entertainers or sports stars visited the church to worship and tried to stay in the ordinary seating, ushers were instructed to take them to a marked-off section up front or to the green room.[29]

The green room culture, unfortunately, is characteristic of many modern famous pastors. Tom Nelson writes, "The green room culture regularly reinforces a distorted telos of pastoral success rather than pastoral faithfulness—much more about furthering a brand than furthering the kingdom, more about amplifying a person than exalting Christ. The green room often promotes a toxic celebrity Christian culture."[30]

Over the years, my (Kevin's) dad has asked leaders a simple question: Are you an empire builder or a kingdom seeker? The idea of a celebrity pastor is the antithesis of faithful, biblical leadership. That does not mean being the pastor of a large church is inherently a problem. Jim and I have both known godly, faithful people who ministered through large platforms yet kept the essence of a biblical shepherd-leader—people like Chuck Swindoll, Jack Hayford, Billy Graham, Ken Shigematsu, and Tim Keller. However, in today's selfie-driven culture where success is sometimes measured by the number of "likes" one gets, there's a subtle but damaging temptation to embrace the rock star mentality.

Lest you think, "Well, I pastor a small church in Sedona, Arizona; Fairfield, Iowa; or Hood River, Oregon. I don't have to worry about becoming a rock star pastor," Nelson reminds us, "The crowd need not be big nor the stage prominent for the celebrity pastor to emerge. Celebrity is not necessarily tied to the size of the audience, but rather the size of the ego longing to be stroked."[31] An inflated ego is not only found in megachurch contexts; it can reside in any human heart.

Holly recently recounted her first call as an associate pastor in Florida:

> The senior pastor went on sabbatical six months into my first call. While he was away, I preached many Sundays, moderated leadership meetings, and generally kept the church running during a typical slow season in the year. Upon his return, a well-meaning elder shared that he could go on sabbatical anytime, as the church was in good hands with me. From that moment on, I was not allowed to officiate any official duties nor preach in his absence. He said that he "didn't want anyone to get the impression that I was the pastor." We stumbled through the next year, but then I left the church and took a new call.

Pastor, as you think about your role as shepherd, ponder these questions:

- How well do I express love to people in the congregation?
- Do I listen well, or am I always in a hurry to get through to the next person?
- How well do I care for the vulnerable and "least of these" in our midst—especially those who are most annoying?
- What can I do more or less of to make each person know they matter?

Neal Jones understands how to foster community. He pastored the largest Baptist church in Virginia in the Washington, DC, suburb community of Falls Church. He baptized Chuck Colson. His church members included Super Bowl champion coach Joe Gibbs and a dozen or more congressmen and senators. He served on the Board of Regents at Baylor University as well as at Prison Fellowship. And I (Kevin) married his beautiful daughter, Caroline!

But famous people in the pews did not define his ministry. Rather, handwritten notes did. Neal told me, "More than fifty years ago, I sensed the Lord nudging me to begin writing with paper and pen to encourage people. Since then, I averaged about forty notes per week—on the back of napkins, paper menus, paper towels, and yes, stationery." This habit become central to his pastoral theology:

> While developing a strong vertical relationship with the Lord, I knew I needed to build meaningful horizontal relationships with people.

> Today, living in a retirement community, I continue to write. Sometimes it's expressing sympathy to a neighbor whose husband died unexpectantly, motivating a woman involved in prison ministry, or encouraging someone who just moved in next door or got home from the hospital. I also like to pick leaves off trees and put them in people's mailboxes. It's a simple way to let them know I'm praying for them.

As I walk through his retirement community, I hear stories of Neal's prayer leaves. I see them in mailboxes and on doorknobs. He makes sure that everyone knows they matter.

In case you think this mode of communication is too outdated, one survey found that 87 percent of millennials rate handwritten notes as the most treasured form of communication.[32] Yet college and seminary professor Donald Whitney says that most of his students have never received a personal, handwritten note other than on holidays.[33]

Neal understood that effective ministry does not just happen to the masses. It takes place one person at a time. He sought to know people as individuals, reach out to them specifically, and pray for them. To foster community, the pastor must become a shepherd.

What Platforms or Programs Should We Consider?

Community doesn't just happen. Leaders have to be intentional, just like we are in our marriages and families. In a church setting, programs and platforms don't create community—though they do create a context for community building, which is an important environment for leading attentive churches. Unfortunately, far too few churches have any intentional plan to create a context that allows community to develop.

Sunday school was the primary vehicle for fostering community and teaching the basics of the faith prior to the Attractional Era[34] of the church. If worship was primarily about the message and sacraments, Sunday school became the context in which people could mingle. In fact, the primary draw to Sunday school is typically not the lesson but the conversations that occur before and after.

During the Attractional Era, a more casual approach through small groups often replaced the traditional Sunday school. Typically, when newcomers connect with a group of seven to fifteen people within their first three months, they are much more likely to stay involved over the long haul. Our own research shows churches that intentionally emphasize small groups foster church health. But it doesn't require one particular model of small groups. They can take any number of shapes and forms: small group Bible studies, quilting groups, mountain-biking clubs, and breakfast meetings, as long as they have an outward focus and foster true community rather than mere hobby sharing.

When we lead a discovery process for a church, we often ask people who they would call if they had a crisis at 3 a.m. If they say they would call someone from church, which often involves a small group relationship, then we know the church is pretty healthy. At the same time, we find that the level of participation in small groups is not extremely high, even in healthy churches. Some people just don't enjoy these settings. In my (Jim's) experience, the unwritten contract between me and the local church is that I don't have to be in such a group. I am free to pick and choose as I desire without any expectation. This is appropriate because different people connect differently. Everyone needs intimate relationships, but they don't have to occur in small groups. If people have one or two close friends at church, then the "intimacy factor" is secure. Finding connections for people in congregations is one way we must learn to be attentive. How can we help move people toward community?

Where Do We Cultivate a Place to Belong?

As part of your plan, consider your facilities. Older church buildings were often built for a classroom era, which may inhibit community today. If you've been to any church leadership conference in the last twenty years, you've probably heard the term *third place*. It's worth unpacking a bit more as you consider your intentional strategy for creating community.

Some churches tend to overemphasize intimacy. Not every relationship in a congregation must involve a deep connection, however. The development of casual relationships is every bit as important. While casual relationships can develop anywhere, our research indicates there is a correspondence between a church's buildings and its effectiveness.

In his book *Celebrating the Third Place*, sociologist Ray Oldenberg suggests the lack of casual relationships in our society puts too much strain on family and work relationships. First place is home. Second place is the workplace. Third place is where casual relationships occur—at a coffee shop, football field, or recreation center. Sometimes it's an open and inviting lobby. A basic principle of organizational dynamics is that structure creates behavior. If a church meets in an elementary school, it must find a place where people naturally gather apart from Sunday morning. If the church's narthex or fellowship space isn't conducive to interaction, it must creatively find an alternative.

But too often, the physical space itself becomes a roadblock to community, and the alternatives are insufficient. When churches start to grow, the unfortunate tendency is to add multiple services, which further cripples casual relationships.

The concept of third place means people have a place to hang out, meet new friends, and talk with old ones. The Latin word *trivium* was the intersection of three roads, a place where people on a journey would stop to talk and socialize. We get our words *trivia* and *trivial* from it. The content of the discussions included everyday things. Small talk is not unimportant. Rather, it is an essential part of community.

Andy Bauer pastors Fireside Church in the Boston area. They meet weekly in a rented elementary school, yet the hub of the church is the fireside gatherings in members' backyards, where meals and studies often occur. When Covid-19 hit and the elementary school was unavailable, the church survived and thrived because their core place was a backyard fire pit. I (Jim) urged Andy to call the participants in the church "embers" instead of "members." The third place was the table on the deck of the participants' homes. I preached there just after Covid-19 and discovered they lost nothing in the pandemic. They only grew.

Our world has become increasingly more suburban. We work in one place, live in another, and worship in yet another. What's missing in American culture, according to Oldenberg, is a place to hang out. In Munich, they do so in the biergartens. In Tokyo, it's the teahouses. In London, it's the pubs. We long for a third place but rarely find it. That's why so much of what's on TV is popular. It helps us meet a need vicariously. *Cheers* is a place where everybody knows your name. In *Friends*, the gang hangs out at Central Perk. In *Seinfeld*, they gather at the diner. On *The Office* it's, well, the office. The *Grey's Anatomy* gang hangs out at Seattle's Emerald City Bar. Companies like Starbucks and Panera have developed profitable businesses catering not only to people's desire for a good cup of coffee or a great salad but also to their even deeper hunger to find a place to connect. Many churches throughout the United States are starting to build a third place. The real question is, "Where do we cultivate a place to belong?"

As you begin to connect people to the church's mission and help them develop intimate relationships, don't ignore the importance of casual relationships. Look around on Sunday morning. Are people hanging out before and after services? Do people gather informally on Tuesday afternoons or Friday mornings? The concept of third place doesn't have to be limited to your church's facilities. You can find third place anywhere. It just has to be easily accessible, help strangers make new friends, and be where old friends can catch up.

My (Jim's) mother was always the last one to leave worship on Sundays. She was like a sheepdog circling around people to help them find safety and a home. I was usually annoyed that we were missing the Sunday afternoon football game's kick off, but my mother stayed to see community emerge in our congregations. I see now how important such people are in the network of the community of belonging.

Forever Changed

Today, Hope Chapel thrives under the leadership of a new pastor. In 2018, I (Kevin) got a call from the board chair. I hadn't heard from the church since Dan resigned in 2014. He filled me in.

> We got phone calls from other rock star pastors around the country offering to help. One even told me that he had the pastor of every church with over ten thousand people on speed dial and asked who we wanted. He said he could make it happen within a few weeks. It was a genuine gesture, which I appreciated. But we knew this was a once-in-a-lifetime chance to pivot, to do something different. We realized that the consumer model was doomed to fail. We knew that we hadn't connected people together in a missional community. But we also knew that God could do a new thing.
>
> The board met in our board room night after night for several months. Finally, we made a decision. It was really fairly simple. We wanted a pastor who would build a team—someone who would focus on developing a strong internal culture that encouraged people to connect to each other. Someone who could lead others into missional living. Steven had been on staff for a few years, and he's a sweet, humble guy who loves Jesus. Not a rock star. So, we asked Steven to be our new pastor. The last several years have been the most rewarding and fulfilling ministry we've ever had.
>
> Our people are more engaged than ever. We are doing more to help other churches than we have ever done. We are building a network in Arizona that is addressing real needs. Yes, we still have twenty-five thousand people. But we have clearly started the journey of building a real community, one where people belong and share in our mission.

A few months after this conversation, the board chair invited me (Kevin) to come back and do some governance coaching with the board to help them create a healthy relationship with Steven and the staff. I immediately knew the church was moving in a different direction. The staff had a new set of core values they built together. The board was moving out of the weeds and focusing on regional and statewide issues.

As we concluded our final meeting, the board introduced their newest member, Winston. I interrupted the discussion because I wanted to hear

Winston's story and what Hope Chapel meant to him. With tears in his eyes, Winston talked about how the church has made a difference in his life.

> I was homeless, addicted to drugs, and in jail when I first met someone from Hope. I met Jesus there, and my life has forever changed. I'm now running a coed ministry that helps people reenter society after incarceration. This church? This church walks the walk. They make disciples. Even though we have thousands of people, each person matters. I'm living proof of that.

Creating a focus on community within our congregations is an essential step toward being healthy. God created us for community, which often provides a context for lives to experience change. As we seek to lead attentive churches, we must shift our leadership from a culture of narcissism to a culture of belonging. Community doesn't happen on its own. It's built around a shared True North. It also requires attention to the kind of culture that will align with that True North. Our churches need to move from a culture of *me* to a culture of *we*.

Questions for Reflection and Discussion

- "To create" is the opposite of "to consume." Consider the ways the laity within your congregation "creates" by developing and leading ministry in and through the congregation.
- Do you think the congregation you serve is creatively owning the ministry God has given them as a community, or is the congregation more inclined to consume programming provided by paid staff?
- What did Covid-19 reveal about the value of community to your congregation? Were there any surprising ways that greater community was nurtured even as people were physically isolated? Has it been challenging to call people back to in-person worship and community? What does this suggest about the value of community within your congregation?

- As you reflect on your role as a pastor or ministry leader, are you stifling the fostering of community? Are you helping to create community? Or perhaps, if you are honest, are you doing some of both?
- How have you experienced the tension between the rock star model and the shepherding model of pastoral ministry? Just as Neal Jones embraced writing handwritten notes, what is one specific way you can increase your touch as a shepherd?

7

What Is Our Ethos?

"ANDESA IS A FIRM THAT has a soul."

These words are the beginning of a mission statement for an amazing company called Andesa Services in Allentown, Pennsylvania. Dr. John Walker, an economist and former professor, founded Andesa on very clear values. At a time when corporate America was often driven by the ideas that the end justifies the means and that employees exist to serve the business, John had a vastly different idea.

John is a friend of mine (Kevin) and serves on LFM's Strategic Advisory Board. He is an incredibly attentive leader in the marketplace. He was also a client of mine when I worked in business. The Walker Department of Economics at Clemson University is named after him. With John's financial support, the university also named the Walker Golf Course at Clemson after his father. John recently said, "People are not just resources or typewriters. They can't just be used. The only way to protect an employee or member of an organization is to make sure that the company's goal can withstand any scrutiny from an ethical point of view."

In a day when many companies used and abused people, John developed an eagle eye to be sure about his ends. He says, "If you become married to your ends without thinking about the consequences of how you're going to achieve that end, you will fall prey to using inappropriate means. And then you can no longer see they are inappropriate. You're blinded by the ends."

John understood that building a great culture in his company was critical for long-term success and health. So he made a radical decision.

In his words, "The only way to protect the people in the company is to make them the ends."

Most businesses or ministries will say that profit or some benevolent cause is their end. However, John saw a subtle danger in this thinking. He believed that while organizations should serve purposes and meet their own needs, they should also strive to exist for their employees.

So he set about building a successful company that served the life insurance and annuity industries while keeping his own employees at the center. He wanted to create a place that would help his people grow in their careers and lives by serving other companies in their field. Andesa adopted a people-first culture. They created an environment in which employees could advance their skills, switched ownership into their hands, and allowed them to participate in building the company.

It's true that John embodies the values that make Andesa great. He has had a tremendous ripple effect on his company. When I (Kevin) talked to the employees about John, this is what I heard:

"It's clear that the heart of Andesa is manifested in him."

"His passion for this company is unmatched."

"He is a man of culture and values like I've never met in my life."

After a careful search for his replacement, John stepped down as CEO several years ago. Things seemed to go well for a while, but after a few years, it became apparent that something had gone awry in Andesa's culture. By then, the board had cycled through a couple of CEOs trying to find John's replacement. The board then promoted Andesa's CFO, Ron Scheese, to lead the company into the future as a long-term replacement. One of Ron's first initiatives was to conduct an employment engagement survey, which revealed discouraging news. Andesa scored in the thirty-sixth percentile for employment engagement, a punch in the gut for a firm that prided itself on being people first.

Something was desperately wrong. Ron reached out to John, who cried over the devastating news. He realized that the management had lost touch with the employees. After a period of grieving, he knew it was time to get busy and fix the problems. He said, "I knew it would be solved.

Period. No question in my mind. It was going to be expensive and it was going to take time, but I was committed."

John became active again at Andesa and came alongside Ron Scheese to mentor him. In some corporate cultures, such negative news would have resulted in the dismissal of the CEO, even if it wasn't his fault. But not at Andesa. John and others saw this as a learning experience to improve. This board wanted to invest in leadership, not dismiss it.

They began an intense, systematic examination of their entire company, starting with the managers. They adopted the mindset that "the problem is inside this room." Managers took personal responsibility for challenges they faced. Then, they strategically engaged employees in conversations about their vision and values. They held focus groups, all of which Ron sat through. They started talking again about how they could grow their people.

"Andesa forever" became their new rallying cry. After listening intently to their people, they reimagined their mission statement in an effort to become an employee-first company. Today, that statement reads, "Andesa is a firm that has a soul—that is to say, it has incorporated into its operating procedures strong core values, which for us include honesty, respect, integrity, responsibility, courage, and initiative."

Their employees, ranging from recent college graduates to decades-long workers, embrace this mindset. And they take investing in people seriously.

Andesa has been back on track for years, embracing a culture that helps its people grow while serving other businesses in the life insurance and annuities community. They thrive because of a great environment where individuals can belong, contribute, and make a difference.

The results are nothing short of amazing:

- Revenue is up 20 percent.
- Net income is up 27 percent.
- Annual employee retention improved to over 90 percent.
- And the company value? Up over 60 percent.

Every year, Clemson University invites John to give a guest lecture. He reminds students that spiritual grace is the most important thing in leading a company: "Spiritual grace is that I know I have been accepted by the Creator of the entire universe, who I am deeply indebted to. I am accepted and can do no wrong in his sight. That gives me incredible freedom. I'm no longer afraid of making mistakes or failing."

Andesa is a firm that has a soul. Ron Scheese, who is also a member of LFM's Strategic Advisory Board, says, "A business does not exist to make a profit. Rather, profit allows a business to make a difference in the lives of our employees and clients. Putting people first at the heart of our vision and culture allows me as a Christian to live my values and serve others every day."

What Is Culture?

The last time I (Kevin) visited Chick-fil-A, I found a clean, attractive restaurant, including restrooms that were well taken care of. Workers greeted me in a friendly manner with their standard, "My pleasure." Chick-fil-A's food is consistently of good quality, and customers keep returning by the droves. I still recall devouring my first Chick-fil-A sandwich at SouthPark Mall in Charlotte as a child. I've been hooked ever since. The American Customer Satisfaction Index (ACSI) recently reported the chicken sandwich restaurant as number one for incredible customer satisfaction in the fast-food industry, with a customer satisfaction score of 84.[1]

Compare that to other fast-food experiences I've had recently when I was greeted by the cashier's blank stare, my order wasn't right and took way too long, and no one offered any apologies. Bill Moore and Jerry Rose wrote, "Culture eats strategy for breakfast."[2] As many businesses, schools, and churches have found, strategy is destined to fail if it does not fit the organization's culture.

We all know businesses have cultures—some good, some bad. But did you know that your church also has a culture? As we help our congregations swim upstream against the currents of cultural narcissism, seeking to lead them toward attentiveness, we need to help them discover their unique culture. A positive, healthy, shared culture moves people from "me first" to "we're in this together."

Ethos

The Greek word *ēthos*, used by Aristotle, means culture. Sometimes we have a positive or a negative culture. Often, it is neutral. In the Bible it refers to a custom, manner, or ritual.

The book of Hebrews uses this word, reminding the Jews to "let us consider how to stir up one another to love and good works, not neglecting to meet together, as is the habit [*ēthos*] of some, but encouraging one another, and all the more as you see the Day drawing near" (Hebrews 10:24-25 ESV). The habit or spiritual culture of some faithful believers was to regularly gather to help each other. The culture of others was all about neglecting to gather.

Leading an attentive church results in part from a church's attention to its culture. A positive ethos acts as a filter for what the congregation is and what it becomes. It keeps out programs and endeavors that don't fit the ethos while supporting ones that do.

The Uniqueness of Ethos

Every church has a unique internal culture. A church's ethos is positive if it makes the people feel like they are home. Part of ethos is the place itself. Studies show that the average American decides within three seconds if a store, a restaurant, or a church is a fit for them. We need a place where our people love being together, where they linger and talk to each other.

Several years ago, we worked with Orchard Hill Church in Grand Rapids, Michigan. Their foyer included various displays of artwork, all of which came from within the congregation. The church employed a full-time visual arts director and hosted regular art shows on the weekends. We often show pictures of this church to groups and ask them to guess what kind of organization it is. People often guess it is an art gallery, a hotel lobby, or a museum. They are astonished when we tell them it's a church! What types of people walk into that church and say, "I'm home"? People with an artistic, eclectic bent. Their worship services include strong creativity and visual enhancement, blending both traditional and contemporary elements. They often change things around in their presentation so participants are never sure what they'll get that week.

Black Hills Cowboy Church in Beulah, Wyoming, holds worship services in a horse barn to set a relaxed tone. They desire to plant a network of cowboy churches throughout the West. Their initial strategy is to hold ranch and rodeo activities and then eventually hold services. Meeting needs through practical means is key at Black Hills, which resonates with the no-nonsense, self-reliant culture of Wyoming and South Dakota. For example, one idea for a serving opportunity through the church is training border collies. Black Hills stays true to its ethos.

A church in Austin boasts of "no perfect people allowed," which describes a huge piece of their culture. Conversely, an unspoken norm for another church we know of is that they are "a successful church for successful people." Think about how these two different cultures affect those congregations and expectations.

The uniqueness of your ethos should be embraced and celebrated. Healthy families have their own unique and creative culture. Yours may enjoy playing board games, eating Chinese takeout, and watching movies together. Another family likes Broadway musicals, art galleries, and fine dining. And yet another loves college football, whitewater rafting, and camping. As you discover your ethos you find reasons to celebrate, bond with each other, and create lasting memories from shared experiences.

A healthy ethos creates focus, motivation, connection, cohesion, and spirit. Every company—and many churches—spends time and money on strategic planning. Only a select few spend time, and much less money, on "culture planning."

What Are the Unwritten Laws and Cultural Structure?

In the late 1990s, Chrysler struggled with keeping its Jeep Wrangler strong in the American market. Larger, more luxurious SUVs were crowding the field, so Chrysler gave the Wrangler a major overhaul. The changes included more luxury without removable doors. To combat decreasing sales, Chrysler also hired French anthropologist, psychologist, and marketing guru Clotaire Rapaille.

Chrysler had focused on functionality and not feelings. But Rapaille knew that feelings sold vehicles. He created consumer groups of Jeep owners, asking them about their earliest memories with Jeeps. They told stories about riding freely, driving on the open road, and exploring places unavailable to an ordinary car. He discovered that Jeep owners don't want luxury but toughness. That resulted in one of Chrysler's more memorable ad campaigns—the Jeep Wrangler perched on top of a rock at dealerships.

To help Nestle sell coffee in Japanese culture, Rapaille investigated Japanese people's emotions and the cultural meanings attached to coffee. Japan valued tea over coffee. So, Nestle created coffee-flavored desserts for children. The strategy was to make a positive emotional imprint related to coffee on Japanese children, who would then carry these feelings with them into adulthood. In this way, Rapaille helped Nestle "carve a niche for themselves" in the young Japanese psyche.[3]

When Procter & Gamble hired Rapaille to help them boost sales for their Folgers coffee, he once again used archetype research to break the emotional-psychological code. He explored the imprints children experience in different countries and cultures related to coffee. In America, he found that children often associate the aroma of coffee in the morning with security and "cozy domesticity."[4] Understanding the strong tie between scent and memory, he told Procter & Gamble to focus not on taste but aroma. The design involved advertisements depicting people waking up at home and smelling Folgers coffee brewing. They also introduced an incredibly successful advertising jingle: "The best part of waking up is Folgers in your cup."

Rapaille built his business, which includes nearly fifty *Fortune* 100 clients, on discovering right-brain tendencies, not just left-brain logic. He says, "I am trying to uncover the unwritten laws. I am discovering the cultural structure of the American mind."[5] An unwritten code in our brains connects with our emotions, driving us to and from certain products.

This unwritten code not only sells products and builds organizations, but it also can be the difference between growth or stagnation for a church or ministry. God has wired each person to be unique. We are "fearfully and wonderfully made" (Psalm 139:14 NKJV). So, God has also wired each expression of the church to be unique.

We desire three aspects of healthy community: we need to belong, we need to contribute, and we need to make a difference. Innate to our existence is the desire to be in healthy community, created in God's image. At church, people need a place to belong. It is believing, "I'm home." Church should also be a place to contribute. It's a healthy sense of believing, "I'm needed." We are not just spectators consuming what the church offers. Rather, we give of ourselves and use our gifts. This leads to the third aspect of healthy community: we need to make a difference by affecting the lives of others in some way. It is believing, "I matter." G. K. Chesterton wrote, "You matter. I matter. It's the hardest thing in theology to believe."[6] *The hardest thing in theology to believe* is not the virgin birth, the Trinity, nor the resurrection of Christ, but that you matter. When a church as God's vessel helps each person know that they matter, the mission is accomplished and the vision is achieved.

Belonging—I'm home.

Contributing—I'm needed.

Making a difference—I matter.

When leading attentive churches, pastors and ministry leaders connect people to all three aspects of community.

Ethos Is Built Around *Aretē*

In chapter five we introduced *aretē*, which can be defined as something's essence, identity, and capability. What makes your congregation unique? What is your church's code? To use Rapaille's language, what is your church's cultural structure, unwritten laws, or emotional imprints? This is more specific than just "We believe the Bible" or "We follow Christ."

What are you passionate about, and how do you strive for excellence? Where do you shine?

Ethos, the culture, is built around *aretē*, the essence. When you know your *aretē*, you know what to say yes to and what to say no to. It helps you decide what to keep and what to let go of, what to start and what to stop. It defines who you are—and who you are not.

Are We Risk-Takers or Not?

When I (Jim) was pastoring First Church—whose history goes back to the 1800s—in Colorado Springs, the elders asked Kevin Ford to help us with a planning process. That's where Kevin and I started our journey as friends and colleagues in ministry. We identified several areas to address, including staffing and strategy. But the complicating issue concerned denominational fit. This congregation had a long history in one denomination. They were one of several congregations along the Front Range of Colorado founded by the church planter Sheldon Jackson.

Two primary options presented themselves. One was to join a denomination with a thirty-year history. The other was to form a brand-new denomination—a project I was already a part of designing. The elders asked me what other churches were in the pool for a new denomination. I replied there was no one else at this point—there wasn't even any water in the pool! The elders took turns sharing which option they thought was best, quickly coming to a consensus that they were not the type of church to dive into something new. They agreed that they tended to approach things cautiously and carefully. I could sense that joining a fledgling new denomination was not in their DNA.

At this point in the discussion, Kevin asked a couple of questions. He asked the elders if it was true that they were a pioneer in singles' ministry, years before most churches even noticed singles. The elders admitted to this. Kevin continued, "Were you also one of the first congregations to begin Divorce Recovery Ministry at a time when most congregations feared having such a program would suggest divorce was acceptable within a church?" Again, the elders admitted this was true but that it was controversial at the time. Kevin then asked, "Is it true that First Church was one of the first conservative congregations to ordain a woman to the ministry?" Again, the elders said yes but added they lost an entire Sunday school class of people over that decision. Finally, Kevin said, "Then is it really true that you are a very cautious congregation—or could it be that risk-taking is in your DNA?"

As a result of this conversation, the leadership discovered a DNA they had not remembered or even acknowledged. This congregation had started as a church plant in 1872 at a time when it was unlikely to succeed. Now, as I led this attentive church, they decided to embrace their core culture and became a leader in forming a new denomination. While denominations come and go, a healthy church's DNA will stand the test of time.

Congregations often have to ask themselves whether a particular program of the church fits their *aretē*. Often, there will be one or two items that no longer fit. One such program in a congregation I (Jim) served was a handbell choir. Handbells can be a beautiful part of worship—but in this congregation there was a decline in participants, especially among younger adults. At some point, a discussion emerged about whether handbells were really part of the DNA of this congregation. I soon discovered handbells were the passion of one person who had experienced them in a prior church. The first solution was to try to recruit more ringers. But after some reflection, I realized that it did not fit the *aretē* of the congregation. Sidelining the handbells was not popular among those who supported it, but after some time the general congregation did not miss them—because they never fit the essence of the congregation in the first place.

In many churches, the composition of who receives what money in a missions budget can be unclear from the outside. Very often, only one or two people may be passionate about a particular line item. Occasionally, it supports a member's niece, nephew, or grandchild. In one of my (Jim's) congregations, we had over one hundred different line items of recipients with no clear plan. Over time our church wrestled with our real passion related to missions, and we discovered we wanted to make a larger difference for a smaller number of recipients. We focused on four major gateway regions for the gospel and put most of our resources there. That meant consolidating the budget and cutting many recipients. We had to work hard to uncover the real *aretē* of our missions passion.

Three Cultures

Every church has three cultures: the founders' culture, the desired culture, and the hidden culture. The founders' culture includes both the positive and negative imprints that the founding members of the church left. Many times, the positive aspects of the founders' culture feed into the desired culture—what the church really wants to be. These could include characteristics such as having a structure that is driven by people's gifts and passions, intentionality about starting new small groups, or a dedication to participate in building houses for lower income families.

However, negative aspects can also be gleaned from the founders' culture that become a part of the hidden culture, or the "unspoken culture"—the one we know exists but lurks in the shadows. In a previous book, I (Kevin) called it "the thing in the bushes."[7] For example, maybe the previous generation of leaders was very intentional about avoiding certain actions because they didn't want to offend a particular wealthy giver in the church. An unwritten rule then became a normal part of the hidden culture: don't offend the big givers. We tend to ignore the hidden culture. However, if unaddressed, it can greatly affect the behavior of the entire system.

For instance, certain congregations highly value excellence. They expect everything—from music to children's ministry—to be done well. This value of excellence ends up competing with another common value of wanting to include everyone in ministry. A church may want lots of volunteers, but they will often defer to staff because they want everything done excellently. Two congregations I have been a part of have utilized professional musicians to perform the music with great excellence. At times, this focus on excellence might prevent volunteers from participating in the life of the church.

These three cultures compete for first place within a church. The desired culture is our *aretē*. It is who we want to be, who we are striving to be, and who we are growing to become. It's who we believe God wants us to be as a specific church in a specific location. As a church grows in attentiveness, they learn to pay attention to all three cultures. As the church matures, they learn to intentionally make both the founders' culture and the hidden culture submit to the desired culture, the *aretē*.

Discovering Our *Aretē*

How does a church discover their *aretē*? It does not come from a senior pastor and staff sitting down for three hours in a meeting and asking, "What's our DNA?" It's a process of discovery. As Rapaille practices, it is a right-brain process more than a left-brain one. It is not primarily concrete, data driven, and logical—it involves traces of intuition, memory, and story. Most of Jesus' teachings came through story. Through his parables, Jesus knew that connecting to the right brain was more powerful than connecting to the logical left brain. Ethos and *aretē* are about identity. It is as much of a narrative force as it is a logical system.

Becoming an attentive church involves an archaeological search to find that *aretē*. During the visioning process, it is not sufficient to simply begin with our goals. We must first discover who we are—not just who we say we are, not just who we want to be, but who we are really. What makes us unique? What makes people come to this particular church and feel they are home?

Rapaille understands this concept. When he worked with Chrysler, he said, "They kept listening to what people said. This was always a mistake." People often respond to questions with what they have been conditioned to say, what they want to be true, or what they think they should say. Uncovering the *why* behind behavior, however, is much more complex. We have to decode the "elements of culture to discover the emotions and meanings attached to them."[8]

Likewise, if logic rules a church's visioning meetings, the leadership may need to ask, "What should be our core values?" Answers likely would flow from stock answers they've been conditioned to embrace based on the values of their denomination or network of churches. The question would not, however, tell them much about their particular congregation's DNA.

Most leaders tend to treat all problems the same way: let's quickly identify a fix and get on with it. But in doing so they often miss deeper issues, which all revolve around conflicts within the culture. These issues are always about competing values. The values of the desired culture clash with the values of the hidden culture.

It is easy to overlook deeper issues and just focus on "practical" ones. But then we wonder why so little progress is made once the new vision or plan is rolled out. It's often because the strategy does not address the competing values, or the strategy is at odds with the church's *aretē*, its DNA.

Aretē is discovered through a process of asking many questions and then listening. It involves time spent together. It shows up in the hero stories of a congregation—especially in the stories involving lay people. One hero of a church I (Jim) pastored in Austin, Texas, was Larry Langley, an attorney with a crusty demeanor. In new member classes when I asked people how they got to that church, about 30 percent of the time it was because of a connection to Larry. He was the consummate inviter. Because he was so crusty, I would have never guessed that he was highly invitational. Larry quietly shaped a positive culture that still exists in that congregation.

Aretē also shows up in stories of failed attempts. Most congregations don't do effective postmortems on what didn't work—but that is where they will discover *aretē*. For example, when evangelism does not work well in particular congregations, people blame the program or the person running the ministry. Yet, the struggle related to training congregations in evangelism is often connected to an emotional issue in their culture. Certain forms of evangelism have contaminated the whole idea for many people. Hence, uncovering the emotional elements in a church's *aretē* means looking for what works well with the people and what doesn't.

The first task of leadership is to answer, "What needs to be preserved? And what needs to change?" Don't start with what needs changing. Start with what is worth keeping, and then make sure you preserve the right things. These two questions are vital for leading attentive churches.

Early in my career, I (Kevin) consulted with a church in Corpus Christi. It was a small church with a lot of property. I encouraged the church leaders to consider what community needs the church could meet. A demographic study revealed a major problem in the community—neighborhood teens had nothing to do after school. Many came from single-parent homes. Both the crime and delinquency rates were well above national norms. As we talked and visioned, the group consensus was to build a gym on the church property, open it to the neighborhood, and use it as a bridge to build relationships. We had three weekends to work on the church's True North.

The same leaders attended all three retreats, including Marilyn. A quiet woman in her eighties, she sat as far away from me as possible. I tried to engage her during breaks, but she made a beeline for the parking lot each time. With twenty minutes remaining in our final meeting, she finally raised her hand. From the glare in her eyes, I could tell she was going to make a statement rather than ask a question. I was nervous about missing my flight out of San Antonio and tried to ignore her raised hand. She persisted. Finally, I acknowledged her.

She started in a low southern drawl. "This church has a long history. My grandparents started the church and I was baptized, confirmed, and raised here. I think we are getting off track with all this talk about a gym and teenagers."

As she spoke, the other leaders in the room interrupted her multiple times. They tried to convince her of the need for a gym and how the church could serve the community. The more they tried to convince her, the more she dug in her heels. Finally, with only a few minutes left, I stopped the group.

I turned to Marilyn. "You represent a lot of people at this church. What do you think they are most fearful of from our three weekends together?"

For the first time, she softened a bit. "The 8 a.m. service," she replied quietly. "That's our family. When Bob died, everyone in that service brought me a meal or visited me. We don't want to lose that service."

I turned to the group and asked what the plan was for the 8 a.m. service. The group responded, almost in unison, "Nothing will change." I asked Marilyn if she thought the people she represented could live with the changes if we left the 8 a.m. service intact. She confidently said yes with a smile. We then closed in prayer, and I made it to the airport on time.

Sometimes, before we introduce change, we need to be clear about what won't change.

To help discover a church's *aretē*, focus on four areas: early memories, meaningful legends, unsung heroes, and tough decisions. The best way to move along in this process is to get people to tell stories. It is a very relational process. We often put leaders in small groups of six or seven people so they can have more intimate conversations. Oh, and please provide a box of tissues.

- Early memories—Tell a story about your most meaningful memory. Maybe it's about a worship service, a mission trip, or a conversation after small group. Don't just describe your favorite things about this church. Tell a story. Be as descriptive as possible.
- Meaningful legends—What are the significant milestone stories that make up your church's history? These are past events that become symbolic and larger than life. Maybe it was a group of people who mortgaged their homes to build the first sanctuary. Perhaps it was a pastor who embraced different races when churches were still segregated. What do these legends reveal about what your church values?
- Unsung heroes—Who are the heroes of your church's past? Many of them may be unsung—the lady who taught third-grade Sunday school for forty years, the man who faithfully opened and closed the church building every Sunday, the senior adult who came early to

cook meals, or the kid with Down syndrome who led everyone in the Lord's Prayer each week.

- Tough decisions—Every church endures times when hard, painful choices must be made. What tough decisions do you remember? What were the circumstances surrounding these decisions? What resulted from these decisions, and what did the church learn?

Resist the temptation to jump to conclusions. Don't rush through these conversations. Be attentive. Allow people to think, remember, and reflect. And keep your archaeological lenses on. If you do a thoughtful investigation into these four areas, you will be well on your way to uncovering your church's essence. What do the stories told about each of these four areas reveal to you about the church's essence, or *aretē*?

Remember, attentiveness includes listening to the Lord and listening to each other. As people share their memories, you can expect some teary eyes, laughter, and moments of silence. Through it all, come with the expectation of the words of Christ: "He who has an ear, let him hear what the Spirit says to the churches" (Revelation 2:7 ESV).

As you listen together, themes will likely emerge. Take note of these. Probe deeper. Ask clarifying questions. Listen. Don't rush. These may be holy moments, especially to those who share.

These related themes will begin revealing to you the essence, the core values, the *aretē* of your church. These are not just a list of things you "should be," like a church that embraces evangelism, missions, or Bible teaching. Rather, these themes will show you who you are as a church. They are enduring qualities, a part of the ministry's essence.

Strategy Flows Out of Ethos and *Aretē*

When I (Kevin) consulted with Memorial Drive Church in Houston, Texas, prior to their elder retreat, we heard from a number of people in focus groups. Two things were repeated over and over by staff members, longtime church members, and newcomers to the church: "We are a house of prayer," and "We practice radical generosity." They practice what they preach. The church organizes a prayer ministry so that every person at the church is prayed for every single day by name. They also honor dollar for dollar mission giving. Half of their budget, which is well over ten million dollars, goes to mission endeavors.

Memorial Drive has a clear sense of who they are. They've built their structure and their brand around it. They have truly discovered their *aretē*, and in being true to it, they are a light in the darkness.

Many churches, unfortunately, have not discovered theirs. Actually, most churches don't even think about strategy. The ones that do tend to jump in too quickly before exploring their congregation's ethos and *aretē*. This is exactly why it is counterproductive to simply go to a trendy megachurch conference that focuses on strategy and try to copy their model in your church, which may be a thousand miles from their setting. The ripple effect God wants to produce through you will be in keeping with what he has already been doing in you and your people—perhaps for generations.

The body of Christ has benefited from churches like Willow Creek near Chicago and Saddleback in Lake Forest, California. Several decades ago, it was common and even a bit faddish to go to one of those churches for their training conferences. For the better part of a week, speakers from the church would explain their strategy and process. Thousands of pastors would return home with hundreds of dollars' worth of notebooks and resources to help them implement that same strategy.

In some cases, churches were able to reproduce the plan well in their settings. However, many pastors encountered great discouragement as they tried to "work the plan." What they often did not take into account is—you guessed it—ethos and *aretē*. Fruitfulness and productivity for one church setting may look significantly different from another. What works beautifully in one of the most established urban cities in the country will not necessarily take root in your city or town. As the old saying goes, we have to learn to bloom where we are planted. In the examples of Willow Creek and Saddleback, their strategies brought tremendous results because they were intrinsically tied to the ethos and *aretē* of those particular churches in those specific places and times.

Strategy is all about using our resources to meet needs in our local community in a unique way. One of our associates at LFM, Rich Hurst, worked with McLean Bible Church in Northern Virginia for several years. Rich shares,

> Early in our work there, the pastor, Lon Solomon, and his wife had a daughter named Jill, who had special needs. Looking around the community, they wondered, "Where do we go to find ministry for someone like her?" At the same time, they wondered who was going to minister to the young twentysomethings in Northern Virginia. Their leadership decided their strategy would be twofold: focus on the secular young people so they could affect the greater Washington, DC, area for the kingdom, and meet the needs of people and families with mental and physical disabilities.
>
> In a church of about eight hundred people, they started Access Ministries with four people who had various special needs. Over the years the ministry blossomed, and today they serve about five hundred families annually. They have a summer camp, a Beautiful Blessings focus for children ages two to fifteen, a Friendship Club for people ages sixty-five and over, a performing arts ministry, and a Signs of Life deaf ministry.
>
> Today, the church operates Jill's House, a respite resort designed to provide short-term, overnight care for children with intellectual and physical disabilities. In Northern Virginia, it costs $2,800 a night to provide childcare for a child with severe disabilities if a husband and wife need to have a night alone. Jill's House serves these families. What do you think people in Northern Virginia think about this church, even if they disagree theologically? Today this church has grown from eight hundred people to about eighteen thousand. McClean Bible Church is using their resources to meet needs in the local community in a unique way.

Our team also partnered with Christ Community Church of Milpitas, California. Once they discovered their *aretē*, they were able to pivot to meet the needs of the local community. In Silicon Valley, where there are thousands of Southeast Asian immigrants, they started an English as a Second Language (ESL) class. Most recently, they offer fifty-two classes each week. The city of Milpitas has even stopped teaching ESL because the church's ministry is so effective. Worship services on Sundays represent the diversity of Silicon Valley.

The church has partnered with other churches in the community to form Milpitas Cares, a movement in the city where each congregation agrees to serve the community based on their unique DNA. One church offers counseling. Another has a food bank. Yet another provides transitional housing. The current leadership explains,

> It started with a group of pastors asking a simple question: "Why can't we take better care of our community?" Indeed, why not? We all agree God deeply cares for our community—and so do we. So, we started Milpitas Cares and encouraged all the churches and people in our community to join with us . . . and you did! Milpitas Cares quickly became the largest community service event in and for Milpitas, contributing tens of thousands of hours of volunteer help to scores of community services each year.

Attentive churches like these know that alignment occurs when strategy and application flow out of ethos and *aretē*. Honoring this results in a healthy state of being. Healthy things grow and accomplish their purpose. Don't violate your *aretē*. Attentive churches understand the need to leverage people's giftedness by putting them in roles where they are strong.

Does culture matter? Absolutely. It can be the one thing that most sets your church apart and makes it unique. It can be the thing that transforms your congregation into a place that makes a difference. People begin moving away from their self-centeredness. They belong to something bigger than themselves. Building your church's culture can result in transformed people saying, "I'm home. I'm needed. And I matter."

Attentive church leadership helps a church discover and align to their True North. That becomes a building block for community. But the community also needs some intangible norms, customs, and behaviors to form an ethos. Ethos creates a sense of belonging to something bigger than oneself. So how do we help people feel like they can really make a difference? That requires shifting from a mindset of entitlement to one of engagement.

Questions for Reflection and Discussion

- Consider the statement, "Every church has their own internal culture, and each is unique." Think about how the church you currently serve or are a part of is unique compared to other churches you have experienced. How do you think these differences came to be?
- Can you articulate any unwritten rules that might define the hidden culture of the congregation you serve?
- As you think about making changes in your congregation, how might you first recognize and articulate the desired culture, based on values that should never change?
- What qualities in your congregation express your church's *aretē*?
- Think of a time when you tried to apply something that did not fit your congregation's DNA. What was the result?

8

Are We Entitled or Engaged?

On a snowy Christmas Eve in the early 2000s, a church service was happening not too far from the Liberty Bell. This church's first Christmas Eve service in 1720 had included many of the nation's founding fathers. Some had signed the Declaration of Independence as well as the church's original charter. Revolutionary War–era soldiers and families were now buried in the cemetery. But this night was unlike any other. Would this be their last service?

After the prelude, the pastor angrily marched up to the pulpit. He glared at the handful of church members who dared to show up and fumed, "This is my church! You have killed my church." After a few moments of silence, he took off his shoes and deposited them on the Communion table. Before storming out of the sanctuary, he blasted them one last time: "You'll never find someone to fill these shoes!" Then he was gone.

Like a petulant child, this pastor reflected the sense of entitlement rampant in today's culture. While it's easy to point the finger at rock star pastors, we can see this same attitude of entitlement in small church pastors, volunteers, long-term members, and even newcomers. The prevailing winds of cultural narcissism have fanned the flame of personal entitlement.

The apostle Paul challenged Timothy to guard through the Holy Spirit the good deposit, the gospel, "which has been entrusted to you" (2 Timothy 1:14 NASB). That call included the following:

- Kindling afresh the gift of God inside him (1:6)
- Not being ashamed of the testimony of our Lord (1:8)

- Standing strong in the grace that is in Christ Jesus (2:1)
- Suffering hardship as a good soldier (2:3)
- Reminding people of God's truth (2:14)
- Pursuing godliness, faith, love, and peace (2:22)
- Staying true to the Scriptures (3:14-17)
- Preaching the Word in season and out of season (4:2)
- Doing the work of an evangelist and fulfilling his ministry (4:5)

Leading attentive churches requires pastors and ministry leaders to be stewards of the gospel. Our friend Alan is helping his church and network do much with what has been entrusted to them. Reflecting on a critical leadership meeting in the history of their church, Alan told us, "We immediately knew we wanted to serve and love our city into the kingdom." In 1992, Alan and his wife began serving a church in Pretoria, South Africa—one suffering from loss of members as well as deep debt due to a series of poor leadership decisions. They desperately needed more than a hero to move them forward. They needed leaders who people could trust again—someone who could mobilize a congregation for something bigger than self-preservation.

When Alan began pastoring the church, he became deeply aware of his own inadequacy and utterly dependent on the Lord as he started becoming attentive. He shared with us, "When God has a plan, he finds a man or woman prepared to trust him, and he fulfills his promise." On one level, that sounds like a naive and pious affirmation. But as Alan and the leadership began to seek the Lord attentively, to their surprise, the church began to experience growth.

Two years into his journey as their pastor, Alan read the Scripture about the gift of faith (1 Corinthians 12:8-9) as he prepared for a leadership meeting. In a holy moment, he sensed the Lord had something to reveal. As he prayed and listened, he perceived the Holy Spirit saying to him, "I now give you the gift of faith to trust me for a city." Alan jotted down in his journal two phrases: *faith for a church* and *faith for a city.*

"I don't know how to explain this," Alan said, "except to say in that moment I became pregnant with the conviction that a whole city, a whole geographical region, could come under the dominant influence of the presence of Jesus Christ."

He went into his meeting that evening with no idea what to say but with a deep awareness that God had spoken. As the team began praying, singing songs, and worshiping together, one senior leader told the group he had something from the Lord to share: "I sense God is saying he is giving us this city." One by one, the other leaders confirmed that they too believed it was from the Lord. Interestingly, up to that point, they had never focused on reaching the city. It seemed to be a fresh stirring from the Spirit that evening.

They did not intend to focus on a political agenda. Instead, they understood God wanted them to serve and love their city, with the result of people coming into the kingdom of God. Growing a large church was not their focus, either. "We were not to feel we had the sole agency to the city, but rather to engage it with faith, love and hope," said Alan.

For the next two years, Alan and his team had no idea what to do to make that vision a reality, so they regularly prayed for wisdom, understanding, and strategy. "I had a vision for reaching the city, but I knew I couldn't do it alone," he said. "The leadership team and I regularly wondered, 'How do we mobilize our people to engage in our mission?'"

In our years working with church leaders, this is perhaps the most vexing question. How do we create a culture of engagement in which every member is in ministry and each person owns the mission? After all, we live in a society where people are becoming more and more disengaged in every area of life. For example, a recent survey of 1,000 American workers by LiveCareer confirmed that 94% of Americans consider themselves to be "quiet quitters." A new phenomenon, quiet quitters show up for work and do just enough to get by. They still earn a salary and benefits but have emotionally checked out. Most quiet quitters also admit to wanting someone else to do their work for them.[1]

Alan knew he would not fulfill God's purpose by saving the day for a group of disengaged people. He wanted every person to be involved to own the mission at a deeply personal level.

He shared,

> Because of the urgency of the moment and the opportunity before us, our church had to rise to the challenge to do what it does in a fresh and new way. We had to change our philosophy of ministry. We had to start thinking differently about church, which fundamentally meant we had to start thinking differently about the people who make up the church. We realized that God wanted to do something through the people. Our discipleship had to go beyond spiritual formation to equipping for mission. We had to start discipling with Monday in mind—connecting Sunday's faith to Monday's life.
>
> The shift was to recognize that people were not just coming to church to be blessed but to be equipped as City Changers, fully fledged disciples commissioned and sent to execute Christ's mission on the planet. They were no longer just attending a program—they became the program!

During this season, they became a more attentive church. The team felt led to relaunch the church with a new name, Doxa Deo, inspired by Habakkuk 2:14: "For the earth will be filled with the knowledge of the glory of the Lord as the waters cover the sea." They intentionally combined the Greek word *doxa* (glory) with the Latin word *Deo* (God) to reflect the bringing together of different peoples and cultures. They wanted to see the multifaceted glory of God revealed in their city.

Their church continued growing, and with their compelling vision, today they have grown to have a burden for connecting with other congregations around the world with a similar vision. The movement, which started at the center, moved outward. This led to establishing the City Changers Movement across Africa, New Zealand, the United Kingdom, Germany, and the United States. The movement has become a catalyst for them to multiply what they were doing through Doxa Deo. Today, three decades into Alan's pastoral tenure, they have twenty-one churches in nine cities around the world. What an amazing ripple effect from these "living stones" (1 Peter 2:5)!

City Changers come alongside existing churches, businesses, and educational institutions to help them become more missional. Alan told us, "We function like an Intel chip to existing groups and individuals of influence. We come alongside them to equip and assist leaders. We specialize in closing the execution gap. There is an enormous need to move people of vision from 'wow' to 'how.'"[2]

Their vision of God revealing his glory is not limited to what occurs inside a church building. Alan and his team long for the

> lordship of Jesus Christ to become a tangible reality not only in our personal experience of salvation, but also in the very construct of our society and world. Therefore education, arts, business, government, sport, the media, social society as well as the Church all have to be aligned to the influence of the lordship of Christ. We therefore do not just want to be a church for the church, but a church for the community. Our people see themselves not as members, but as partners of a dream to see cities and communities transformed.[3]

The vision of the City Changers Movement is not to create self-serving, consumer-driven congregations. Instead, their goal is to raise up missional disciples who see themselves as agents of transformation for the world around them. They prayed and strategized to mobilize their people to accomplish their mission. Their activities, consequently, are outward focused, "engaging intentionally the different spheres of society."[4] In addition to starting their own schools, they created a plan and program to keep an intentional presence in state public schools, engaging over 130 schools daily. They have also established work in African inner-city centers as well as English suburban churches.

Today in Pretoria, Doxa Deo gathers in fourteen campuses, serving about thirty thousand people. Unlike many multisite churches, they don't use digital broadcasting to engage the different locations. Instead, they have focused on raising leaders both to lead and to communicate. They are truly seeing the glory of the Lord fill the earth. Alan said, "Our focus really was never to build a big church but to transform the city."

Focus. That's a good word to describe Alan's leadership. He is leading an attentive church and influencing other attentive churches. He is a strategic leader, a visionary. But effective leaders know that visionary leadership, in and of itself, is not enough.

Lives Changed

The miracle of Doxa Deo is not about building a big church or movement. It is about the power of changed lives. Alan shared one such story:

> A homeless person in Pretoria named Tshwane attended one of our life skill programs called Popup at our social ministry. He couldn't read or study properly. Through our life skill program we introduced him to Jesus, who began healing the pain of his past. He discovered who he is in Jesus' eyes and began overcoming the challenges that held him back. After our three-week ministry program and other preparatory courses, he attained the skill to enroll in a culinary course. Through our job placement ministry, he ended up in the Sheraton Hotel as a chef intern and did so well that today he's one of the formally appointed chefs of the Sheraton Hotel in Pretoria.

Doxa Deo has a passion for orphan care. They partner with a welfare organization to manage a house for children in the orphan program of the South African government. One young lady came to them with incredible emotional pain and turmoil after much abuse, including sexual abuse through the foster care system. Some parents in the church began to care for her. She finished high school and then received a sponsor from one of their church members to attend Metamorpho, a one-year potential development program that helped restore her dignity and confidence. She then found a job, and today she is healthy and successful. Caring people who gave their time, skills, and money helped turn her spiral of devastation into a whole new destiny.

One church member works for an organization called Heartlines in South Africa (HAS). He and a Doxa Deo pastor joined one of the pastor fellowships HAS sponsors, which sparked a movement of reconciliation in Pretoria. He facilitates a program called "What's Your Story?" He reached out to Black and White leaders who did not want to engage the apartheid history in South Africa. Workshops and retreats gained momentum as people shared stories of where they came from and how apartheid affected their past. One Black pastor admitted he hated White people to the extent that he would never have thought he would talk to a White person. He testified how this program brought healing, and now he even calls White men his friends.

Doxa Deo is an example of one congregation that, in the middle of a season of struggle, saw another picture of their calling. This vision for a church came from attentiveness to God. How do we pay this kind of attention to God? And what gets in the way of our attentiveness?

Entitled or Entrusted?

Years ago, I (Kevin) heard my dad preach at a rally in a large coliseum. He asked this simple question: Are we entitled or are we entrusted? Doxa Deo's story magnifies what happens when God's people get a vision beyond themselves—when they flesh out Paul's exhortations to Timothy to guard the good deposit entrusted to him. Sadly, many believers and churches become mired in self-absorption. They prefer to be recipients of blessing more than being fishers of men and women. The key is learning to be attentive to what God is stirring up in their midst.

Our culture has produced a self-absorbed mindset that is all about "me." One study estimates that people across the planet take more than one million selfies each day. The average millennial will likely take more than twenty-five thousand selfies in her lifetime. Another study found the average woman from age sixteen to twenty-five spends five hours a week taking selfies.[5]

Our Western culture of entitlement infects our congregations. I (Jim) have encountered numerous congregations that see themselves as the owners of a faith culture in a particular location. They feel that most people should flock to their congregation because they were the "first" church on the major corner in town. These congregations are not responsive to new ideas for reaching the lost or new ways God may be moving in their location, nor are they helpful to new church plants in town. They simply act as if everybody who is somebody will eventually find a way to their beautiful sanctuary. How does a congregation get a sense of entitlement? It starts with ceasing to be attentive.

Entitlement is "the unjustified assumption that one has a right to certain advantages, preferential treatment."[6] This assumption boils down to one's attitude. As followers of Christ, we are wise to each pay attention to our attitudes. Many of us are comfortable in cultures surrounded by material, spiritual, and intellectual abundance. One barrier to attentiveness to God is a sense of entitlement that comes upon congregations as well as individuals.

My (Kevin's) systematic theology professor at Regent College, J. I. Packer, wrote a book called *Hot Tub Religion*, the term he gave for "Christianity corrupted by the passion for pleasure." He said,

> Hot tub religion is Christianity trying to beat materialism, Freudianism, humanism, and Hollywood at their own game, rather than challenge the errors that the rules of that game reflect. Christianity, in short, has fallen victim yet again (for this has happened many times before, in different ways) to the allure of this fallen world.[7]

Does the relative abundance around us make us feel entitled? Does it allow us to take our faith for granted, to become self-absorbed and cynical, and to appear detached or untouchable?

In 1995, alternative artist Joan Osborne asked, "What if God was one of us?" The incarnation stands as Christianity's central miracle. God becoming one of us remains a sharp rebuke to an attitude of entitlement. If we had planned how Christ should come to this earth, he would not have been born in an obscure village in an unimportant province. Common shepherds would not have been his first visitors. And his parents, who had no money for a lamb for the purification rite, would have been wealthy people of notoriety. But God chose for the grandest person in the universe to arrive in humility. He was one of us.

Paul writes in Philippians, "Adopt the same attitude as that of Christ Jesus" (Philippians 2:5 CSB). If anyone deserved entitlement, it was Jesus. Yet he became a servant. The Creator modeled obedience, and he died. He who was without sin became sin. Abraham Kuyper said, "Christ's self-emptying was not a single loss or bereavement, but a growing poorer and poorer until at last nothing was left to him but a piece of ground where he could weep and a cross whereon he could die."[8]

Certainly, Jesus died to provide atonement for our sins, granting us the gift of salvation. But he also demonstrated the meaning of discipleship on the cross. In the passage from Philippians 2, which was a hymn sung by early Christians, Paul writes, "He humbled himself in obedience to God and died a criminal's death on a cross" (Philippians 2:8 NLT). Hours before his crucifixion, Jesus took the manner of a house servant, washing the feet of his disciples. His model illustrates that we find life, purpose, and fulfillment by yielding ourselves to him, following his path, and using our lives to serve others.

God chose to adopt us into his family as his sons and daughters. We are not to identify as children of affluence but rather as children of adoption. Paul reminds his readers that their citizenship ultimately is not in the Roman Empire but in heaven. This reality should fill us with wonder. Instead of living self-absorbed lives of entitlement, we are to join with Paul: "We don't live for ourselves or die for ourselves. If we live, it's to honor the Lord" (Romans 14:7-8 NLT). We are entrusted with the gospel of Jesus Christ, a matchless gift we take to the world as his ambassadors.

Sadly, churchgoers today often feel a sense of entitlement. Ed Stetzer writes, "Millions of Americans live in the shadow of churches that have become consumer Christian centers, but pastors are ruined and the mission of God is cheated when consumers enjoy goods and services from their local church."[9] Consumerism and entitlement go hand in hand. But community does not form with a group of people who feel entitled. Rather, community emerges when people come together around a common mission. They are entrusted with the mission.

Interest-Based Versus Mission-Focused

In our Western culture, broadly speaking, there are two types of organizations: interest-based and mission-focused. An interest-based organization exists to serve its members. People come together around a common interest, such as a Harley Owners' Group (HOG), a bowling league, or a country club. The shared interest could be a hobby, like a mountain-biking club or an alumni club watching a college football game on a Saturday afternoon. Or it could gather people from similar lifestyles, like Mothers of Preschoolers (MOPS), an activities group for the elderly, or a singles organization.

Robert Bellah's definition of lifestyle enclaves is a good description of interest-based groups: "A lifestyle enclave is formed by people who share some feature of private life. Members of a lifestyle enclave express their identity through shared patterns of appearance, consumption, and leisure activities, which often serve to differentiate them sharply from those with other lifestyles."[10]

Interest-based organizations share several qualities:

- While the members share a particular external interest, they receive the benefits themselves.
- Typically, members pay their own membership fees for online communities, subscriptions to streaming services, or music fests.
- Once the members lose interest—or find a better product—they walk away from the group.

There's nothing wrong with interest-based organizations. They serve a vital purpose in creating casual relationships. Sociologists tell us humans need a combination of casual and intimate relationships. If we don't have casual relationships, we end up putting too much strain on our intimate relationships because we expect them to meet all of our needs. In other words, we need interest-based organizations. Even a church needs to be a place where people can experience casual relationships. But on a fundamental level, a church is called to be more than a social club.

On the other side of the spectrum are mission-focused organizations, which exist to serve non-members. They start where they are and then have an exponential impact on others. Real community doesn't come from a hobby. Instead, it arises from a shared mission. Examples of such groups include World Vision, Acts 29, Orange, and Surge. These organizations share several characteristics.

- The mission is external. World Vision's mission statement reads, "World Vision is an international partnership of Christians whose mission is to follow our Lord and Savior Jesus Christ in working with the poor and oppressed to promote human transformation, seek justice, and bear witness to the good news of the Kingdom of God." The website of Acts 29 states, "We plant churches worldwide by recruiting, assessing, training, and supporting church planters."
- The member is not the beneficiary. Rather, the member serves as a trustee, and the benefit flows outward. Surge, a global church planting movement, explains their purpose: "Plant a self-replicating, Spirit-filled church in every community."[11] The nonprofit organization Orange partners with churches and homes, seeking to "influence those who influence the faith and future of the next generation."[12]
- The members will never lose interest in a mission that unleashes their sense of purpose, like Paul before King Agrippa: "I couldn't just walk away from a vision like that!" (Acts 26:19 MSG).

Many church traditions in American culture were started around a common interest rather than a shared mission. A group of immigrants shared a common tongue and were looking for people who spoke the same language, or they shared a common heritage and wanted to preserve traditions from their homeland. Devotees to Presbyterianism, Lutheranism, Anglicanism, Methodism, the Baptist Church, Congregationalism, and the Moravian Church were the first to settle in America, and many of their traditions continue to this day. This is a tricky topic. We don't mean to suggest that the church should not care for their own people. In fact, the opposite is true. In taking care of our own we are, in fact, stewarding the mission. The two can go together naturally as long as the priority of mission is understood.

But remember, a mission-focused organization exists to serve its non-members. In Western culture, many churches function like interest-based organizations, primarily serving their members. This is in the vein of self-centeredness fueled by cultural narcissism. Stetzer writes, "Believers who think like customers contribute to the underachieving church in America. The damages move far beyond ineptness at engaging the mission of God." The incessant demands of a consumer congregation cause irreparable damage to those who lead such congregations.[13] But the biblical model is for the church to be mission based, serving those on the outside.

Why Engagement?

I (Kevin) consulted with hundreds of businesses and corporations for twenty-five years. At first, I primarily focused on organizational strategy. Over time, however, I learned that employee engagement was far more important than organizational strategy. *Fortune* magazine conducts an annual survey of the one hundred best companies to work for, rating employee engagement as high on their list. If employees hate their jobs, the organizational strategy is doomed to fail. As a result, I helped develop an employee survey called the Engagement Dashboard, which contains surveys of hundreds of businesses and agencies throughout the United States. In our research, we found an interesting correlation: when employees felt a sense of entitlement at work, the level of engagement dropped drastically. But when employees felt empowered—as in, they felt entrusted with the mission—engagement scores improved dramatically. Entitlement leads to disengagement. Empowerment leads to engagement.

Recent Gallup data reveals that only 36 percent of US-based employees are actively engaged in their work, and 15 percent are actively disengaged. The remaining 49 percent are lukewarm about their jobs. Imagine three companies that all do the same thing. The only difference is the level of employee engagement: one has actively engaged employees, the second has actively disengaged employees, and the third has lukewarm ones. If you were an investor, which company stock would you buy?[14]

While it may seem that interest-based and mission-focused organizations are mutually exclusive, they are not. But there is an order. An attentive church's first priority should be their mission. To fulfill that mission, they must care for their own people. The US armed forces, for example, have a sacrificial commitment "to leave no one behind." It is in the Airman's Creed ("I will never leave an airman behind") and the Soldier's Creed ("I will never leave a fallen comrade"). So, it's not an either-or choice. But the mission must come first.

Let me offer an example from my background in business. Years ago, I came across a concept out of Harvard called the Service-Profit Chain: create a positive internal culture, and you will have greater employee satisfaction. Employee satisfaction leads to greater employee retention and productivity. Experienced and productive employees lead to higher product or service quality. Quality products and services lead to customer satisfaction. Customer satisfaction leads to customer retention. Ultimately, customer retention leads to profitability and growth.

Obviously, we need to be careful about importing business concepts into our churches. Yet many businesses have learned how to take care of their employees based on their understanding of Scripture. Sometimes a church can learn biblical truths from how a God-honoring business is run.

We must create a great ethos where we deeply care for each other. Our people experience life-changing Christian community and want to share it with their friends, family, and neighbors. In so doing, our people become engaged in the mission. The danger, however, is mission drift. If we only create a great culture where we care for insiders, then we have simply created a lifestyle enclave. This means attentive churches must balance a focus on the internal culture as well as a focus on the mission.

Bill Robinson was the president of Whitworth University from 1993–2010. He was exemplary in helping Whitworth grow into a top-rated university, but he always kept his eye squarely on a deeply encouraged and appreciated staff. He knew employees and students by name and built a culture where that relational value was spread among many.

Is Our Focus Clear?

We have to be clear about our True North. If we are not, people will default to personal interest. People cannot feel ownership if the mission and vision are unclear. Again, *apostolos* refers to the church's mission, calling, and objective. A church must have a transcendent cause greater than themselves. If not, they will quickly turn inward and play games at the foot of the cross. *Telos* refers to the purpose, end, or vision of something. What specifically are we trying to accomplish? How can we concretely fulfill our mission? Churches need a compelling future in a consumer-driven culture competing for their attention.

Mission is what we do and what we don't do. A solid mission statement helps us say no to good things. Embedded within a mission statement is our purpose, our beneficiary, and our desired result. If mission is what we do, then vision is where we are heading. Mission rarely changes. Vision changes after we achieve it. Take a young basketball player as an example. The basketball player's mission is to be the best player he can be. The vision, however, changes as the ball player grows. It may be to make the junior varsity team. Once realized, the vision changes to make the varsity team. Then to win the conference championship. Then regional or state playoffs. To play college ball. To make it to the Final Four. You get the point. Vision must be achievable, to some extent. And once we achieve it, the mission points us toward our next vision.

Many churches get stuck on tactical issues, unable to get past their own spiritual navel-gazing to look at the fields that "are ripe for harvest" (John 4:35). If your church has a board, for example, take a look at your typical board meeting agenda. How many of those items are strategic in nature? Our experience is that a vast majority of church boards focus almost all of their time on tactical issues—budgets, facilities, and schedules. Many churches spin their wheels focusing only on the barn and never the wheat. Or, as the proverb says, "Where there are no oxen, the manger is clean, but abundant crops come by the strength of the ox" (Proverbs 14:4 ESV).

Strategy requires being clear about how people will be engaged in our shared mission. What specifically has God called your church to do? Values and mission should rarely change. But as context changes, strategy must change. As we typically have no control over our changing context, we must change our strategies in order to fulfill our mission—which often results in a new vision as well. Every time we change our vision and resulting strategies, we have to be very clear about how people will engage with the new direction or focus. This means leadership meetings should typically be built around more strategic conversations and fewer tactical issues.

As a strategic leader, you learn to know both your people and your church's community. Alan helped his congregation become attentive to their community. Exciting pictures of the future emerged as they imagined how their congregation could be engaged to meet specific needs.

Attentive leaders realize that every congregation, like Esther, exists in the kingdom of God "for such a time as this." These leaders work to help their people discover the distinct ways they can meet needs in their communities and beyond. As we obey the commands of Jesus and live them out practically, "every congregation becomes a world-missions strategy center. God can impact the world through one church."[15]

Empowering the Church

While feeling entitled remains a temptation for church members, being overly controlling is a temptation for church leaders. Like the pastor who dropped his shoes on the Communion table before storming off, many pastors feel a need to be the primary decision-maker. But the task for leading an attentive church is to create a culture of empowerment. Inattentive churches default to two archetypes: one of control or one of autonomy. Wise ministry leaders want to add more people to the church's leadership base as the church grows. We want to empower people to do ministry rather than micromanage their service.

The hardest transition for some church leaders is moving from doing everything to giving the ministry away. Instead of organizing our structure for control, predictability, and efficiency, we need to grow people, develop them, and release them to their biblical functions. Our friend Rhett Wilson writes,

> Attentive leaders empower people on ministry teams to make decisions regarding their respective areas. We can delegate decisions, thus nurturing a feeling of ownership and openness. When appropriate, they come to the leadership for input and approval. Every decision does not have to be discussed with the entire congregation. Instead, use congregational discussion times for sharing what they sense to be leadership from the Lord and sharing about things that affect the entire body. Pastors act as overseers and equippers, helping to empower people to do ministry and thus fulfill the church's mission.[16]

We should also clarify that empowerment is not the same thing as autonomy. Many leaders think that giving the ministry away is a laissez-faire type of leadership allowing people to do whatever they want to do. We have partnered with dozens of churches who believed they were empowering people, only to discover years later that each individual ministry had taken on a life of its own. Individually led ministries vie for resources such as space, budget, and staff. Rather than collaborating, autonomous ministries become unintentional competitors.

Empowerment occurs within the boundaries of shared values and mission, clarity of direction, and collaboration. We have found that most churches default to a culture of either autonomy or control.

Clint Tolbert started pastoring First Church in a small town outside of Toledo, Ohio, in 2010. "The growing pains have all been worth it," he said. Prior to his arrival, the church weathered several seasons of turmoil and conflict, marked by differences of opinion and the absence of a common purpose. The last few years of the former pastor's tenure included several times of intense strife, leaving the congregation hurting. An interim pastor helped them pick up the rubble of damaged relationships and begin to rebuild. When Clint came, he knew his role would include leading toward healing, establishing a common purpose, and empowering the members to accomplish their mission.

It didn't take long to realize that the church was not outwardly focused and that two differing theological sides existed within the congregation. Those sides differed on how to approach Scripture and how to love and serve the community. Clint wisely and intentionally began listening to and building relationships with leaders and church members, trying to discover who they were.

The church elders suggested they partner with an outside consultant to help them move past their hurts, discover a way forward, and clarify their values and vision. Clint had heard me (Kevin) speak at a conference and invited me to come. I used our Transforming Church Insight (TCI) survey, asked lots of questions, and spent time over the course of a year with various focus groups and the church's leadership. My purpose was to help them consider a few critical questions to help them frame a new path toward change by identifying their True North, rediscovering their *aretē* (quality of excellence and capability), and clarifying their *apostolos* (missional calling) and *telos* (purpose or end).

Clint recently reflected,

> The turning point of the weekend came when Kevin asked, "If First Church closed its doors tomorrow, who besides the members of the church would notice or care?" Though it was hard to acknowledge, the church leadership could not be confident that anyone within the community would notice or care. We began to recognize that our life together was focused on meeting the expectations of the members of the church, not serving the mission Jesus had given his church within the community and world.

As they evaluated their history, they rediscovered a core value: "At the beginning of our church—and at our best—we are a lay-led congregation with a pioneering spirit." Their key historical figure is Horatio Conant, a lay elder, missionary, and pioneer doctor. As they expressed the stories of their church's past, they realized they were always at their best when the lay people were leading in missional ways within the community.

Through our intentional journey together, they rediscovered a second core value that eventually led to a renewed missional focus. They realized that engaging in the study of Scripture for lifelong transformation and growing a community of faith would be critical if they were to serve their community together. Clint said, "Though we may differ on how to apply any particular passage of the Bible, we all needed to agree that Scripture was the mat upon which we would wrestle with what it means to serve Jesus in the world faithfully."

Once the church rediscovered their *aretē*, a path toward a new mission and vision naturally emerged. And the ripples began expanding. Clint and his ministry leaders made great progress toward leading an attentive church. Congregational leaders felt empowered to look outward to find opportunities to serve their local community and to engage others to help meet these needs. Over the following months and years, they found exciting and meaningful ways to engage the people in their area. Following several conversations with the Maumee Schools superintendent and several school principals, they began an intentional partnership to help meet the needs of students and families. Here are a few examples arising from that focus:

- "Read and Relate" was established as a program for church members to partner with young struggling readers, building positive relationships around the values of reading.
- Music lovers in the church witnessed a lack of access to instruments for low-income students and began a supply bank to offer instruments to those who could not afford them.
- Through conversations with a partner school, Feed My Starving Children was brought in to introduce students and community members to the realities of global poverty while giving them the opportunity to be a part of the solution. Hundreds of community members were involved in this service project.

The church sought to support the leadership of the schools and provide opportunities to engage the community. In addition to the school outreach, First Church aligned with a ministry to families in poverty called Mosaic Ministries, helped families through Baby University, and provided meals and mentorship in various ways. On a global scale, while on a mission trip with Compassion International, church members saw a need for clean water in a small community in the Dominican Republic. They brought the financial request to the congregation and raised funds to send to the local Compassion church. They now have established a water purification plant that supplies water to the entire town and also raise financial support for the Compassion Center.

All of these ministries were an outpouring of one or two individuals following their hearts and inspiring others to help meet the needs of those they encountered. Their actions began tangibly fulfilling the church's newly established mission statement, their *apostolos*: "We are the church family engaging each person to enrich our community for God's glory through Jesus."

Clint shared,

> As the leader throughout this process, my role was to establish boundaries and provide support and encouragement for the mission, while continuing to ground the members of the church in the truth of Scripture. Our church had been paralyzed, not knowing how to move forward. This process gave us renewed purpose and direction to take the gospel beyond the walls of our congregation.

The people at First Church came to understand that sharing the gospel started with helping to meet true needs within their community. Clint and his staff provided context for the church by asking questions like the following:

- What needs are we trying to meet?
- How are these ministries helping us to fulfill the mission to which we are called?

- Are we merely giving financial resources, or is this ministry helping us to engage our church family and the community?

In their journey to clarify their mission and vision, the church has had a significant effect on their community. The gospel extended beyond their walls and in ways that will continue for years. Just as importantly, a change occurred in the hearts of those within the church to know Jesus more fully and embrace the mission.

One passage in Scripture that helped First Church define the beauty of the church working together on mission is 1 Corinthians 12:18-20 BSB: "But in fact, God has arranged the members of the body, every one of them, according to His design. If they were all one part, where would the body be? As it is, there are many parts, but one body." This truth has become an important focus for the church to encourage each part of the body to do its work. As a leader, Clint encourages each member to know their importance—whether it is speaking up front, singing in the choir, or being the hands and feet of Jesus in the community. All are valuable. He says, "We had the financial resources to benefit others and had done this in a variety of ways. However, rather than just extending a check, we also began to use our resources to help our members engage in the ministry through commitment and passion."

This church in Ohio, with fewer than four hundred active members, serves as a tremendous example of the transformation that occurs when a congregation rediscovers their values and clarifies their mission, thus becoming an attentive church. Clint summarizes,

> God has called each one of us to be a part of his mission, sharing his love and forgiveness with the world. Our church knew this call beginning over two hundred years ago. It has been my privilege to remind our church of this call and to empower them to take the gospel into the community by identifying and meeting specific needs while also sharing the love of Christ. While change is not easy, our church has grown in numbers, but more importantly, in compassion for others.

On our journey of leading attentive churches, creating a culture of engagement begins by clarifying True North and creating mechanisms for people to engage. But what happens when directional clarity is not enough? What do we do when people are not just casually disengaged but actively resistant? If True North is so vital to mobilizing our congregation and creating a shared culture, we are wise to ask, "What gets in the way of their fulfillment?" In the next couple of chapters, we'll address issues related to facing resistance and managing conflict as we seek to mobilize and motivate our churches toward their compelling future.

Questions for Reflection and Discussion

- How do you see the struggle between entitlement and entrustment in your ministry?
- In what ways have you witnessed entitlement negatively affect the church?
- What mechanisms or structures do you have in place that naturally allow people to be engaged?
- Consider taking your leadership group—staff, elders, deacons, etc.—through a discussion of what it means to be an interest-based group versus a mission-focused one. How might that change the trajectory of your ministry?
- What has leadership done, intentionally or unintentionally, to create a culture of entitlement?
- In what ways can you work at intentionally empowering other people to do ministry rather than assuming all of the responsibility?
- Spend some time in prayer asking the Lord to move your church to a place of empowerment rather than entitlement so that lives will be changed.

9

How Do We Facilitate Real Transformation?

"I'm so frustrated," Pastor Chris proclaimed. "I want to see our congregation become an authentic community. I want to see people growing into mature disciples of Jesus. But we can't get past our board's leadership dysfunction. When I remain in a posture of humility, they say I'm being passive. When I try to be bold, they call me controlling. The irony of this overwhelms me at times."

Clearly, Chris had lost his board's trust. But more significantly, the board had lost the congregation's trust. Many people left the church. Quite a number who remained were highly cynical. As we partnered with them, we recommended a structure that would begin managing the system's distrust. Building trust takes time, often years. One element of this plan clarified accountability for Chris: he became answerable to the elder board's chair, which allowed the board to speak with one voice to him through the chair.

In one of our meetings early in the process, Chris was clearly angry about the new structure. "I shouldn't need a supervisor," he fumed. "It feels remedial." We explained that authority is conferred, not taken. Regardless of what "should be" or what the contract says, the trust people have in the leader limits that leader's authority. It's a relational covenant, not a legal contract. Establishing trust authorizes a person to lead, and they do so by maintaining healthy boundaries, meeting basic expectations, and establishing order.

Chris wanted to lead. He wanted to see people come to know Jesus. He desired to lead an attentive church. He had a great vision—to build a community of mature disciples. The problem, however, is that nobody can lead if they are not authorized. Authority is almost always informal. While some of the blame fell on Chris, the real leadership dysfunction came from a poorly designed leadership structure. People fell through the cracks. Congregational requests for pastoral care were never returned. A staff person had an affair with a volunteer. Staff members complained of a hostile work environment created by a former employee. So the congregation assigned the blame to the most visible person they knew: Chris. And seeking to be an attentive congregation was not yet on their radar.

Over time, a new governance model was introduced and implemented. The board clarified a handful of key policies for board members and Chris. They published their meeting minutes for the congregation. Board meetings shifted from lots of tactical issues to life-giving conversations. Eventually, the board members formed a deep sense of community. Trust was restored.

After a couple of years in the new structure, Chris emailed us.

> I'm amazed at how much better things are with my board chair and our board in general. I was ready to find a new job, but I think God has planted me here for at least a few more years. But I'm still frustrated on one level. While leadership is much healthier, we are not seeing it translate to the congregation. By and large, we still have spectators who come for the worship experience and children's ministries. I want to see real transformation. Help!

Chris was discovering that leaders establish trust when they follow through on commitments and maintain healthy boundaries. But trust doesn't create transformation. It's simply the soil in which transformation is nurtured.

Investing Trust

Tod Bolsinger is the senior congregational strategist and associate professor of leadership formation at Fuller Theological Seminary. He recently shared with us,

> Technical solutions do something. They build trust. But trust is not transformation. As leaders we have to invest trust into transformation. So, our success is not just about having integrity and performing our duties. We must help our congregations move from consumerism to community, because consumerism is a way of outsourcing transformation instead of taking on responsibility.

Tod became the senior pastor at a church in San Clemente, California, in his thirties after the church experienced the turbulence of marital infidelities by two pastors. A dynamic and capable young leader, he came with a clear sense of purpose. He also brought a strong tactical competence that allowed him to build trust and help the church slowly recover and stabilize. By every outward metric, the church seemed to thrive for years. They tripled in size, the budget grew four times its amount, and they redid the entire campus and buildings. By the North American church growth model, they were a smashing success.

After his ninth year, he took a sabbatical. When he returned, he realized that morale among leaders was waning—"Key people were getting cynical and checking out." Tod couldn't understand. He worked hard, executed great tactical skills, and was an effective communicator. But something was amiss.

When he reached out to me (Kevin), he had just fired his previous coach who told him he had a vision problem. As we journeyed through our discovery process, I realized what was happening. I told Tod that he was the problem. As a competent, strong leader, he became the hero in the church, the one they paid to watch and to do ministry. He had rescued the church during a tumultuous time, and in the process, the church became far too dependent on him. He was too central.

Tod said, "I had unintentionally made the ministry about me. That's what I knew about leadership. Bring the solutions and wins to the people, and they follow me. For several years people were talking about me a lot. I was the center. I knew it wasn't healthy, but I didn't know any way out." Tod realized that some of the very things that produced success on one level were stopping them from thriving on another level. He says in retrospect, "I didn't know how to make the church bigger than me."

I told Tod at the time that he had solved most of his problems with tactical solutions, which made him appear very capable and trustworthy—which he was. But what he and the church needed now was transformational leadership, or adaptive leadership, which Ron Heifetz defines as "the practice of mobilizing people to tackle tough challenges and thrive."[1] We prefer the term *transformational leadership* to *adaptive leadership* because as Jesus' followers, we believe transformation is the ultimate goal. This type of leadership embraces change while building on the past rather than jettisoning it. It relies on diversity, occurs through experimentation, and takes time.[2] Unlike the one-size-fits-all approach, it pays attention to the people in the church and its unique context.

What Is the Goal?

The goal is not just to see bigger church budgets and larger attendance (nickels and noses, as people used to say). The goal is for individuals, transformed by God's grace, to become a community of fully devoted followers of Jesus. The Bible challenges believers to be "transformed by the renewing of your mind. Then you will be able to test and approve what God's will is—his good, pleasing and perfect will" (Romans 12:2). Paul uses the Greek word *metamorphoō*, from which we get the word *metamorphosis*. The word can be translated as "be transfigured, be changed, be transformed."[3] It conveys the idea of a caterpillar being changed into a butterfly. As we practice attentive church leadership, the goal of our ministry should include divine life-change. The real work of transformation is through the power of the Holy Spirit. But as leaders, our job is to clear the way—to become facilitators of transformation. We can never control or monitor God's work, but we can certainly control and monitor our own work. We can also make adjustments when we realize that our methods are blocking true transformation.

How easy it is for us leaders to give attention to the tactical, which often is simply a focus on external metrics. As the Lord told the prophet Samuel, "The LORD sees not as man sees: man looks on the outward appearance, but the LORD looks on the heart" (1 Samuel 16:7 ESV).

A transformational leader does not just manage people and programs. She manages the process to get the roadblocks out of the way so that authentic change can take place, moving people from self-centeredness to authentic community. Let's look at that process and how leaders can lead transformation.

Competing Values

What is the greatest roadblock to transformation? Me. My selfish desires get in the way of a life-giving biblical community. "Me versus we" is the essence of competing values. Like iron sharpening iron, competing values bring about transformation.

Church leaders experience competing values in every aspect of congregational life. I (Jim) once got a strange question from a group of ushers: "What do you want to do with the smugglers in the sanctuary?" Baffled, I asked, "What's being smuggled into the sanctuary?" In unison the ushers replied, "Coffee. Starbucks coffee." As in many traditional churches, a prominent sign hung at the entrance reading, "No food or drink in the sanctuary." Yet every week after the third service, the ushers picked up empty Starbucks cups. Like many congregations we had ample coffee for free in big urns, but it was usually Folgers, purchased on sale. Our third service targeted young adults, whose taste in coffee was much more sophisticated than Folgers. While the ushers successfully stopped people from bringing the free coffee into the sanctuary, a five-dollar cup of Starbucks was not so easily relinquished.

I could have simply told them to allow coffee in the sanctuary. Years before, I had exercised that power with the "no baseball hats in the sanctuary" rule. On my second Sunday in that church, a college student emailed asking how much a baseball cap was worth to me. I asked her for more context. She explained that she frequently attended and for months had tried to get her boyfriend to come to church, but he was uninterested. In May of that year, I arrived and she tried again, inviting him to come see this new pastor. He came that Sunday wearing his signature baseball cap. An usher told him he would need to take it off to enter the sanctuary—and that if he preferred to wear it, he would need to watch the service on closed-circuit television downstairs. The young man took one look at his girlfriend and walked out. How much was a baseball cap worth? Rather quickly, I let the ushers know that we didn't need to enforce that rule at church. It was a simple tactical change that did not cause any significant ripples.

The baseball cap and coffee situations are related to how we understand and express sacred space. Regulating the proper use of such spaces comes from a value system that appreciates reverence before God. For many, neither the presence of hats nor coffee expresses appropriate reverence. Children running in the sanctuary also elicits a rebuke in many congregations.

This event around coffee in the sanctuary actually provided an opportunity to teach lessons about transformational change. I asked the ushers to come to the next elders meeting to talk about the smugglers. The elders, most of whom did not attend that third service, were mortified there was coffee in the sanctuary. They saw the implications that would follow. One elder posited that the goldfish crackers for children would be next. The ushers quickly said they had chosen not to fight the goldfish battle because that service went past noon and the children were hungry. The next elder, realizing there was a pizza place one block from the church, brought up the fear of a delivery person entering the sanctuary and calling out, "Who ordered the pepperoni?" Another elder who saw catastrophe coming said, "I refuse to smell french fries in this sanctuary!"

Courageously, two young adult elders spoke up to defend the coffee in the sanctuary. They explained that having a cup of good coffee during worship brought feelings of bonding and was appropriate for building community. Suddenly, we uncovered the needed ingredient for transformational change—the presence of two competing values, reverence and hospitality. Coffee suggested invitation and a welcoming, warm community. Reverence meant taking God's presence seriously. How could they both be expressed? For three months, the elders discussed this challenge. They concluded that "no food or drink in the sanctuary" is not in the book of Leviticus. They discovered that meals were a part of early church worship. What's more, they learned their view of reverence might be too narrow and their view of hospitality could expand.

If I had just told the ushers to allow the coffee in the sanctuary, we would have missed a fantastic learning experience. The smugglers helped us become a more attentive church.

Remember, we want people to move from entitlement to engagement. Tactical leadership establishes trust, but it also reinforces entitlement by creating dependence on the pastor or leaders. When a pastor overfunctions within the system, they allow the rest of the church to underfunction. Transformational leadership is the only way to move from entitlement to engagement by shifting the real work to the people. That begins when we identify the competing values and then engage our people in them.

Authority Versus the Status Quo

Transformation can't happen without trust, but trust alone doesn't create transformation. Trust comes from reliable leadership and predictable behaviors. Trust is built when we know what we can count on. But transformation occurs when the status quo is challenged. When we challenge it, we begin making withdrawals from the investments made in our "trust bank." Those investments could result in exponential returns, or they could bankrupt our portfolio.

Isn't that what Jesus did? He challenged the disciples and the Pharisees. He disrupted the status quo. "You have heard it said, but I say to you" is a phrase Jesus uttered many times to correct the use of Scripture in an abusive context.

Leaders must be attentive to the difference between exercising their perceived authority and using their position for power. Too often, leaders unintentionally abuse their position. If they aren't attentive to this distinction, the results can be messy. The assumption of authority can quickly create distrust within the congregation. This is a dance that requires keen awareness of self and others. The limits of a leader's authority are constrained by the limits of the trust people have in the leader. Because trust is relational, authority is never what is written in a contract.

Brad Longhorn pastored Goose Creek Church in Lexington, Kentucky. His two-hundred-year-old church had been located in the same place for all those years. After a fire in the 1920s the church was rebuilt, but in 2007, the building was in disrepair. Deferred maintenance would cost several hundred thousand dollars, which seemed impossible since their membership was in decline. And the church's primary demographic no longer matched that of the surrounding neighborhood.

Brad convened his leadership team to explore options. Over the course of several months, they quietly conducted demographic studies and consulted with realtors. They sensed it might be time to relocate to a fast-growing northern suburb. At one service, between Sunday announcements about the men's breakfast and Mothers of Preschoolers (MOPS), he casually mentioned the idea of relocating. He assured the congregation that he wanted to hear from them to test out the idea before any decision was made. But by the following week, dozens of people let Brad know they were leaving the church.

Afterward he called me (Kevin), clearly frustrated. "We just lost dozens of people in one week. I even told them we wanted their input. I'm not sure what happened. I've been blindsided."

I explained to Brad that the people perceived a decision had already been made. Brad, as pastor, started with a solution. If he had started with the problem, he would have engaged the people. Instead, they felt pushed aside by a decision from the leadership.

The issue went far deeper than deferred maintenance. A potential relocation represented competing values—preserving their past versus securing their future; tradition versus innovation; meeting internal needs versus meeting community needs. Brad thought he was simply exercising his authority by communicating a general idea. What he didn't realize was that church members believed a decision had already been made—an abuse, albeit unintentional, of his position as pastor. Whenever competing values are present, the leader needs to shift the conversation back to the people. Competing values require transformational—not tactical—leadership.

Transformational leadership begins by engaging our people in existing problems and issues. Too often, leaders feel like they need to be the ones with the answers. This well-intentioned posture stunts transformation.

Overprotective parents want to protect their children from danger. But the unintended consequence is often a child who becomes overly dependent on the parent, incapable of functioning independently. The same is true for a pastor who thinks she must be the one with all the answers for the congregation.

We told Brad it wasn't too late. He still had enough of the congregation left to do a reboot. We asked him to go through a yearlong process of discernment with the church, putting the issues back on them: What do we do about our deferred maintenance? Why is our membership in decline? How do we address the differences between our congregation and our neighborhood?

After a year of engaging the entire congregation, a new solution emerged. Rather than relocating, they realized a unique opportunity for a multisite, multicampus church. They would rebuild their existing facility to meet the needs of the neighborhood. They could establish a site in the fast-growing northern suburb while establishing a third site near the university. When Brad announced the new direction on a Sunday morning, the congregation stood to their feet and cheered!

Brad and his leadership team might have landed in the same place without congregational input. But involving other people gave them new ideas they had never considered. More importantly, if Brad had presented a multisite plan to the congregation without their involvement, he would have experienced the original result—people feeling like leadership was ramrodding a decision. The process itself was the secret sauce.

Transformational leadership helps navigate competing values. Brad assumed that he and the leadership team had the authority to consider a relocation, but they didn't realize at first that their authority did not address competing values. The two go hand in hand, but they are not the same thing.

Authority, Leadership, and Power

It is important to distinguish between these three concepts. As we mentioned earlier, authority is conferred regardless of position. Sometimes people assume that someone is automatically a leader because of their position. In reality, to identify the leaders in an organization, simply ask, *Who is exerting influence, and who are people following?* In a small church, the pastor may stand in front of the people and speak, but the real leader, or influencer, may be a seventy-year-old matriarch who sits in the back row. When real decisions must be made, the people ask her and not the pastor for advice. Pastors who want to exercise authority must build relational equity. Regardless of the employment agreement or contract, authority only exists based on a trusting relationship.

So what about power? In its most negative form, power is abusive. We've all seen pastors, politicians, and CEOs who use their positions for personal gain. But often, the use of positional power is unintentional—and just as problematic. At Goose Creek Church, Brad Longhorn unintentionally misused his position. If one member had turned to another and said, "We should think about relocating our building," the comment would have been laughed off. But because Brad was the pastor, his words carried more weight than the average member's did. A leader's unintentional abuse of power decreases their authority because the people start to lose trust in them. On the other hand, a leader's authority increases as their people trust them more. Somewhere in the middle is where we find transformational leadership. Leaders must have enough trust to raise competing values, but they must do so in a manner that doesn't abuse their position.

In business, there's an old adage: "It takes money to make money." The same is true for trust and transformation. We leverage trust so that we earn the right to raise the competing values. Once we've raised those competing values with our people, and they experience true transformation, then we earn even more trust.

Too often, however, leaders are not aware that they are dealing with transformational matters. Here are four questions that may help you identify issues requiring transformational leadership.

- **Is there a gap between our stated values and our actual behaviors?** If we say we value evangelism but our behavior says we hang out with insiders, then we have an adaptive challenge. Or perhaps leaders say they value each person equally, but they really pay attention to the biggest giver. That's also an adaptive issue. But when behaviors and actions line up with the stated values, it's simply a tactical challenge.
- **Are there competing values, even if they are both good values?** We recently talked with a pastor whose church was growing. They had two Sunday morning services with coffee hour in between. To accommodate growth, leadership decided to cancel the coffee hour and add a third service. Within six months, the church was in decline. They failed to navigate the competing values of external growth and internal fellowship.
- **Are our leaders focusing on distractions rather than the real work?** In your leadership meetings, do you focus on short-term decisions and projects rather than on underlying tensions and conflict? We worked with a leadership team of a ten-thousand-member church that asked us to help them navigate a pretty severe disagreement about the leadership of the children's ministry. When we sat in on a typical staff meeting, we noticed that the senior leadership team spent almost an hour editing a brochure for an upcoming event. There was no mention of the conflict or the children's ministry.
- **Do our problems tend to repeat themselves over time?** Take a minute or two to jot down the problems your church currently faces. Which problems were there five or ten years ago? What solutions have you attempted? We find that blaming and scapegoating are expedient solutions that prevent a church from dealing with

underlying issues. Dealing with these types of problems requires transformational leadership.

Engaging the People

It's been said that an expert is someone who flies in from across the country with a briefcase. We've all experienced "experts" who fly in, give their professional solutions, and fly out. This may work if you are trying to fix an HVAC system or a piece of machinery. But it does not work well in organic systems composed of people.[4]

Pastors are no different. Jack Peebles pastored in Yakima, Washington. He called me (Kevin) a few years ago and complained that his congregation was not the missional community he wanted them to be. When I asked what he had done to try to move them toward a missional posture, he said, "Well, I just did a twelve-week sermon series on missional living, and nothing has changed."

In Jack's theological heritage, the centrality of the preached Word is highly valued. He said, "I assumed the Holy Spirit would show up, and transformation into missional living would just occur—people would get it and run with it." Like the expert flying in and out for professional solutions, Jack assumed he could simply preach a great series and see transformation occur. Through some coaching on transformational leadership, he was able to pivot and begin engaging people in conversations about the competing values in everyday life. He realized the paradigm shift from the attractional model to a missional one is drastic, requiring changes from our consumeristic tendencies. "Preaching was the tactical solution, but we also needed to engage in transformational change as we rethought our ministries," Jack said. "We began rethinking our entire discipleship and spiritual formation strategy, not thinking of formation as an end unto itself. Rather, we asked, 'If we want to form missional disciples of Jesus, what does that require?'"

Jack and his leadership began challenging their people to see that as they lived their lives, through their families, neighborhoods, and vocations, God was sending them into those places and relationships for his purposes. For Jack, this wasn't a quick fix or an easy answer. He and his leadership had to engage people in a different way. Preaching alone was insufficient.

Asking Questions

The transformational leader doesn't make decisions or establish strategic plans but instead facilitates a series of conversations among key stakeholders. She doesn't jump in with the solutions and say, "Do it my way." An effective leader gathers the right people together and begins listening. Attentiveness is crucial to transformational leadership.

Engaging in conversations flies in the face of the Lone Ranger, "I am the hero" style of leadership. We know a pastor who said to his congregation, "I am the only person in this church God speaks to. Your responsibility is to follow what I say." Such a narcissistic approach to shepherding the church is the opposite of the kind of attentive leadership we are suggesting. You cannot lead your church alone. Effective, lasting change necessitates that you bring both positional leaders and influencers to the table.

As you do, begin a practice of asking questions more than offering solutions. Your goal is to learn, and you learn by listening. In our coaching, we use the 3-D Method to tease out competing values in three phases: dialogue, discussion, and decision. Most leaders, particularly young ones, want to jump too quickly into making decisions. However, the first two stages are critical for gleaning the wisdom and understanding needed to make sound decisions.

In the dialogue phase, we ask people to share their opinions and perspectives without giving feedback or interruption. This displays value for each individual and allows you to gather needed information. The Greek origins of the word *dialogue* suggest a "togetherness in discourse." We are together when we listen to each other.

The discussion phase helps us to understand one another. The word *discussion* has Latin origins and means to "shake up" or "break apart." At this time, participants can disagree and express why they disagree. The goal here is not consensus but understanding. Keep asking why until you get to the ultimate value at stake for each person. As the opinions from the dialogue phase are "shaken up" in the discussion phase, you will eventually discover the competing values.

Finally, after the discussion phase, the leadership can move toward making decisions—but only after a lot of listening. While the decision phase does not guarantee consensus, it does mean that the decision is well-informed, people have been heard, and competing values have been considered. Leaders still must make decisions that are best for the entire community. Individuals may experience loss in this process, but the goal should always be what's best for the church's mission. Consensus rarely happens on the front end of a decision around competing values. But, if it's the right decision, consensus will occur later as people come to recognize that the right decision was made. Trust will then increase after a series of good, but difficult, decisions have led to transformation.

The value of the 3-D Method is not just in the information but in the process itself. It helps people move past the either-or mindset that permeates so much of our society these days. By examining competing values, people start to see the issue in a wider spectrum and experience less polarity.

Manage Anxiety

In transformational leadership, you will experience anxiety—both in the congregation and in yourself. We discussed the importance of managing anxiety in chapter three. When anxiety comes from the outside, it can be enormous, and so can the resulting changes. Just think of the impact of the pandemic in 2020. The question is what you do with that anxiety. Most leaders have a default—some become more urgent and demanding. Some talk and talk and talk. Others walk away. In times of heightened anxiety, leaders need to work on bringing the anxiety down. People need a calming presence when facing a war, a pandemic, or an economic disaster.

Yet, in times of low anxiety, leaders need to bring the anxiety up. A good leader learns how to shift the appropriate level of anxiety back to the people.

Moderate levels of anxiety allow transformation to occur. Martin Linksy writes, "Leadership requires disturbing people—but at a rate they can absorb."[5] Ron Heifetz put it a different way at a gathering we hosted: "Leadership is disappointing people . . . at a rate they can tolerate." Good leaders do not try to rid the system of all anxiety. Instead, they lead at a rate the people can handle. A seminary professor once told a class of students, "Leadership means getting far enough ahead of your people so that they recognize you as the leader, but not getting so far ahead of them that they mistake you for the enemy and shoot you in the bottom!"

For example, some well-meaning pastors storm into a church during their first year and decide to do a major overhaul. They give away the hymnals, change the dress code, rewrite the constitution, and alter the schedule right out of the gate. Many times, such drastic shifts come back to bite them, creating distrust and putting too much anxiety into the system at one time.

Embrace Conflict

Conflict is your friend. It means you're exercising leadership. What matters is what you do with the conflict and how you treat the people involved. Our colleague Jim Osterhaus writes,

> We realize that the word conflict is loaded emotionally. Many people associate conflict with destructive images, of people shouting at one another, of gangs shooting at each other, of countries bombing one another. Certainly those are conflicted situations. But conflict, at its core, involves disagreement, differing ideas and opinions, discrepant evaluations and judgments. People are different. Each person walking this earth has a different slant on things, different ways of seeing what is unfolding, differing priorities, different strategies for dealing with all the situations life throws at us.[6]

Managing yourself is critical in leading change. It's essential that you remain a non-anxious presence. In some ways, transformational leadership requires being a grief counselor as much as a vision caster. You have to carefully and prayerfully comfort people as they embrace change, which means letting go of some things in order to embrace new ones.

Heifetz shares, "When you lead people through difficult change, you take them on an emotional roller coaster because you are asking them to relinquish something—a belief, a value, a behavior—that they hold dear. People can stand only so much change at any one time."[7]

When you experience pushback, it may allow you the opportunity to step back, gain some perspective, and consider other courses of action. It does not have to completely derail the system. But it may help you to make the process better and build trust with the person who is pushing back. Listening to them respectfully can build a bridge of trust.

When Tod Bolsinger began embracing transformational leadership, he slowly drew key people around him, engaging them in conversations. During that time, his biggest pushback came from some of his best leaders who had seen him thrive during his first nine years. They thought he was losing the fire in his belly by not wanting to manage everything himself. In reality, though, he wanted strong people to be able to use their gifts. Tod wanted to see people grow and develop—not just make the machine of the church function. He said, "Now I see leadership as transforming a community of people so that they can accomplish the ministry."

Reframe the Problem

I (Kevin) was leading a focus group at Messiah Church near St. Louis. One participant was upset at the new pastor, Paul Schult. "He acts like he is the CEO of a business," she said. "Are we a family, or are we a business?"

This was a congregation in a fast-growing suburb. The first pastor was relational, personable, and an effective church planter, building a culture that was often referred to as a family. After ten years, he decided with the congregation to have Paul help with the increasing workload.

In a recent conversation, Paul recalled,

> As the congregation continued to grow, so did expectations of expanded and improved programs that continued to effectively

include more people in the process of helping people be and make disciples of Jesus. The growth also created more demands for new systems for business operations.

When I arrived, I possessed natural strengths in the areas of strategy and designing systems. Some members of the congregation were excited that the ministry structure and systems could be improved, an important priority for the congregation to continue growing and reaching more people. As the work began, some founding members became frustrated by new ways of doing things. It felt like moving from a mom-and-pop family business to a growing operation that needed to be more organized, effective, and efficient. It wasn't long before the changes were perceived as a challenge to the family culture. Over time, the new organizational systems and programs were labeled as being too corporate, too much like a business instead of a church.

Eventually, people in the congregation began to take sides and attach the two pastors to the two different values. As a result, a set of competing values formed that was being discussed as a case of right versus wrong, good versus bad.

Paul said, "Rather than having productive and healthy conversations about the different values, the benefits of both, and how to best manage them, the conversations became divisive and personal." Eventually, Paul contacted me (Kevin) to facilitate an extensive visioning and planning process. After completing our discovery phase, the competing values began to emerge. I raised the issue with leaders of the church who were finally positioned to talk about the conflict that was increasingly dividing the church and harming their work and mission. At the end of one planning session, the same participant from the focus group said, "Are we a family, or are we a business? I asked you this question a few weeks ago, and you never answered me!"

Rather than answer her question, I decided to let the group argue about it for a while. The tension in the room grew as people took sides.

Once a healthy level of anxiety was present, I suggested that they were asking the wrong question. They stared at me, stunned.

Eventually, one leader asked what the right question was. I replied, "The question is not 'Are we a family or a business?' but 'How is a church different from both a family and a business?'" I then had the group create a list of how a church is different from a family, and how the church is different from a business. Over the course of a couple hours, the mood in the room softened. Excitement emerged as they began to see things from a new perspective.

"From that moment on," Paul recounted, "the people of the congregation were finally positioned to talk about these critical values openly, honestly, and effectively without making them personal and divisive."

In John's Gospel, the Pharisees tried to trap Jesus. They brought him a woman caught in adultery and reminded him that Jewish law commanded they stone her, even though they also knew Roman law forbid such a punishment. They framed the problem in such a way to trap Jesus with two competing values.

Yet, Jesus was a master at reframing. He moved the issue away from the competing values of two different legal systems and reframed it as a personal issue. He bent down and wrote in the ground, perhaps outlining the sins of the Pharisees. "Let any one of you who is without sin be the first to throw a stone at her," he said (John 8:7). Eventually, they all left.

The woman was left alone with Jesus. In one of the most powerful moments in all of Scripture, Jesus straightened up and asked her, "Woman, where are they? Has no one condemned you?" (John 8:10)

"No one, sir," she said.

"Then neither do I condemn you," Jesus declared. "Go now and leave your life of sin" (John 8:11). The ultimate reframe results in transformation.

As we dialogue with our people and discover competing values, it's important to listen intently to how they are framing the problem. Once we understand that, we can look for a reframe—a different way of viewing the same problem. Good leaders learn the art of reframing so that instead of seeing a challenge as an issue, they view it as an opportunity to learn and grow. At Messiah Church, I didn't dismiss their conflict. Rather, I rearranged it. I changed the question. Doing so allowed the group to discern new solutions and ideas.

As you listen to people's complaints, pay attention to what you don't know. Make sure you understand their frame before challenging assumptions. Once you are clear about how someone is framing an issue, you can explore a possible reframe.

A successful reframe includes several components:

- Don't accept the frame as presented, but don't dismiss it entirely. While the current frame may not be the way forward, it provides clues that allow a reframe to emerge.
- Let the temperature rise. A healthy level of anxiety creates a posture that will accept a new way of looking at things. People have different types of anxiety, whether over learning new things or over current realities. When learning anxiety exceeds current anxiety, people become open to a reframe.
- Provide a valid alternative viewpoint to the same problem. I didn't tell the leaders at Messiah Church that the problem wasn't real. I simply suggested that they were asking the wrong question.
- Be surprising or provocative. Everyone in the room expected me to answer the question as presented: "Are we a family, or are we a business?" My response surprised them.
- Be plausible. My reframe wasn't out of the blue. It was a genuine attempt at finding a better question. It emerged from their current view of reality.
- Generate energy. If the alternative frame isn't generating energy, then it's probably not the right reframe. Follow the energy until the person or group is engaged.
- Create hope. A reframe should suggest a positive future, a way forward. It also helps the person or group save face because they couldn't solve the problem with the previous frame.

- Allow for a new set of solutions. If the reframe doesn't lead to new thinking and new solutions, don't pursue it. But once people own a new frame, they begin to dream of new solutions.

Competing values often create a frame that seems unsolvable. That's why reframing is so important—it creates a way forward. Attentive leaders learn to function in three modes: strategic, tactical, and transformational. Strategic challenges involve responding to the world outside of our church, the changing context. We can't build community without paying attention to the changing world. We also can't build community without establishing trust. We have to pay attention to our people and understand their needs and expectations. Tactical leadership requires expertise and integrity, and when we perform diligently, trust grows. Finally, transformational leadership addresses competing values and the associated behaviors and attitudes. The apostle Paul reminded the Ephesian church to use their spiritual gifts to serve others

> until we all attain to the unity of the faith and of the knowledge of the Son of God, to mature manhood, to the measure of the stature of the fullness of Christ, so that we may no longer be children, tossed to and fro by the waves and carried about by every wind of doctrine, by human cunning, by craftiness in deceitful schemes. Rather, speaking the truth in love, we are to grow up in every way into him who is the head, into Christ, from whom the whole body, joined and held together by every joint with which it is equipped, when each part is working properly, makes the body grow so that it builds itself up in love. (Ephesians 4:13-16 ESV)

Attentive church leadership facilitates real transformation. Like a stone thrown into a body of water, the movement of the church, healthy leadership, and attentiveness work together to create a multitude of ripples. People will take ownership of their spiritual journey. They will become engaged in a shared ethos. They will move past entitlement. Like iron sharpening iron, new realities will emerge.

As you become a transformational leader of an attentive church, your perspective will broaden. You will start to become more generative in your thinking. Your vision will grow beyond your own church. Your vision will grow for the kingdom of God—the rule and reign of Jesus Christ everywhere.

Questions for Reflection and Discussion

- Think about a particular issue that has become a focal point of conflict in your church. How is that issue currently being framed? What competing values can you identify?
- What do the authors say is the goal of transformational leadership? What will that mean for your ministry setting?
- How do the four questions that identify issues requiring transformational change challenge you in your role and ministry?
- How might you engage people on a deeper level to begin shifting the anxiety to them? What presenting issue might be a good case study to test out the 3-D Method with your leaders (and then key stakeholders)?
- What reframes might be helpful to mobilize your leadership core?

10

How Do We Pass the Torch?

A quote often attributed to Dietrich Bonhoeffer says, "A righteous person is one who lives for the next generation." Attentive church leadership includes the divine imperative to entrust the gospel to individuals who will invest it into others.

A Giant Embodies Mentoring

Few people in the twentieth century shaped the body of Christ as significantly as John Stott did. A prolific preacher, evangelist, teacher, and author, he defended what he called balanced, biblical Christianity, was a pioneer in lay mobilization, chaired the group that wrote the Lausanne Covenant, and became a key shaper of the evangelical movement, right up there with Billy Graham, Bill Bright, Carl Henry, and J. I. Packer.[1] He lived as an attentive Christian, and the ripple effect of his life still continues for the kingdom.

One of Stott's influences was Eric Nash. The son of a clergyman, Nash came to Christ at age nineteen, entered Cambridge at twenty-four, and studied theology later at Ridley Hall. Serving on staff with the Scripture Union, he pioneered and supervised youth camps, helping many of the nation's young people come to faith in Christ. Many of the attendees of these camps came from the rich and privileged of English society, and many would later become the leadership of the country. One author noted, "High-ranking servicemen, politicians, bishops, clergymen, headmasters and a host of others spoke of him with reverence—even with awe."[2]

Those who knew Nash best said he was a man of prayer, deeply devoted to Christ. But what truly set him apart was the fact that he prioritized building friendships and creating community. He fostered significant relationships with headmasters of many of the nation's schools, becoming "a 20th century missionary to England's 30 or so top independent schools."[3] Nash possessed a natural winsomeness and worked diligently at nurturing friendships with both influential adults and up-and-coming youth.

John Stott met Nash when the youth worker came to speak at Rugby School's Christian Union. After Nash's sermon, Stott had many questions, which Nash patiently answered. That evening, at his bedside, Stott opened the door of his life to Jesus Christ. The elder mentored the younger over the next five years. "Identifying and mentoring the next generation of leaders" marked Nash's ministry, and it would be "a trait that would characterize Stott's own ministry in a remarkable way."[4]

After Rugby School, Stott studied at Trinity College, University of Cambridge, graduating with double first-class honors. Like Nash, he studied theology at Cambridge in Ridley Hall. At age twenty-eight, he became the rector of London's All Souls Church, Langham Place, where he began to earn a reputation as someone committed to the careful exposition of God's Word as well as a minister who engaged with his people. Stott led a thriving, multifaceted ministry in the church that was considered innovative and pioneering for its time. He provided regular evangelistic training, follow-up discipleship courses in homes, a weekly prayer meeting, monthly prayer services for the sick, and a children's ministry, to name a few. He even once disguised himself as homeless "and slept on the streets in order to find out what it was like."[5]

In a day when evangelicals had little influence over the Anglican church, Stott gradually began exerting national influence as an attentive leader, eventually serving key roles in the church, university, and crown. He established the Evangelical Fellowship of the Anglican Communion, served as chair of the Church of England Evangelical Council and the National Assembly of Evangelicals, and as president of Scripture Union and the Evangelical Alliance. Stott served four terms as president of the Universities and Colleges Christian Fellowship. He became an honorary chaplain to Queen Elizabeth II for over thirty years. An intellectual to the core, he strove to wed scholarship with evangelistic zeal. Historian David Edwards argued John Stott was "the most influential clergyman in the Church of England" of the twentieth century, apart from William Temple. Also, "theologian Alister McGrath has suggested that the growth of post-war English evangelicalism is attributable more to John Stott than any other person."[6]

Stott grew to have great influence internationally as well, recognized for serving as the Bible expositor six times at InterVarsity Christian Fellowship's Urbana Student Mission Convention. He played a key role in the 1974 International Congress on World Evangelization in Lausanne, Switzerland. At that time, Billy Graham said, "I can't think of anyone who has been more effective in introducing so many people to a biblical world view," and he credited Stott's work as "a significant factor in the explosive growth of Christianity in parts of the Third World."[7]

My (Kevin's) father worked closely with Stott to craft the Lausanne Covenant and the Lausanne Movement. "When I was selected as chair of the international Lausanne Committee for World Evangelization," Dad recalled, "I was relatively young and inexperienced in leading a diverse group of global leaders. John Stott was very much my senior in that regard, yet as a colleague on the committee he provided me guidance and support—and a caution or two when needed! Without his wise and collegial spirit Lausanne would have been much poorer."

A prolific author, Stott mastered the art of fostering friendships, which he did with leaders around the world. A website dedicated to him surmises, "It is little wonder that *Time* magazine in 2005 named John Stott as one of the world's one hundred most influential people, that Billy Graham called him 'the most respected clergyman in the world today.'"[8]

One of Stott's lesser-known practices was to hire study assistants to work by his side for three years at a time. He was known as "Uncle John" to many of our friends like Mark Labberton and Corey Widmer. John Yates III worked for Uncle John in the 1990s in London. Today, Yates is the rector of Holy Trinity in Raleigh, North Carolina. His role under Stott encompassed a variety of responsibilities, including running errands, cooking, correspondence, research, and editing. During his first week on the job, he had a significant experience and important conversation that would shape his time working for Stott.

Yates shared with us,

> On my first day of work, a handwritten manuscript was left on my desk to review. It was a written interview to be included in a book on singleness that would be published in the US.[9] I was twenty-two and single at the time, and John had left a note with the manuscript asking if I had any feedback or comments that might be helpful. After reading through the interview, I made half a dozen comments ranging from suggestions about word choice to encouragement to add another sentence or two on a related topic. The following day I found the manuscript on my desk once again with a note attached that read, "What do you think now?" Reading through the interview I saw that he had followed every suggested change and addition that I had made. I was stunned. If John Stott was going to take me this seriously, then I was going to have to be serious about the work I was doing.

Later that week, the two men sat down in Stott's study and talked about the parameters of Yates's role. Stott was clear that Yates was not there to be mentored. They wouldn't be meeting every week for training or intentional discipleship. He was there to join in the work and to support Stott's ministry. However, Stott told him that if he paid attention and did the work conscientiously, he would learn more through observation and action than he ever could through instruction. And when Yates had questions or concerns, Stott would always be available for conversation.

Yates said,

> That first week taught me some important lessons about mentoring that would be proven by experience over the next three years. The first lesson is that the best mentors invite you into their lives and allow you to watch and learn from the inside. John was open and

> transparent with me. He trusted me and gave me responsibility well-beyond what my age and experience would have suggested was wise. He allowed me to ask questions about process and goals. He wanted me to learn not just what to do, but why to do things a certain way. The second lesson is that the best mentors invite you to walk alongside them, rather than simply to sit at their feet. In order to learn I needed both to watch and to do. By walking alongside John on a daily basis I got to see how he led, studied, prayed and planned. I also got to participate in all of these areas of his life and to step out and do many of them on my own on his behalf.[10]

What an incredible testimony of the process of mentoring. So many values can be transmitted by a deep life-on-life investment. Yates summed it up by saying, "My time with John Stott was a time of watching, learning and partnering. There wasn't much direct instruction or guided reflection. But during those years I learned more than at any other time of my life."

Who Are Your Friends on the Journey?

Uncle John modeled as well as any leader in the twentieth century the need to foster friendships. Today, the need for leaders to create a thriving community is as desperate as ever. With people often lacking real connections, a ripe opportunity lies before pastors and leaders. But it's not enough to just have information, degrees, and skills. In becoming attentive leaders and leading attentive churches, we've got to love people and become friends on the journey. That also means we need to have friends on the journey.

Barna Research reveals that 61 percent of pastors have few close friends and feel lonely. Sadly, for years it was common for pastors to be told that they should not have friends within their own congregations. This adds to an isolationist mentality that does not model healthy biblical relationships. The pastor becomes a silo expected to feed the consumers.[11]

Dr. Charles Stone suggests five key factors that inhibit pastors from developing close friendships:

- Lack of formative modeling—some pastors weren't close to their parents, and/or their parents never modeled how to create intimate relationships.
- Some pastors developed a loner tendency—they'd rather be alone.
- Personality—some personalities may unintentionally push people away.
- Wounds from the past can compel some pastors to put up walls with others.
- Fear of sharing loneliness with others—some pastors think that if people knew they struggled, hurt, or had problems, they would receive less respect, which would hinder their leadership effectiveness.

Stone challenges pastors, "Don't minimize the importance of friends in the ministry and in your church. Push through your loneliness and find some friends."[12]

Jesus modeled healthy relationships along the journey. He developed relationships at different levels: the seventy, the Twelve, and the three. Though he certainly could have done ministry with the silo mentality, he brought a few men and women around him. He didn't just build working relationships with them; he built friendships. Jesus told his disciples near the end of his earthly journey, "I no longer call you servants. . . . Instead, I have called you friends" (John 15:15). When the apostle John reflected on his relationship with the Savior, he called himself "the disciple whom Jesus loved" (John 13:23; 19:26; 20:2; 21:7, 20).

We can't build community by programs alone. And we can't create deep relationships by simply training people in studies and classes. While these things are needed, real community happens both organically and intentionally. Community in a church occurs when a pastor purposely becomes a friend on the journey and allows relationships to flourish. We've been amazed at how few pastors have ever been mentored or discipled by another person. Is it any wonder they don't know how to replicate this with other leaders in their own churches?

What Does Mentoring Look Like for You?

The relationship between Stott and Yates illustrates that mentoring takes many forms. It is not a one-size-fits-all strategy. Bobby Clinton, a retired senior professor of leadership at Fuller Theological Seminary, defines mentoring as "a relational experience in which one person, the mentor, empowers another person, the mentoree, by sharing God-given resources."[13] The relationship may be long term, but many times it is seasonal, meeting a specific need during a fixed time.

Mentoring is certainly not limited to the spiritual realm. Rather, it is part of the fabric of life. Sadly, the church has often attempted to do ministry without embracing mentoring roles.

The word *mentor* originates from Homer's *The Odyssey*. When King Odysseus leaves his wife Penelope and son Telemachus to lead his army during the Trojan War, he assigns the overseer, Mentor, to be a guardian for Telemachus. Odysseus's intent is for Mentor to serve as his guide.

In the real world, mentors exist in a multitude of forms, roles, and jobs. Steven Spielberg greatly influenced the up-and-coming J. J. Abrams, which opened up influential doors for the young filmmaker. Spielberg once said, "The delicate balance of mentoring someone is not creating them in your own image, but giving them the opportunity to create themselves."[14] Audrey Hepburn mentored Elizabeth Taylor for years, and they remained close friends until Hepburn's death in 1993. As far back as 400 BC, Socrates invested in Plato, who later mentored Aristotle.

While still a very young man, my (Kevin's) father, Leighton, invited Billy Graham to speak at a Youth for Christ gathering in Chatham, Ontario. When the invitation to receive Christ was given, almost nobody responded. Uncle Billy could tell that Dad was deeply disappointed. So he walked up to him, put an arm around his shoulder, and said, "Leighton, I can see that you have the heart of an evangelist. I will do whatever I can to support you in the years to come." That began a mentoring relationship between Uncle Billy and Dad that continues even after Uncle Billy's death. The "arm around the shoulder" embodies what mentoring is all about. It's not a program or a study. Dad's personal mission is to be "an artist of the soul, a friend on the journey."

The apostle Paul challenged his mentee, Timothy, "And the things you have heard me say in the presence of many witnesses entrust to reliable people who will also be qualified to teach others" (2 Timothy 2:2). Paul taught Timothy, who entrusted to faithful people what he had learned, who then taught Christ to others.

My (Kevin's) grandmother, Morrow Graham, was a devoted follower of Christ. As a child, I remembered seeing her highlighted and well-worn Bible open on her desk every day. She taught Sunday school, sang in the choir, and became a charter member of what was then known as Calvary Presbyterian Church in Charlotte (now the nondenominational Calvary Church). Just before her final moments, she mustered her strength and wrapped her arms around my mother's neck. "Pass it on to every generation," she whispered. Soon after, she joined her husband, Frank, in the Lord's presence on August 14, 1981.

My mother went on to have a significant spiritual influence in the lives of a number of people. Dad said,

> My wife, Jeanie, has certainly been my number one mentor, confidant, and guide, both personally and in our ministry across the years. Not one significant decision have I made without her wise input. When we were seeking to discern how to pursue a new ministry with young leaders, she had a dream in which I was helping to serve and develop leaders around the world. It was so vivid that she flew to Montreal where I was preaching to share that dream with me—a dream that became reality.

For many years, she taught a weekly Bible study for forty to fifty women in Charlotte, North Carolina. Dad says "she gently led them through the Scriptures, asking probing questions which would help them apply these teachings to their lives. Many of these women speak of the impact these sessions had on them."

And the river of God keeps flowing.

Ripples of Multiplication

On October 15, 1988, while eating breakfast at a diner in Dublin, California, I (Kevin) noticed a young man reading his Bible. I awkwardly approached him and said, "I'm Kevin Ford, and you're the first person I've seen reading a Bible here."

"Hi, I'm Lon Allison," he grinned. "I'm pastoring a new church plant nearby." Neither of us could imagine at the time what a providential connection this was. We became great friends, and I later introduced Lon to Dad, who invited him to become an original member of the Point Group in 1989. This mentoring community is LFM's longest-standing one and continues meeting to this day.

Lon participated in Dad's Arrow Leadership Program, eventually becoming an instructor for Arrow training leaders in evangelistic preaching. On several occasions, Lon told me that Dad's real impact occurred most frequently during their walks together. To Lon, Dad was a friend on the journey.

In 1998, Lon started the Star Group right after he became the director of the Billy Graham Center at Wheaton College in Illinois. His desire? To create safe times, safe places, and safe people for emerging evangelists. The Star Group included Wesley Paul, a young evangelist from India. Through Wesley's international ministry, many people have come to Christ and many believers have been encouraged in the Caribbean, India, and United States.

Mentoring relationships tend to pass from one generation to another. So in December 2019, Wesley hosted his first mentoring retreat for the new "Arrow Tribe" with emerging national and global leaders from India, Nigeria, Kenya, Pakistan, Australia, and North America.

One young leader from the tribe, Rishi, makes an incredible impact in southern India, where Christians are experiencing enormous persecution. A young pastor, he helps oversee one hundred churches and more than one hundred missionaries across Nepal and India. He lives in a large urban center, which includes a thriving prostitution business run by organized crime. Rishi and his wife meet with the prostitutes and give them personal hygiene kits and food they requested. They also talk to them about spiritual matters and pray with them.

Rishi and his wife discovered the mob uses teenage boys who have crossed paths with the law to run the brothel business. Because of their criminal record, they aren't allowed to participate in normal functions like school and recreational activities. People with Rishi's ministries developed a burden for this group of young men. They asked the boys, "What would you really like to do?" Many of them responded they wanted to play soccer and learn to dance.

So, their ministry began a soccer league across the city to teach these boys how to play. The boys also indicated their desire to read, write, and get an education. Rishi's ministry started a school, teaching them basic academics, spiritual realities, and fundamentals of business. As the boys progressed and graduated, the ministry helped them form self-supporting businesses to keep them from going back into the brothel business.

Another longtime member of Lon's Star Group is Rike Huettman. She and her family live in Marburg, Germany, and she has been very involved with the Lausanne Movement, hosting Lausanne Younger Leaders gatherings in Europe, speaking at evangelistic events for women, and leading in the Christian Coffeeshop Network. At LFM, we're excited to be partnering with Rike to start our fiftieth global mentoring community.

Rike told us,

> My heart burns for creating spaces where people in our city have a possibility to meet others and God. I've been walking alongside younger women for over two decades now. I love to see them bravely taking hold of possibilities to build God's kingdom. The Star mentoring community in our lives was a safe place to be honest, and it was a place where God met us deeply. It changed our sights, feelings, and behavior and encouraged us to trust. It probably saved our faith and our ministry during a deep crisis. And we made deep friendships. I want to create the same for other women.

Rike also hopes her missional group can encourage these women to step out of their safe circles and build relationships with people who do not yet know the gospel. She hopes to see them create spaces, formats, and ideas that connect with people in our post-Christian society.

Notice the threads through these stories. An arm around the shoulder. A friend on the journey. Safe times, safe places, and safe people. None of this is programmatic. Mentoring is life on life. It requires no degrees or formal curriculum. My grandmother Graham challenged her family to entrust the gospel to future generations. Uncle Billy put an arm around Dad's shoulder. Dad and others took that summons and invested it into individuals like Lon Allison, Rishi, and Rike, who passed it on to other faithful people. The multiplication factor continues today, as the Bible says: "This same Good News that came to you is going out all over the world. It is bearing fruit everywhere by changing lives" (Colossians 1:6 NLT).

And the river of God keeps flowing.

Where Does Mentoring Occur?

"Could God use your dorm room Bible study to touch the world? That was one question I had never considered," our colleague Rhett Wilson Sr., recently shared with us. Rhett, a writer and editor who serves as LFM's senior communications director, has been in pastoral ministry for three decades.

Attending an evangelistic Christmas conference for college students in 1993, he heard Paul Stanley, former international vice president of the Navigators, share about how he mentored Romanian pastors in small groups before the fall of the Iron Curtain, when Bibles were scarce. Stanley challenged students with this simple question: "Are you asking God to use your small dorm room Bible study to touch the world? If not, why not?"

In Rhett's freshman year of college, a senior with a heart for mentoring invited several underclass men and women to join him on Monday nights in his dorm room. For the semester, he led them through a study of LeRoy Eims's *The Lost Art of Disciple Making*.

Rhett remembers, "Gene had a vision of seeing a disciple-making movement spring up among students on that campus. He decided the best way to invest his time for the kingdom his senior year was to mentor a small group of younger students who hopefully would catch the vision."

Throughout the summer, Rhett asked God to give him one man to pour his life into when he returned to campus for his sophomore year. His first day back, he providentially met a freshman named Chip who had recently become a believer. After a couple weeks of establishing a relationship, Rhett asked Chip, "I see God at work in your life. I've walked with the Lord for a few years, and I'd love to spend some one-on-one time with you this year helping you learn how to walk with God." Chip enthusiastically said yes, and for the next year-and-a-half, they met weekly for Bible study, prayer, and mutual encouragement.

Rhett became president of the Fellowship of Christian Athletes, the main evangelical presence on the campus. For two years he led dorm room Bible studies and helped facilitate mentoring relationships for young men and women. Through the church he attended in the same town, he connected with a godly woman in her eighties who loved to mentor young women. Alma Galloway, also known as Mama G, had a large room built in her house specifically for prayer, Bible study, and hosting groups for spiritual direction. She called it her "Son Room"—a place where Jesus was welcome. For years, college students spent time in her home.

Mama G regularly mentored women one on one or in small, intimate groups. For several years, Rhett occasionally called or visited her with similar requests: "Mama G, I've met this young woman who is a new Christian and trying to get close to the Lord. Do you think you could meet with her some and help her?" Her normal reply was, "Oh yes, honey. Just give me her name and number." She was always eager to do so and had a great ministry of influencing women.

Returning from the Christmas conference his junior year, Rhett began asking God daily to use this small group of students within his scope of influence to touch the world. Little did he know how quickly God would answer that prayer.

The Lord soon moved deeply in Chip's life. One day in the school cafeteria, Chip looked directly at Rhett and said, "God is calling me to be a missionary, and I'm fighting it." Over the next few weeks, they spent hours discussing God's call and the cost of following him.

In the following years, God led several of those young people into vocational ministry. Chip prepared to be a career missionary. Thomas, another man in their midst, also sensed a call to mission work. Both Chip and Thomas grew burdened for the Muslim world. Ten years later, both men—with their wives and children—accepted positions with two different missionary-sending agencies. Among the world's thousands of ethnolinguistic groups, both families were assigned not only to the same country but to the same people group. Both families left for their assignments within two weeks of each other. And the river of God keeps flowing.

Rhett shared, "What an amazing God. He touched the hearts of these two young men while they were college students, knowing that a decade later he would send them both via different agencies to the exact same people group to the same area of the world. Yes, God can use your small group to touch the world. Ask him to do so."

Jesus' primary method of spreading the gospel was through mentoring. Unfortunately, the Western church has lost this practice. Notice the pattern in the stories we've shared thus far. John Stott and John Yates. Billy Graham and Leighton Ford. Jeanie Ford and women in Charlotte. Lon Allison to Wesley Paul and Rike Huettman. Rhett and Chip. Each of these stories occurred outside the local church.

Parachurch ministries have often filled a gap that the local church has neglected. When we work with a church leadership team, we often ask the leaders about their own spiritual journeys. Most of them point to a mentor outside their church. Sadly, our churches have lost the art of mentoring relationships and replaced them with programs. We love what so many parachurch ministries have done here in the United States and around the world. But we believe a new era is emerging as the Western church reclaims the lost art of mentoring.

What Is the Best Way to Foster Community?

When Jesus came to this earth, he focused on pouring himself into twelve men who would go on to reach the masses. Yet in today's ministry methodology, we often focus our time and resources on events or efforts aimed directly at the masses. What would your ministry look like three years from now if you made it a priority to pour yourself into a few potential leaders? Who in your circle of influence might you mentor? Why not ask God to give you a vision for multiplying yourself into the lives of a few and then ask him to open your eyes to who they are? The exponential widening of influence may eventually astound you.

My (Kevin's) dad left the Billy Graham Evangelistic Association in 1986 on good terms. He was the vice president and associate evangelist preaching to crowds of ten or fifteen thousand in auditoriums from Sydney to Montreal. But he had a concern about the future of the church. Traveling the globe, he observed a leadership vacuum. The "Builder Generation" of Billy Graham, Bob Pierce, and Bill Bright created tremendous ministries. But who would lead the church of tomorrow? And who was pouring into the up-and-coming Christian leaders? In 1991, Dad founded the Arrow Leadership Program, where a group of twenty to thirty younger leaders would come together for two years. They did personal assessments, sat in classrooms with international gurus, and participated in doctoral-level projects. But Dad found along the way that the real power was not in the program but in relationships. The walks outside in between classes. The visits by the fireside. The one-on-one breakfast gathering before worship. It was the arm around the shoulder, the listening, that mattered the most.

Mentoring is all about friendships. In one of Arrow's newsletters, John Mallison writes, "Mentoring was a way of life in Bible times. A few of the more prominent mentoring relationships were Jethro with Moses; Moses with Joshua; David with Jonathan; Barnabas with Paul; Lois and Eunice with Timothy; Priscilla and Aquila with Apollos; and Paul with Timothy. Jesus, with his disciples, provides our prime mentoring model."[15]

In today's often cookie-cutter, large group approach to informing the masses in our churches, the personal, relational power is often overlooked. However, "The New Testament is full of 'one another' and 'together' passages pointing to Christianity as relational, about community, the power of togetherness."[16]

As Leighton continued to see the value of mentoring relationships, he eventually established LFM as a catalyst for mentoring healthy leaders around the world. At LFM, we help launch and sustain mentoring communities for kingdom leaders, facilitate personal retreats, and provide one-on-one mentoring and counseling. We also partner with churches for visioning, coaching, and organizational development. Our goal is to help churches thrive.

How Could a Focus on Mentoring Relationships Affect Your Church?

Healthy models of mentoring inside churches do exist today. Some pastors, like Mark Toone, intentionally invest in others. Mark pastors Chapel Hill Church in Gig Harbor, Washington, just across the bridge from Tacoma. Some large congregations will never be able to hire all the staff they need. But there are willing, high-capacity leaders ready to be trained for important ministry. Mark mixes both spiritual growth and leadership training that readies their large staff leaders and lay leaders for effective service. Character issues capture a significant portion of the training. How to be on time, how to complete assignments, and how to avoid whining and complaining are all part of the curriculum. Mark selects people in the congregation who might end up in staff or pastoral roles. One byproduct of the training is the deep shaping of a shared culture.

But training has its limitations. Mentoring happens on a much deeper and more personal level. Most of the time, the best and most effective type of mentoring takes place informally without a rigid structure. As the old saying goes, "More is caught than taught." Ellis White is one of Mark's mentees. After meeting in the United Kingdom and a few short conversations, Mark gave Ellis a business card and told him to email him after Ellis completed his university studies. Mark saw a potential staff member in the young man, and six months later Ellis and his family moved to Gig Harbor, where he served as Mark's intern. Ellis shared with us, "Mark gave me opportunities to learn and grow in a variety of different areas in the church." Ellis was not looking for a mentor at the time. But moving to the other side of the world made it difficult to maintain pre-existing relationships. Mark stepped into the gap and provided mentoring in ministry, faith, and life.

Ellis explained, "Perhaps more than anything I needed someone who would allow me to fail and then have my back when I did. Mark has never publicly criticized me, even though I have done many things wrong. Privately he has coached me and given feedback, which at times has been hard to receive, but through it all I knew he had my best interests at heart."

This relational mentoring allowed Ellis to develop as a leader. Mark provided him safe times, safe places, and a safe person—himself. Authentic mentoring includes vulnerability in being self-revealing. Ellis said,

> The most helpful thing Mark has done as a mentor is to open up his personal life. He has shared transparently his own struggles and invited me to pray and support him in that. He has opened his home to me and my family, becoming a surrogate grandfather to my children. And he has sought to engage with my own family, visiting them in the UK when he was there for a trip, and always inviting them over for dinner when they visited the US.

By opening himself up in this way and becoming a part of Ellis's personal life, Mark as a mentee saw "how he relates to his own family, how he manages his finances, how he stays physically healthy, and what his own personal spirituality looks like." Such lessons are worth the price of a seminary education.

Early in their relationship, Mark approached Ellis and said he saw a call to pastoral ministry in his life. He challenged him to start seminary while remaining on staff at the church, which was relatively novel in their denomination at the time. Mark pushed him to begin as soon as possible and said the church would support him with time and money as well as provide opportunities for him to grow and develop in ministry. Ellis shared, "Seminary was on my radar, but I wouldn't have considered doing it in a hybrid model at that point in ministry without Mark's support and encouragement."

Another person greatly affected by Mark Toone's mentoring is Jeremy Vaccaro, who came to Chapel Hill to serve in the church's youth ministry. In the early years, Jeremy remembers, Mark and his team "allowed me to be in the room where stuff was happening at an executive level. Just being part of those conversations and interactions was a leadership lab, and I soaked it up." Mark, along with his copastor Stuart Bond, intentionally invested in Jeremy's leadership development. One of the best methods was simply including him in their work. After five years on staff, Jeremy became the senior associate pastor, a role in which he walked closely with Mark in his daily work.

Jeremy told us,

> We worked together constantly. Every week we worked together on his sermon. We strategized for whole church initiatives. We worked through issues with elders. We processed staffing needs, budget issues, congregant struggles, church vision, and much more. And in the midst of that we shared life. We encouraged each other. We prayed for one another. We exhorted one another. I believe we were often a great encouragement to one another.

At the time, Jeremy thought this behavior was normal. But as he interacted with associate pastors at other churches, he realized how unique his experience was. Jeremy now serves as a senior pastor in Fresno, and he attributes much of his growth in skill, wisdom, and understanding to his relationship with Mark. Even in his current role, Mark continues encouraging Jeremy, who says, "It's come through phone conversations, emails, and time together in person when possible. He has been an ongoing help, and I believe that I have sometimes been an ongoing help to him."

Mentoring Staff Members

Steven Koski, who pastors in Bend, Oregon, also incorporates mentoring into his ministry. I (Kevin) have journeyed with Steven for over twenty years and have seen the fruits of his ministry around the world. One young woman named Morgan Schmidt worked under him as director of youth ministries. Over time, she grew into the role of pastor for youth and their families. During the pandemic, she took the lead in their emergency relief work, including overseeing a ministry with more than twelve thousand participants. Eventually, she felt called to run for public office to help their marginalized neighbors and develop policies to help the community flourish. When the church blessed her as she stepped forward, Steven reminded the church to recognize "their role in mentoring Morgan. I commended the congregation for providing the space where Morgan could identify her gifts, clarify her sense of call, develop her voice, and gain the confidence and courage to pursue her sense of vocation."

Greg Bolt preceded Morgan as youth pastor, and Steven remembers it as Greg's "first call and the creative space where he could learn, experiment and grow as a leader and pastor."

Greg said,

> Working with Steven was always extremely collegial. While we all knew our roles, it didn't feel like a hierarchy of creativity. During staff meetings every staff member was encouraged to contribute to the process of the day-to-day operations of the church. He also allowed me to be creative and try new things within my ministry, and was always there for counsel or correction. I always felt like he had my back, which was very helpful for me as a newly ordained pastor.

Steven recently gave the charge at Greg's installation service, where Jenny Warner, who we mentioned in chapter five, delivered the sermon. Jenny's first place of service was as the associate pastor for spirituality and community under Steven for seven years. Steven says he reminded his congregation "of their ministry of mentoring such strong, creative, capable and gifted leaders like Greg and Jenny. The role of creating space for young leaders to learn, grow, discover their voice, and lean into their sense of vocation is a vital gift the congregation offers the wider church."

We've also partnered with Jenny's church in Portola Valley, California, and have witnessed her continue the journey of mentoring in her new church. "The place is important," she told us, "but it's not an end unto itself. We are trying to be countercultural to the Silicon Valley pace of life. I want to see people slow down, focus outward, and connect authentically. That just doesn't happen much in Silicon Valley."

Leadership Incubator

As we want to lead attentive churches as pastors and ministry leaders, we are wise to ask how to incorporate mentoring into our lives. Robert Kelly, one of my (Jim's) former doctoral students, pastors Beacon Church in Long Island, New York. He developed a "Leadership Incubator," which helps high-capacity leaders understand the mission, vision, and values of their congregation. The Incubator also focuses on processes that aid in spiritual growth, theological rootedness, and leadership skills, all directed to their congregation and its mission. Robert designed the Incubator to allow lay leadership opportunities for multiple roles both inside and outside of the congregation. All of their pastoral care team and ministry volunteers are urged to do this training. It requires one Saturday morning per month for a year to grow in strategic skills, character development, and visioning, and involves a comprehensive assessment of deployment within the mission of the congregation. They receive assigned readings and written homework through the process. The students appreciated the training so much that the staff developed a second year of it.

Congregations are wise to enlist and train high-capacity leaders within their own ranks—without having to continue hiring multiple staff positions. Sadly, few "leadership incubators" exist today in North American congregations. What could a focus on mentoring do for your church? How could that change the broader culture? Let's get practical.

Church programs can be effective. But real community is fostered in mentoring relationships. As we coach pastors, we encourage them to consider Jesus' model of investing in a few leaders—and then model it for those leaders so they can then invest in a few others.

Most of the time mentoring involves simply being present, putting an arm around their shoulder and praying. But we also encourage leaders to ask questions. Mentoring is not about giving answers but asking and listening. Too many leaders think they have to give advice and be a subject matter expert. An effective mentor, like a chaplain, is comfortable with silence.

While being present is at the heart of mentoring, we encourage the mentoring relationship to have ongoing conversations around things such as:

- Spiritual vitality
- Personal wellness and balance in life
- Family health (spouse, children, parents, extended family)
- Self-regulation (being well defined)
- Cultural intelligence (learning how to become a good citizen in the community; earning the right to be heard)
- Leadership and change

Most of the time, however, mentoring relationships are about listening to someone's story and looking for where God is already at work. Ken Van Vliet is the pastor of Monte Vista Chapel in Turlock, California. In 2009, he sensed God shifting their focus away from the attractional model to one focused more on formation and transformation.

Recently, he shared,

> Core to formation is the need to know ourselves—that which actually needs to be transformed into the image of Christ. Unfortunately, our informational way of discipleship in the attractional model taught people to state propositional truths about themselves. They would assert what *should* be true, despite that assertion being far from their actual experience. For example, someone would state an intellectual truth such as, "I am loved and accepted by God." But

that was typically at the expense of what was actually going on in her real, lived life—"I don't feel loved" or "I am working hard for God's approval." We began to notice that proposition was often an enemy of transformation.

So, the leaders of Monte Vista Chapel started a new approach that focused on mentoring relationships in a group context—story groups. Ken said, "Our story groups addressed that problem as they served to help people become present with themselves, with others, and with God in the same space." Turns out, this is an environment that is highly conducive to transformation. Ken added,

> These small groups, usually four to six people, are intentionally designed to facilitate spiritual and emotional awareness and growth. Through the sharing of our stories, we learn to be attentive to the Holy Spirit as we listen to what he may be doing in our lives and the lives of others. If you are looking for a safe space to deepen your relationship with God and others, a story group may be just the place for you.

The majority of people who enter these groups have gone through "The Journey," a yearlong formation process in which they learn the importance of vulnerability in their small groups. They have a desire to continue them, but the church cannot continue to provide another program around which they gather. So these story groups serve as a very helpful way to stay connected in each other's lives without needing some type of program around which to gather. Their stories are the program.

Even smaller churches can answer, "How do we help a newcomer get connected with four to six people in our church, involved in some type of small group experience, and engaged in some type of ministry?" Consider your plan. Of the strategies we've mentioned, where will you spend the least amount of money to reap the greatest benefit?

Sunday school classes and small groups help create a context for community for roughly 20 percent of the congregation. They require a good deal of coordination, management, and supervision. Larger churches will need to dedicate staffing and facilities to this ministry.

Creating a third place in your church building—a space that allows people to connect—is another great way to foster community. However, someone has to purchase the space and manage it. We are fans of third place, but recognize there is a significant investment required.

Mentoring costs nothing, unless you are a paid staff person. You can do it anywhere. And our research suggests that the impact is much more significant than a program or a building.

Where Do I Start?

Mentoring takes place in various ways and on many levels. Paul Stanley writes with Bobby Clinton about several types of mentoring in their book *Connecting: The Mentoring Relationships You Need to Succeed.* Mentoring relationships can include coaches, counselors, teachers, and models.[17] Every one of them is important and needed for different purposes. And these mentoring styles are all very personal—one life touching another in some way. As the church continues to move through the twenty-first century, we are wise to ask, "How can we incorporate these models into our discipleship and leadership development?"

One type of mentoring relationship is the intentional discipler. One person spends a lot of time with another, usually one on one, intentionally building into them the basic habits and beliefs of the Christian life.

Historically, intentional disciple-making through mentoring relationships has held significant value. In the eighteenth and nineteenth centuries, the spread of Methodism through England became one of Christian history's most impressive movements. Along with the impassioned preaching of John Wesley, Francis Asbury, and Thomas Coke, and the rich hymnody of Charles Wesley, the most compelling feature of Methodism was the way regular people received mentoring and equipping for ministry through three different sized groups. These associations became known as bands, classes, and societies, and they helped to create a dynamic spiritual community.

The shaping experiences that happened through intentional and relational mentoring gave the movement both depth and resiliency. These mentoring habits formed the "method" of Methodism. Sadly, such a practice no longer operates in most parts of that family of faith—or most others. The practice of mentoring shaped their mission and vision, fashioned character and values, and stimulated healthy behaviors and attitudes.

The early church prioritized the development of its leaders. In some ways, eighteenth- and nineteenth-century Methodism brought back a lost practice. The process for spiritual growth in the early church began with new converts spending three years with a mentor. This resulted in great life change among early Christians. Their belief, belonging, and behavior all transformed. It was a patient process. These early believers had come out of a Greco-Roman cultural context that was inconsistent with the kingdom of God. Through believing, belonging, and behaving, they learned a new set of values—kingdom values. This mentoring helped produce the fastest growing period of church history.

In 1980, like Rhett, I (Jim) read LeRoy Eims's *The Lost Art of Disciple Making*. What a telling title! In most congregations it is still a lost art. As with Rhett, God used it to hook me with a passion for authentic discipleship. In the summer of 1981, I entered my first discipling relationship. I was doing ministry among minor league baseball players. We provided chapel every Sunday when they were at home and a Bible study during the week. But one young player, Dave Valle, asked me if we could spend more time together because he yearned to grow and be transformed. He asked for an intentional, relational investment in his life around Scripture. There was one problem: I did not know exactly how to do it. No one had officially discipled me, but I had accumulated a few ideas here and there. That summer transformed both of us. I slowly learned a practice that I have continued to this day, and Dave eventually began a ministry outside of baseball that also continues.

From there I began working in a congregation in San Antonio, Texas, and began a ministry of discipleship with individuals and small microgroups. It began the real calling of my life. Forty years later I'm still doing this kind of personal ministry. *Discipleship depends on relationships rather than programs.* Real change, and the ever-widening ripple effects, flows through people more than classes. This can be a hard paradigm shift for churches. Most congregations in the past century expected that the combination of classes and small groups would result in a community of maturing followers. In our own research, through the Transforming Church Insight (TCI), we have discovered that classes and small groups rarely produce this desired result. Poet Maya Angelou, who was amazed by God's love for her, wrote, "I've learned that people will forget what you said, people will forget what you did, but people will never forget how you made them feel."

As we have stressed throughout, the North American church's Attractional Era church unconsciously wed itself to consumerism, which bred cultural narcissism. The goal for the consumer was to find the highest inspiration at the lowest cost. It grew difficult to get most people beyond Sunday morning worship. And if they did join a class or a small group, they wanted minimal investment.

I (Kevin) am not a regular volunteer in many of our church programs, other than playing bass on our worship team. But I am very intentional about one-on-one time with my pastor. We have lunch. We take walks together. This relationship requires no line item in the budget, no facilities, and no board decisions. The church in America doesn't need more programs. It needs more mentors. Life-on-life relationships. A handful of people invested in each other for the long haul. We need to see more pastors become friends on the journey, offering an arm around the shoulder. Our hope is that you will become a leader who is attentive to the person in front of you.

Jesus' ministry was not a ministry of programs. Nor was it primarily a ministry to the masses. It was a ministry of one—the person in front of him. Someone once said that "Jesus' ministry was a ministry of interruptions." In fact, he was "interrupted" thirty-five times in Mark's Gospel. What does that tell us about who Jesus valued? The goal? The task? Or the individual, the person in front of him? At its core, mentoring is paying attention to the person in front of you.

Could it become normal in a congregation's culture for a movement of mentoring to flourish? We think so. In recent decades, the church has often leaned on programs and classes rather than invest in the more difficult but transformational task of mentoring. Remember, people disciple people. Many, and perhaps most, seminary-trained pastors have not actually had an intentional and relational mentoring investment in their own lives.

Our world desperately needs real connections. Author Ken Boa observes, "When I go to a conference, the times between sessions are essentially silent breaks now. These times used to be for meeting new people or catching up with those you haven't seen in a while." Unfortunately, he shares, "Now, everyone avoids eye contact and spends time catching up on email or social media—'connecting'—while utterly disconnecting to the people standing right beside them."[18]

Attentive church leadership is an overarching concept, but leaders need to mold it and shape it to their unique context. We first learn to be attentive as individuals, accepting and caring for ourselves, and then learning how to respond to the anxiety within our churches. As we practice healthy boundaries as leaders we build trust with our people, which is necessary to shepherd them through changes. As we lead our churches to be attentive, we help them clarify their True North and create a shared culture that fosters community. We embrace our church's ethos and move people to engagement. Finally, we learn to facilitate real transformation and embrace a movement of mentoring, seeing lives changed. The effects of your one life invested in attentive church leadership will create a ripple effect that will go on for eternity.

Jesus Christ invested himself in a select few people who would lead the masses and change the world. Coming to him as to "the living Stone" (1 Peter 2:4), we as "living stones" (1 Peter 2:5) can make an eternal splash in the lives of a few. And those ripples will continue spreading. As you seek to be an attentive leader for an attentive church, remember to heed the apostle Paul's exhortation to take the gospel you have received and "entrust these to faithful people who will be able to teach others also" (2 Timothy 2:2 NASB).

Questions for Reflection and Discussion

- How have you experienced various types of mentoring? Remember how those relationships enriched or helped you.
- Do you have healthy, filling relationships in your life? If so, what can you do to strengthen them? If not, how can you intentionally develop some friends on the journey?
- As you reflect on your current ministry or church, is it primarily program driven? Do you see life-on-life healthy kingdom relationships growing?
- Consider Paul Stanley's question, "Could God use your dorm room Bible study to touch the world?" Ask the Lord to take your sphere of influence to touch the world with the gospel.
- Based on the stories in this chapter, how might you foster authentic community in your church and ministry?
- Who could you intentionally begin mentoring in some way?
- Spend some time in prayer asking the Father to help you become a more attentive leader and to shepherd your congregation toward being a more attentive church.

Epilogue

In 2013, we were asked to journey with University Place Church near Tacoma, Washington, during a pastoral transition. Our team included Jim Osterhaus, Tod and Beth Bolsinger, and me (Kevin). We found a church with a great history, but it was in decline.

University Place Church began as a small mission Sunday school for children on Day Island in 1927. It became a gathering of children and adults from the neighborhood, and a community of believers called Wayside Chapel was born. In 1941, they relocated across the street to the auditorium of University Place Elementary. Officially organized with forty members in 1943, the church grew, constructed a building, and eventually had between two and three hundred children and adults enrolled in Sunday school. The church thrived in the midst of American Christendom. From the early days in a tomato shed to now, University Place Church emphasized Bible study, children, and Christian outreach through missions. However, as the decades rolled along, the church shifted into a state of decline. It followed the same trajectory as so many Christendom-era churches in America.

We conducted a study of the local community, as we typically do in any visioning process. The city of University Place, a stable community, provided a great opportunity for the church to invest in relationships. Like much of the Northwest, it was a highly unchurched area. More than eighty thousand people within five miles of the church were not involved in matters of faith at all. The need for a godly faith presence was tremendous and represented a significant opportunity and challenge.

Through our Transforming Church Insight (TCI) congregational survey, we discovered several things going really well. They enjoyed great facilities, which the community used for activities such as afterschool programs, support groups, divorce recovery workshops, and the high school baccalaureate, to name a few. They also scored high in their overall financial health, which included a high level of trust from church members. This indicated an atmosphere of integrity and transparency—a strong foundation for their next season of ministry.

We also identified several challenges and concerns. While they scored low on our TCI in several important areas, the one that stood out most was a lack of ownership and connectedness within the congregation. Congregants felt limited in their ability to affect the direction, mission, and vision of the church. Many felt uninformed about church happenings, decisions, and larger denominational issues related to theology and practice. Very few people thought they could make a difference in the church. They didn't believe their actions influenced the church. We are created in God's image with an innate desire to belong, to contribute, and to make a difference. This was not the case at University Place Church. But this lack of connection and ownership was merely a symptom of a larger issue—the absence of a clear, compelling, and shared vision.

Thankfully, the church viewed their leadership in a positive light, and members wanted it to continue in the current trajectory. They were open to a new vision and a new pastor.

In our recommendations to the church leadership, we focused on their need to create the following:

1. A clear, shared True North
2. A pervasive culture of shared healthy collaboration and empowerment
3. An infrastructure that supports a clear, shared strategy for ministry

As we met with their leadership and various church members through a few visioning retreats, a new True North emerged for University Place Church. We had the leadership in breakout groups, sharing their most meaningful memories of the church. They talked about unsung heroes and past decisions. The groups were astounded to realize they all had similar themes, which formed their newly minted core values:

As a family of faith, we

- Love kids
- Share
- Are in this together
- Embrace the messiness
- Create
- Make room

They then defined their mission as, "We strive to be the love of Jesus locally, intentionally, spontaneously and tangibly."

We also had them brainstorm BHAGs (big hairy audacious goals). They landed on five:

- Create a community center to meet the emotional, physical, recreational, and spiritual needs of people in Pierce County.
- Demolish the consumer mindset by connecting every person in service together.
- Make God's love real to every child in our community.
- Be known regionally as *the* church for single-parent families.
- Engage 20s and 30s in a setting where they can meet Jesus through us.

After finishing their initial work on True North, they continued their search process. It didn't take long to realize that the right person was already on staff. Aaron Stewart checked all the right boxes. He knew the area well. He had a strong background in leadership. Aaron had a constellation of spiritual gifts and talents that offered a unique, holistic perspective. He was a stabilizing leader who was relational, motivating, energizing, and thoughtful. He was the kind of leader who would make other leaders better. He was not in ministry for his own ego. With clear leadership that values the whole team success over any individual credit or glory, he would help the church move into a new era.

After Aaron was hired, we wrote in our report back to leadership, "If this team can continue to function as a healthy team of teams—all the while incorporating lay leaders into those teams—there is great potential for energizing an exciting new season of growth and ministry for University Place Church."

Once they knew their True North, hiring Aaron was a natural next step. Four years later, when I (Kevin) revisited them, they enthusiastically recounted what God had done through their church:

- Turned the Sunset Christian Preschool into the largest preschool in the state.
- Built the Mothers of Preschoolers (MOPS) ministry to serve over one hundred women, many of whom are single parents or unchurched mothers.
- Developed the youth ministry to a substantial size, serving hundreds of students a week.
- Served three thousand individual clients a month through the food bank.
- Launched a refugee ministry and established the University Place Presbyterian Church (UPPC) safe haven house.
- Remodeled the facilities to align to their True North.

When they took the TCI again, their overall score rose from the 48th to the 74th percentile. And their vision score, one of their key areas of inattentiveness, moved from the 22nd percentile to the 78th. An amazing turnaround! Pastor Aaron told us,

> Things at church are going as well as I could hope. You'd be amazed at the physical transformation of our building and how much it's changed. It is a really good picture into how our values and code shape our space for the sake of our mission. I may have told you this previously, but our preschool is now the largest in Washington State

> and has served as the primary way that new families with children become a part of our church.
>
> Attendance in worship has increased dramatically for the first time in thirteen years, and over a seven-day period in December, we had five thousand people attend services. We are grateful and a bit overwhelmed too!
>
> Of course, we owe so much of our journey to our partnership with you. I love that your philosophy is to help churches find their own distinctive voice and identity. That has been the secret sauce for us, as it has given our people a confidence and boldness for ministry initiatives.

Maybe you are a church planter. Maybe your church is in decline and you need a reboot. Maybe your church is healthy and thriving, but you recognize there are unknown challenges in the future. Be attentive. God is so great at taking our mistakes and failures and using them for his good. He can still fill "in the valleys, and level the mountains and hills. Straighten the curves, and smooth out the rough places" (Isaiah 40:4 NLT). And when he does, "the glory of the LORD will be revealed" (Isaiah 40:5 NLT).

In the introduction we mentioned Will Torres, who considered giving up as he moved a grand piano after the church's worship service in an elementary school. While moving the piano and contemplating his future, he noticed students' artwork displayed on the walls of the school.

Will said, "As I turned the corner pushing the piano into place, I looked up at the wall, and God spoke to my heart as clearly as I have ever heard him. Taped on the wall in front of me was a child's poster that simply said, 'Don't give up.' Tears filled my eyes as I felt a sacred moment that God used to encourage me to continue."

Will's church pressed forward with renewed commitment, not knowing what the future held but knowing they served the One who holds the future. One month later, Will met Pastor Andy Hagen of Advent Church in Boca Raton, which was supporting a small church meeting at a facility they owned. Andy posed the idea of uniting Proclaim Church with the other group under the umbrella of Advent Life Ministries. "It was an amazing gift from God," Will said. "We would not only unite with Advent, but we would get a building with over seven thousand square feet of ministry space and financial support. And they changed the name of the location to Proclaim Church." This would not have been possible if Will had given up and walked away. He said, "The lesson we learned is that perseverance pays off. When we are faithful to God, he is more than faithful to us. Even if the end of the story didn't look like this for us, I know that he would have taken care of us. I can't wait to see what the future holds. If he brought us through this, I know whatever comes next, we will be all right, because he is with us."

As you practice attentive church leadership, God will be with you too. And the ripple effects will go on and on and on.

In a world screaming for our attention in a thousand different directions, it is essential for God's people to become attentive—to him, to their congregation, and to their community. We are reminded to "lead with [our] ears" (James 1:19 MSG). One basic reality of walking with God is that we need to be committed listeners—expectantly seeking to hear what God has to say to us every day of our Christian life. Jesus began many of his teachings with the same exhortation: "Listen!" (Mark 4:3). And he reminded the people, "Whoever has ears to hear, let them hear" (Mark 4:9).

It is our prayer that you will be an attentive Christ-follower, an attentive servant, and an attentive pastor or leader, paying attention to the person in front of you. As you do, you will become a friend on the journey, building a thriving community for the glory of the Lord and the good of the people.

Acknowledgments

From Kevin

Before acknowledging those who helped make this book a reality, I want to give deep appreciation to my family. My parents, Leighton and Jean Ford, raised me in a wonderful home dedicated to the Lord. I am eternally grateful that God allowed me to marry my best friend, Caroline. My daughters, Anabel and Leigh, make me a thankful dad. I can't wait to see how God will continue to hold them in his tender care as they journey through life.

This book represents the collaborative effort of many people to whom we are indebted. First, I am grateful for the friendship I've developed with Jim Singleton over the last number of years. He has been patient with me as we have created this book together. Jim is a church historian and has brought a rich perspective to this book that I could not have done without him. Not only is he a great ministry colleague, he is also a friend and mentor to me. I am also grateful for the people who have made this book possible. Rhett Wilson, the senior communications director for LFM, has been invaluable. Rhett is a gifted writer and communicator who helped make two voices come together as one. He has such a great servant's heart and is a joy to work with. Another talented writer, Tom Bowers, who is also my cousin, read through the book several times and helped make the book much more readable. In addition to Rhett and Tom, Lee Weeks was a helpful editor. Jim and I are so thankful for this great team.

We have many thriving ministry partners whose stories illustrate the key points in this book. I've appreciated their willingness to share their stories, even if we had to change a few names and places. I am also thankful to the team at LFM—our staff, board of directors, and strategic advisory board members. Many of them are mentioned by name in the book. Al Hsu and the team at InterVarsity Press have been delightful. I couldn't ask for a more attentive editor and publisher.

Most importantly, I thank God for a lifetime of second chances. Although I don't deserve them, I need them. I pray this book brings glory to him.

From Jim

As we finish a book about congregations, I must begin with thanksgiving for having grown up as a child of pastoral parents who loved their congregations. They taught me how to both appreciate the congregation as it is and hope for its development. My wife Sara is also the child of a pastor who carried a similar love of congregations. Eventually Sara became a pastor, and I had the privilege of watching her lead a congregation in such loving ways. Each of the four congregations I had the privilege to pastor taught me enormous things about the nature of the church, including the hopes and disappointments that can be present. At my ordination service, my father charged me to love my congregations before trying to fix them. Sadly, I did not always heed his advice, but now I see how vital love is to the process of change. I must not fail to mention how much it has shaped me for the ten years I spent at Gordon-Conwell Theological Seminary teaching nearly one thousand students about life in the church. It was a privilege to help shape the dreams of these amazing students from whom I learned so much.

Attentiveness is something Sara Singleton and Leighton Ford have been trying to help me learn for years. I am still learning so much about how to discern God's leading in a particular gathering of his people. Having the opportunity to join with Kevin Ford at LFM is a rich gift and continues to shape how I see this glorious gathering we call the church can be more like it was intended to be. Thank you, Kevin, for the gift of this season of work in my life.

Notes

Introduction

[1] Steve Farrar, *Manna: When You're Out of Options, God Will Provide* (Nashville, TN: Thomas Nelson, 2016), 186.

[2] *Merriam-Webster's Dictionary*, s.v. "Attentive," accessed May 19, 2023, www.merriam-webster.com/dictionary/attentive.

[3] *Webster's New World Dictionary* (New York: Pocket Books, 2003), s.v. "Attentive."

1. How Did We Get to a World We've Never Known?

[1] Robert Wuthnow, *The Restructuring of American Religion: Society and Faith Since World War II* (Princeton, NJ: Princeton University Press, 1988).

[2] Dan Miller, *No More Dreaded Mondays* (New York: Crown Currency, 2009), 180-81.

[3] Steve Farrar, *Battle Ready: Prepare to Be Used by God* (Colorado Springs, CO: David C. Cook, 2009), 190.

[4] Thom Rainer, "73% of American Churches are Declining," accessed May 17, 2023, https://churchleaderinsights.com/73-of-american-churches-are-declining-by-thom-rainer/; Wendy Wang, "The Decline in Church Attendance in COVID America," Institute for Family Studies, accessed May 17, 2023, https://ifstudies.org/blog/the-decline-in-church-attendance-in-covid-america.

[5] Paul Chenoweth, "Dr. Karen Swanson Discusses 'Worship Behind Bars,'" Belmont University News and Media, October 22, 2014, https://news.belmont.edu/dr-karen-swanson-discusses-worship-behind-bars/.

2. How Do I Become an Attentive Person?

[1] Statistics provided by The Fuller Institute, George Barna, Lifeway, Schaeffer Institute of Leadership Development, and Pastoral Care Inc, accessed August 3, 2023, www.pastoralcareinc.com/statistics/.

[2] Bertrand Russell, *The Basic Writings of Bertrand Russell* (London: Taylor and Francis, 2009), 348.

[3] René Descartes, *A Discourse on Method* (Sydney, Australia: ReadHowYouWant.com, 2006), 48.

[4]Anthony J. P. Kenny, "Philosophy of Mind of Aristotle," Britannica Online, accessed August 3, 2023, www.britannica.com/biography/Aristotle/Philosophy-of-mind.

[5]"Kant's View of the Mind and Consciousness of Self," Stanford Encyclopedia of Philosophy, July 26, 2004, https://plato.stanford.edu/entries/kant-mind/.

[6]David Hume, *A Treatise of Human Nature in Two Volumes*, vol. 1, Everyman's Library, ed. Ernest Rhys (London: J. M. Dent & Sons Ltd., 1920), 238.

[7]Ken Shigematsu, *Survival Guide for the Soul* (Grand Rapids, MI: Zondervan, 2018), 40.

[8]Paul Tillich, quoted in Ken Shigematsu, *Survival Guide for the Soul* (Grand Rapids, MI: Zondervan, 2018), 36.

[9]Henri J. M. Nouwen, *Life of the Beloved: Spiritual Living in a Secular World* (New York: Crossroad, 1992), 31.

[10]Timothy Keller, *The Meaning of Marriage: Facing the Complexities of Commitment with the Wisdom of God* (New York: Penguin, 2013).

[11]Shigematsu, *Survival Guide,* 52.

[12]Richard Foster, *Celebration of Discipline* (San Francisco: HarperSanFrancisco, 1978, 1998), 7.

[13]Garrett Kell, "The Pattern Among Fallen Pastors," The Gospel Coalition, May 26, 2015, www.thegospelcoalition.org/article/the-pattern-among-fallen-pastors/.

[14]Bob Burns, Tasha Chapman, and Donald C. Guthrie, *Resilient Ministry* (Downers Grove, IL: InterVarsity Press, 2013).

[15]Wayne Cordeiro, *Leading on Empty: Refilling Your Tank and Renewing Your Passion* (Minneapolis, MN: Bethany House Publishers, 2010).

[16]Ken Shigematsu, *God in My Everything* (Grand Rapids, MI: Zondervan, 2013).

[17]Ken Shigematsu, "The Unbearable Pressure to Do Great Things for the Lord," *Christianity Today*, March 11, 2019, www.christianitytoday.com/pastors/2019/spring/unbearable-pressure-great-things-lord-significance.html.

[18]MaryKate Morse, *Lifelong Leadership* (Carol Stream, IL: NavPress, 2020).

[19]We explore the subject of mentoring more deeply in chapter ten.

3. How Do I Manage Anxiety?

[1]Jim Osterhaus, personal correspondence with author, September 24, 2022.

[2]Jim Osterhaus, "The Well-Defined Leader," Leighton Ford Ministries, accessed September 5, 2023, https://leightonfordministries.org/articles/the-well-defined-leader-2/.

[3]Bill Gaultiere, "Triangulating Hurts You and Your Loved Ones," Soul Shepherding, accessed May 11, 2022, www.soulshepherding.org/triangulating-hurts-you-and-your-loved-ones/.

[4]*Encylopaedia Britannica Online*, s.v. "defense mechanism," accessed April 12, 2023, www.britannica.com/topic/defense-mechanism.

[5]*Encyclopaedia Britannica Online*, s.v. "defense mechanism," accessed August 4, 2023, www.britannica.com/topic/defense-mechanism.

[6]C. S. Lewis, *Mere Christianity* (San Francisco: HarperOne, 2001), 136-39.

[7]Osterhaus, "The Well-Defined Leader."

[8]Jim Osterhaus, *Thriving through Ministry Conflict* (Grand Rapids, MI: Zondervan, 2009).

[9]Osterhaus, *Thriving*, 27.

[10]Osterhaus, *Thriving*, 23-24.

[11]Edwin Friedman, *A Failure of Nerve* (New York: Church Publishing, 2017), 244.

[12]Friedman, *Failure of Nerve*, 232-33.

[13]Osterhaus, "The Well-Defined Leader."

[14]This material comes from our friend Jim Osterhaus.

[15]Jim Collins, "The Hedgehog Concept," Jim Collins, accessed April 14, 2023, www.jimcollins.com/concepts/the-hedgehog-concept.html.

[16]Jim Osterhaus, *Avoiding Pastoral Pitfalls* (Peabody, MA: Hendrickson Publishers, 2021), 15.

[17]Osterhaus, "The Well-Defined Leader."

[18]"Window of Tolerance," Good Therapy, updated August 8, 2016, www.goodtherapy.org/blog/psychpedia/window-of-tolerance.

4. How Do I Increase My Trust Quotient?

[1]Stephen M. R. Covey with Rebecca R. Merrill, *The Speed of Trust* (New York: Free Press, 2008), 333.

[2]"What Is Pastor Burnout?," Gravity Leadership, accessed June 17, 2023, https://gravityleadership.com/pastor-burnout/.

[3]Robert J. Morgan, *The Jordan River Rules* (USA: Cover to Cover LLC, 2021), 51.

[4]Robert Frost, "Mending Wall," Poetry Foundation, accessed April 18, 2023, www.poetryfoundation.org/poems/44266/mending-wall.

[5]Ron Heifetz, *Leadership Without Easy Answers* (Cambridge, MA: Harvard University Press, 1998), 56-57.

[6]Frances Hesselbein and Alan Shrader, eds., *Leader to Leader 2* (San Francisco: Wiley, 2008), 348.

[7]Kevin Ford and Ken Tucker's book, *The Leadership Triangle* (New York: Morgan James, 2014), addresses three necessary sides of leadership: tactical, strategic, and transformational.

[8]"The Policy Governance Model," PolicyGovernance.com, accessed June 5, 2023, www.carvergovernance.com/model.htm.

[9]Here are just a few examples: *1001 Illustrations that Connect* by Laron and Ten Elshof, *750 Engaging Illustrations for Preachers, Teachers, and Writers* by Craig Larson, *Tony Evans' Book of Illustrations* by Tony Evans, and *The Tale of the Tardy Oxcart* by Charles Swindoll.

[10]Eugene Peterson, *The Contemplative Pastor* (Grand Rapids, MI: Eerdmans, 1993), 115.

[11]J. Oswald Sanders, *Spiritual Leadership* (Chicago: Moody, 1994), 67.

5. Is the Tail Wagging the Dog?

[1]"AT&T Stadium," Arlington Convention & Visitors Bureau, accessed December 3, 2021, www.arlington.org/things-to-do/attractions/att-stadium/.

[2]"Art," AT&T Stadium, Arlington Convention & Visitors Bureau, https://attstadium.com/art/.

[3]Johannes Blouw, *The Missionary Nature of the Church* (England: Lutterworth, 1962).

[4]See LFM's website at www.leightonfordministries.org.

[5]Lee Bolman and Terrence Deal, *Reframing Organizations* (San Francisco: Jossey-Bass, 2003), 43.

6. How Do We Create Community in a Narcissistic World?

[1]"Narcissus: The Self-Lover," Greekmythology.com, accessed June 6, 2023, www.greekmythology.com/Myths/Mortals/Narcissus/narcissus.html.

[2]Cambridge Dictionary, s.v. "Consumerism," accessed May 29, 2023, https://dictionary.cambridge.org/us/dictionary/english/consumerism.

[3]"Consumerism," Tech Target, accessed May 29, 2023, www.techtarget.com/whatis/definition/consumerism.

[4]Alan Kreider, *The Change of Conversion and the Origin of Christendom* (Eugene, OR: Wipf and Stock, 1999).

[5]Neil Postman, *Amusing Ourselves to Death* (New York: Penguin Books, 2005).

[6]For one example, see Sarah Konrath, Yioryos Nardis, and Elliot T. Panek, "Mirror or Megaphone?: How Relationships between Narcissism and Social Networking Site Use Differ on Facebook and Twitter," *Computers in Human Behavior* 29, 5 (2013): 2004–2012, www.sciencedirect.com/science/article/abs/pii/S0747563213001155.

[7]Kathryn Carver, "Cultural Narcissism: Is Social Media Making Us Narcissists?," LAPP, accessed June 5, 2023, www.lappthebrand.com/blogs/perspectives/cultural-narcissism-is-social-media-making-us-narcissists.

[8]Bushman and Baumeister write, "The results showed that the combination of narcissism and insult led to high levels of aggression toward the source of the insult. Narcissism did not affect displaced aggression, which was low in general. Self-esteem (measured this time with the Janis & Field, 1959 scale) proved irrelevant to aggression." Brad J. Bushman and Roy F. Baumeister, "Does Self-Love or Self-Hate Lead to Violence?," *Journal of Research in Personality* 36, 6 (2002): 543-45, www.sciencedirect.com/science/article/abs/pii/S0092656602005020.

[9]Carver, "Cultural Narcissism."

[10]Valentina Fernandez, "Social Media, Dopamine, and Stress: Converging Pathways," Dartmouth Undergraduate Journal of Science, August 20, 2022, https://sites.dartmouth.edu/dujs/2022/08/20/social-media-dopamine-and-stress-converging-pathways/.

[11]Fernandez, "Social Media."

[12] Fernandez, "Social Media."

[13] Fernandez, "Social Media."

[14] Carver, "Cultural Narcissism," bold in source.

[15] Archibald Hart and Sylvia Frejd, *The Digital Invasion: How Technology is Shaping You and Your Relationships* (Grand Rapids, MI: Baker Books, 2013), 44.

[16] Chuck DeGroat, *When Narcissism Comes to Church* (Downers Grove, IL: InterVarsity Press, 2020), 35.

[17] "Teen Depression," Mayo Clinic, accessed June 5, 2023, www.mayoclinic.org/diseases-conditions/teen-depression/symptoms-causes/syc-20350985.

[18] Leslie Davis and A. W. Geiger, "A Growing Number of American Teenagers—Particularly Girls—Are Facing Depression," Pew Research Center, July 12, 2019, www.pewresearch.org/short-reads/2019/07/12/a-growing-number-of-american-teenagers-particularly-girls-are-facing-depression/.

[19] "The CDC Says Teen Mental Health Is in Crisis. Who Is Most at Risk?," USA Facts, updated October 4, 2023, https://usafacts.org/articles/the-cdc-says-teen-mental-health-is-in-crisis-who-is-most-at-risk/.

[20] Hart and Frejd, *The Digital Invasion*, 43.

[21] Hendrik Kraemer, *A Theology of the Laity* (Vancouver: Regent College Publishing, 1958), 50.

[22] Kraemer, *A Theology*, 58.

[23] Thom Rainer, *I Am a Church Member* (Nashville, TN: B&H, 2013), 12.

[24] Greg Ogden, *The New Reformation, Returning the Ministry to the People of God* (Grand Rapids, MI: Zondervan, 1991).

[25] Stanley Grenz and Jay Smith, *Created for Community: Connecting Christian Belief with Christian Living* (Grand Rapids, MI: Baker Books, 2015).

[26] Don Everts, *The Reluctant Witness* (Downers Grove, IL: InterVarsity Press, 2019).

[27] Max De Pree, *Leadership Is an Art* (Lansing: Michigan State University Press, 1987), 25.

[28] Ed Stetzer, "The Problem with Pastors as Rock Stars," September 14, 2015, https://outreachmagazine.com/features/4968-consumer-church-problem-with-pastors-as-rock-stars-celebrity-culture-ed-stetzer.html.

[29] David French, "The Crisis of Christian Celebrity," French Press, December 6, 2020, https://frenchpress.thedispatch.com/p/the-crisis-of-christian-celebrity?s=r.

[30] Tom Nelson, *The Flourishing Pastor* (Downers Grove, IL: InterVarsity Press, 2021), 15.

[31] Nelson, *The Flourishing Pastor*, 15.

[32] Ken Garfield, "The Write Idea," South Park, January 2, 2020, https://southparkmagazine.com/the-write-idea/.

[33] Donald Whitney, "Why Are Handwritten Notes Important in a Digital Age?," The Ethics & Religious Liberty Commission, February 14, 2017, https://erlc.com/resource-library/video-explainers/why-are-handwritten-notes-important-in-a-digital-age/.

[34]The Attractional Era basically mimics the television medium in that it was prominent from the 1950s through the 1980s.

7. What Is Our Ethos?

[1]Kate Taylor, "Chick-fil-A Continues to Dominate Customer Satisfaction Rankings as the Fast-food Chain Takes over America," Insider, June 30, 2020, www.businessinsider.in/retail/news/chick-fil-a-continues-to-dominate-customer-satisfaction-rankings-as-the-fast-food-chain-takes-over-america/articleshow/76717609.cms.

[2]"Culture Eats Strategy for Breakfast," Quote Investigator, May 23, 2017, https://quoteinvestigator.com/2017/05/23/culture-eats/.

[3]"Clotaire Rapaille—A Glimpse into the Genius's Ingenious Marketing Ways," Illuminz, accessed August 17, 2022, www.illuminz.com/blog/clotaire-rapaille-a-glimpse-into-the-genius's-ingenious-marketing-ways.

[4]"Clotaire Rapaille."

[5]Jack Hitt, "Does the Smell of Coffee Brewing Remind You of Your Mother," *New York Times Magazine*, May 7, 2000, www.nytimes.com/2000/05/07/magazine/does-the-smell-of-coffee-brewing-remind-you-of-your-mother.html.

[6]G. K. Chesterton, *The Father Brown Omnibus* (New York: Dodd, Mead & Company, 1945).

[7]Kevin Ford and Jim Osterhaus, *The Thing in the Bushes* (Carol Stream, IL: NavPress, 2001).

[8]"Clotaire Rapaille."

8. Are We Entitled or Engaged?

[1]Nina Paczka, "Making Noise for Quiet Quitting | 2023 Study," LiveCareer, January 17, 2023, www.livecareer.com/resources/careers/planning/quiet-quitting.

[2]For more information about City Changers, check out their website at https://citychanger.org/.

[3]Jackie Georgiou, "Alan Platt—Urban Influencer, " Joy!, accessed September 5, 2023, https://joymag.co.za/article/alan-platt-urban-influencer/.

[4]Georgiou, "Alan Platt."

[5]Julia Glum, "Millennials Selfies: Young Adults Will Take More Than 25,000 Pictures of Themselves During Their Lifetimes: Report," International Business Times, September 22, 2015, www.ibtimes.com/millennials-selfies-young-adults-will-take-more-25000-pictures-themselves-during-2108417.

[6]*Dictionary.com*, s.v. "Entitlement," accessed September 12, 2022, www.dictionary.com/browse/entitlement.

[7]J. I. Packer, *Hot Tub Religion* (Carol Stream, IL: Tyndale House Publishers, 1987).

[8]Abraham Kuyper, *The Work of the Holy Spirit* (New York: Funk and Wagnalls, 1990), 107.

[9]Ed Stetzer, "How Christian Consumers Ruin Pastors and Cheat the Mission of God," Ideas for the Common Good, accessed September 13, 2022, http://208.106.253.109/blog/how-christian-consumers-ruin-pastors-and-cheat-the-mission-of-god.aspx.

[10]"Lifestyle Enclave," accessed September 13, 2022, https://en.wikipedia.org/wiki/Lifestyle_enclave.

[11]"About," Surge, accessed August 4, 2023, https://surge.org/about.

[12]Reggie Joiner, "What is Orange?," Orange, January 19, 2021, https://orangeleaders.com/2021/01/19/what-is-orange-2/.

[13]Ed Stetzer, "How Christian Consumers Ruin Pastors."

[14]Jim Harter, "U.S. Employee Engagement Data Hold Steady in First Half of 2021," Gallup, July 29, 2021, www.gallup.com/workplace/352949/employee-engagement-holds-steady-first-half-2021.aspx.

[15]Henry, Richard, and Mike Blackaby, *Experiencing God: Knowing and Doing the Will of God* (Nashville, TN: Lifeway Press, 2022), 226.

[16]Rhett Wilson, "Church Structure: Organizing Around Your Mission," *RHETT-orical: Musing About Faith, Family, and Freedom* (blog), April 11, 2013, www.wilsonrhett.com/2013/04/church-structureorganize-around-your.html.

9. How Do We Facilitate Real Transformation?

[1]Ronald Heifetz, Alexander Grashow, and Marty Linsky, *The Practice of Adaptive Leadership* (Boston: Harvard Business Press, 2009), 14.

[2]Heifetz, Grashow, and Linksy, *Practice of Adaptive Leadership*, 14.

[3]William Arndt et al., *A Greek-English Lexicon of the New Testament and Other Early Christian Literature* (Chicago: University of Chicago, 2000), 639.

[4]In partnering with churches for many years, LFM does not take the fly in and fly out approach. We desire to walk with a church and their pastor(s) for several years, believing that a relationship will most help the church and their leaders.

[5]Ronald Heifetz and Martin Linsky, *Leadership on the Line: Staying Alive Through the Dangers of Leading* (Boston: Harvard Business Review Press, 2002).

[6]Jim Osterhaus, *The Red Zone, The Blue Zone: Surviving and Thriving in Church Conflict,* Leighton Ford Ministries, June 2021, https://leightonfordministries.org/wp-content/uploads/2021/06/Red-Zone-.pdf.

[7]Heifetz and Linsky, *Leadership on the Line.*

10. How Do We Pass the Torch?

[1]We use the term *evangelical* as it was originally intended—to indicate a strong commitment to the good news of the gospel and the basic beliefs of biblical Christianity—not to refer to a partisan political group.

[2]Georgina Giles, "Bash," Evangelical Times, September 1, 2011, www.evangelical-times.org/bash/.

[3]Giles, "Bash."

[4]"John Stott," accessed December 23, 2022, https://johnstott.org/life/.

[5]"John Stott."

[6]"John Stott."

[7]"John Stott."

[8]"John Stott."

[9]John Stott, "Appendix: John Stott on Singleness," in Albert Y. Hsu, *Singles at the Crossroads* (Downers Grove, IL: InterVarsity Press, 1997), 176–81.

[10]John Yates III, personal correspondence with author, December 13, 2022.

[11]Charles Stone, "Pastors Who Lack Close Friends: 5 Reasons Why," Church Leaders, June 21, 2023, https://churchleaders.com/pastors/415312-pastors-who-lack-close-friends-5-reasons-why.html.

[12]Stone, "Pastors Who Lack Lose Friends."

[13]Bobby Clinton, "Constellation Model," accessed December 15, 2022, https://bobbyclinton.com/downloads/articles/ConstellationModel.pd.pdf.

[14]Morri Yancy, "The Powerful Impact of a Mentor," U.S. Chamber of Commerce Institute for Organization Management, February 1, 2017, https://institute.uschamber.com/the-powerful-impact-of-a-mentor/.

[15]John Mallison, "Mentoring to Make Disciples and Leaders," Lead On: Inspiration from Arrow, May 2020.

[16]Mallison, "Mentoring."

[17]Clinton, "Constellation Model."

[18]Ken Boa, *Life in the Presence of God* (Downers Grove, IL: InterVarsity Press, 2017), 124.